Duff —
Happy 65th!
what a wonderful spot.
Enjoy the shore birds.
fondly
Bob and Susan
March 1990

FLORIDA'S BIRDS

FLORIDA'S BIRDS

A HANDBOOK
AND REFERENCE

Herbert W. Kale, II, and David S. Maehr
Illustrated by Karl Karalus

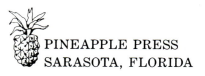

PINEAPPLE PRESS
SARASOTA, FLORIDA

To the birders of Florida—past, present, and future.

—Herbert W. Kale, II

To Clifton and Erin.

—David S. Maehr

To the two Helens in my life—my wife and my mother—and to my daughter Charlene; to June and David Cussen, patient publishers and dear friends; and to William and Kathy Cummings and Reeve and Sharon Abraban, friends who were always there.

—Karl Karalus

Inquiries should be addressed to: Pineapple Press, Inc.
P.O. Drawer 16008
Southside Station
Sarasota, Florida 34239

Library of Congress Cataloging-in-Publication Data

Kale, H. W.
    Florida's birds: a handbook and reference / by Herbert W. Kale,
II, and David S. Maehr; illustrated by Karl Karalus. — 1st ed.
      p. cm.
    ISBN 0-910923-67-1: $26.95. — ISBN 0-910923-68-X (pbk.): $19.95
    1. Birds—Florida—Identification. 2. Birds—Florida. I. Maehr,
David S., 1955–   . II. Title.
QL684.F6K35 1990
598.29759—dc20
                                  89-16334
                                  CIP

First Edition
   10 9 8 7 6 5 4 3 2 1

Design by Joan Lange Kresek
Printed in Singapore through Palace Press
Typography by E. T. Lowe Publishing Company, Nashville, Tennessee
9/11 Century Exp.

CONTENTS

ACKNOWLEDGMENTS

We are grateful to our many friends and colleagues in the Florida birding community and in our respective organizations, the Florida Audubon Society and the Florida Game and Fresh Water Commission, for encouragement, suggestions, and criticisms. A debt of thanks is owed Diane Maehr who typed early drafts of the manuscript. We offer special thanks to Dr. William Robertson for his thoughtful review of the final manuscript. Finally, we appreciate the guidance and abundant patience of June and David Cussen of Pineapple Press.

PREFACE

One of the most frequent requests of Florida bird watchers is for a reference that deals only with Florida birds—one that helps to identify them with pictures and descriptions, along with information on distribution, habitats, habits, and breeding biology. Usually, the birder is referred to one of the standard bird guides (see the Introduction) which cover all or part of North America. Alexander Sprunt's *Florida Birdlife*, a 1954 revision of Arthur H. Howell's 1932 classic, has long been out of print (although occasionally available from dealers specializing in natural history books).

Florida's Birds was written for the average citizen or visitor to Florida who wants to identify the birds he or she is likely to see in the course of a day—for instance, the birds that frequent a backyard feeder, the gull or sandpiper standing on the beach, the waders in a roadside ditch. Although we include accounts of nearly all of the native species that occur in Florida, we have not illustrated some species, such as the less common transients that are rarely seen except by avid birders who spend hours afield searching for them. Some readers may be disappointed by this decision, but with the plethora of excellent field guides to North American birds readily available, this should not present a hardship to anyone. Experienced birders from out-of-state not familiar with Florida habitats will also find this guide useful.

The format of *Florida's Birds* is straightforward. Following an introduction is a chapter describing Florida's habitats. This is followed by the individual species accounts and the color plates depicting most of those species. Each account lists the English common name, scientific name, other common or colloquial names that the species may be known by either currently or in the past, a description of the bird, its range and habitat in Florida, habits, food, and breeding biology, if it breeds in Florida.

The remaining chapters are devoted to beginning bird watching, bird study, bird finding, bird conservation, attracting and feeding birds, care and rehabilitation of sick, injured, or orphaned birds, and human/bird "problems" and suggested solutions. A final section, preceding the index, is a checklist of the birds of Florida.

We hope this book will be of interest to all who have a love for Florida's birds, and that it will help foster an appreciation and concern for these birds and their natural habitats.

Herbert W. Kale II
David S. Maehr
Karl Karalus

FLORIDA'S BIRDS

INTRODUCTION

Novices to bird watching often feel overwhelmed by the variety of birds and the difficulties of bird identification. For some groups of birds, such as sparrows and fall warblers, these feelings may be justified, but it does not take long before the beginner acquires the skills and confidence to readily identify many species. In a book of this nature it is impossible to illustrate each of the various plumages that may be worn by some species at different times of the year. For some species, the plumages of the juvenile and the adult male and female may be identical or very similar. A Blue Jay is easily identified regardless of age or sex. In other cases the sexes show color and size differences, termed sexual dimorphism. The Northern Cardinal is a good example of this, the male red and the female brown. Or juveniles and adults may differ. Young American Robins and young Northern Mockingbirds bear speckled breasts, while the breast of the adult of each species is plain without spots. In some species the winter (nonbreeding) plumage differs from the summer (breeding) plumage. We point out these differences in the written account for each species, even though we may illustrate only one of the adult plumages on the plate.

The general sequence of plumages for most birds is a natal down at hatching, followed by a juvenile plumage acquired as the young bird develops and begins flying. The next molt, usually in late summer, may result in a completely new plumage that resembles the mature adult, or, in some species, an immature or subadult plumage. This fall plumage may be fringed with drab-colored feather tips that gradually wear away over the winter months leaving the bright spring or breeding plumage, or it may be replaced by another molt in early spring.

In some species the soft parts, i.e., facial skin and legs, become extremely brilliant and colorful during courtship. This is especially evident in the herons, ibises, and gallinules.

Listing Order

Some readers may wonder about the sequence of the birds presented herein. It follows the order of the American Ornithologists' Union Check-list (6th edition, 1983, and supplements No. 35, 1985, and No. 36, 1987) which places species in the sequence of what is considered to be their natural relationship, termed phylogenetic order. Each species is assigned a two-word scientific name in Latin—a genus and a species. Related genera (plural of genus) are grouped into a family, and related families into an order. All the orders of birds comprise the class Aves, one of the five classes of the Vertebrata. The other vertebrate classes are mammals, reptiles (including snakes, lizards, turtles, and crocodiles), amphibians (including frogs, toads, salamanders), and fishes.

Several of the larger bird families are subdivided into subfamilies. For example, the large family Emberizidae is comprised of the subfamilies Parulinae (wood-warblers), Thraupinae (tanagers), Cardinalinae (cardinals, grosbeaks), Emberizinae (towhees, sparrows), and Icterinae (blackbirds, orioles). A population of birds that differs from other populations of the same species may be described as a subspecies or race of that species. For example, the Seaside Sparrow in Florida is represented by at least five distinctive subspecies.

The species accounts are in phylogenetic order, but anyone desiring to look up the account or illustration of a particular species will also find it listed in alphabetical order in the index.

Bird Identification

To identify birds one needs to look for certain identifying charcteristics or patterns, called field marks. Sometimes it is a simple task—the all-red bird with a top knot or crest is, of course, without question, a male Northern Cardinal. Some species of birds look very similar to other species, and more subtle marks need to be looked for. A few closely related species are so similar in appearance that they can be identified in the field only by their call notes. We briefly list the most distinctive field marks opposite the picture of each species depicted and present more detail, if necessary, in the text. In order to understand our descriptions it will be necessary to know the body parts and terms describing them, as illustrated below.

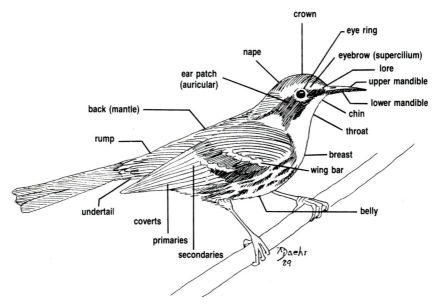

Note: The eyestripe, not illustrated here, is usually a thin dark line that extends through the eye. A stripe only in front of the eye is called a preocular stripe; one behind the eye, a postocular stripe. The space between the bill and the eye is also called the lore. The scapulars are feather tracts along each side of the back above the wings, and they may partly cover the wings. (A sleeping bird tucks its head under the scapulars, not under the wing.) The speculum is a rectangular patch of color—usually white, blue, purple, or green—on the trailing edge of the secondaries (the inner flight feathers) of the wings of many duck species.

One way to identify a bird is simply to look at pictures in a guide until you find the bird. If the species is distinctive and unlike any other species then you will probably make a correct identification. In many cases it will not be that easy. Therefore, you should make an effort to note or record several bits of information as you are observing the bird:

Size: Is it sparrow-size (about 5-6 inches), robin-size (about 10-12 inches), crow-size (about 20 inches), or larger? What size is it in relation to a nearby species that you have already correctly identified?

Colors, patterns: Note all colors and patterns (stripes, contrasts, wing bars, eye ring, etc.)

Shape: Wings may be long and pointed or short and rounded, etc. The bill may be stout, finchlike (sparrows, grosbeaks); thin, pointed (wrens, warblers); hooked (hawks, owls); long, decurved (ibis, curlews); etc. You may also note the shape of legs and feet: long legs and toes, webbed, hooked talons, small, weak, etc.

Season: The avifauna of Florida is comprised of species that are permanent residents, i.e., year-round occurrence; summer-only residents; winter-only residents; and transients, i.e., migrants that pass through the state only during spring and fall migrations to and from their northern breeding grounds and southern wintering grounds in Central and South America. The calendar bar opposite each species plate indicates when the species is in the state, and if it breeds in Florida, the months it does so.

Habitat: Forest? Field? Marsh? Beach? You would not expect to see, deep in the woods, a species whose habitat is a marsh or open field. For each species depicted in this guide we have indicated the habitat (described in detail in the habitat chapter) in which that species is expected to occur.

Behavior: Walking? Hopping? Soaring? Wading? Climbing a tree trunk? If it is singing, try to describe the song, better yet, tape record it. A recording presenting the songs of 100 speces of Florida birds has been prepared by Dr. John W. Hardy, Curator of Birds at the Florida Museum of Natural History in Gainesville, and is most helpful in identifying a singing bird. This recording is available from the Florida Audubon Society (1101 Audubon Way, Maitland, Florida 32751) or from the museum (Florida Museum of Natural History, University of Florida, Gainesville, Florida 32611).

Books Dealing with Bird Identification

We highly recommend readers to obtain a copy of one or more of the following (listed in alphabetical order) excellent and complete field guides to the birds of eastern North America, usually available through most bookstores unless indicated otherwise:

A Field Guide to the Birds East of the Rockies by Roger Tory Peterson. Houghton Mifflin Co., Boston. 1980.

Birds of North America by Chandler S. Robbins, Bertel Bruun, and Herbert S. Zim. Golden Press, New York. 1983.

Field Guide to the Birds of North America edited by Shirley L. Scott. National Geographic Society, Washington, D.C., 2nd Ed., 1987. This guide is available only from the National Geographic Society or selected nonprofit organizations.

More advanced students may desire to acquire the three-volume *Audubon Society Master Guide to Birding* edited by John Farrand, Jr. Alfred A. Knopf, New York. 1983.

In recent years, a number of guides dealing with specific groups of birds have appeared. These are most helpful in identification of similar-appearing species that are difficult to separate in the field in some plumages. Among these references are:

Hawks of North America by William S. Clark and Brian K. Wheeler. Houghton Mifflin Co., Boston. 1987.

Hawks in Flight: The Flight Identification of North American Migrant Raptors by Pete Dunne, David Sibley, and Clay Sutton. Houghton Mifflin Co., Boston. 1988.

Shorebirds: An Identification Guide to the Waders of the World by Peter Hayman, John Marchant, and Tony Prater. Houghton Mifflin Co., Boston, 1986.

Seabirds: An Identification Guide by Peter Harrison. Houghton Mifflin Co., Boston. 1983

Gulls: A Guide to Identification, 2nd Ed., by Peter J. Grant. Buteo Books, Vermillion, SD. 1986.

FLORIDA BIRD HABITATS

An animal's habitat is its "address" or the place where it lives. Florida bird habitats range from isolated islands of the Dry Tortugas to remote interior swamplands and our increasingly numerous suburban backyards. And, while many of the Sunshine State's birds are year-round residents, many more find refuge each winter from icy northern climes. We have estimated that 179 species are known to breed in Florida while nearly 300 species are spring and fall migrants or reside during winter. Although Florida is often pictured as a coastal palm-shaded resort, many other unique and attractive landscapes are tucked away in the state's vast interior. Further, the vast majority of bird habitats are seldom seen by sun-seeking vacationers. It is in these areas where many of Florida's most spectacular birds reside.

Florida lacks the topographic variation typical of many other states. However, the patterns created by subtle changes in elevation, water drainage, and climate are apparent in the dizzying variety and combinations of vegetation. A drop or rise in elevation of only inches can explain the sudden occurrence of a cypress pond within a pine flatwoods or a longleaf pine sandhill within a live oak hammock. Water drainage is a major influence on the development of soils, which in turn determine the distribution of plant species and plant associations on a site. Very often, vegetation is useful in predicting the resident bird species to be found in an area. One would not expect to find a Brown Pelican at the edge of a hardwood swamp; however, during spring it would be unusual not to find the cavity-nesting Prothonotary Warbler and nocturnal Barred Owl there. During winter the Prothonotary's absence is more than compensated for by the influx of American Robins, Cedar Waxwings, American Goldfinches, Ruby-crowned Kinglets, and other northern migrants. Most Florida bird habitats display a seasonal variation in species occurrence. It is this constant turnover of breeding, wintering, and migratory birds that makes Florida such an exciting place for bird watching at all times of the year.

It is useful to have an understanding of a bird's habitat requirements. Similarly, it is helpful to know what bird species are typical in a particular habitat type. Insight such as this will aid the observant birder in knowing what to expect, while allowing rational judgments to be made concerning unusual sightings and rarities. The habitats listed opposite each species' plate illustration are those in which it is most likely to be found. This information can be helpful in identifying the bird.

Coastal Beaches

The coastal region of Florida supports the densest human use of any habitat in the state. As a consequence, Florida's coastline also has experienced the most development and habitat alteration. It is, perhaps, as much a statement about human aesthetics as it is about the tenacity of birds that a large proportion of bird watching occurs before an endless backdrop of resorts and condominiums.

Those few undisturbed stretches of coastal beach remaining reflect the natural molding forces of wind and surf. Vegetation is often sparse and short and is specialized to withstand the stresses imparted by a salty, sandy environment. A series of dunes are characteristic of beach habitats, and these support a characteristic array of plant species. Annuals such as sea oats, morning glory, railroad vine, and dune panic grass are found closest to the shoreline, while more woody vegetation tends to dominate the back dunes. Scrub live oak, cabbage palm, saw palmetto, wax myrtle, coco plum, and sea grape may be found in these more protected dunes. Life on Florida's beaches and dunes is well suited to this harsh and ever-changing environment. The persistence of these plant species following a hurricane's wind, rain, and sea surge attests to their tenacity.

Bird species to be looked for on open beaches and inlets are GULLS, TERNS, PLOVERS, SANDPIPERS, LOONS, SEADUCKS, PELICANS, and CORMORANTS. On the vegetated dunes, especially when these are interspersed with shallow pools of water, look for PUDDLE DUCKS, EGRETS, and SAVANNAH SPARROWS in winter, and WILSON'S PLOVERS and WILLETS in spring and summer.

Salt Marshes

Salt marshes are highly productive marine systems and are found on the east coast behind barrier islands from Daytona Beach northward into Georgia and on the Gulf coast from Tarpon Springs to Apalachee Bay, where they extend out into the Gulf of Mexico because of the shallow water and relatively insignificant wave action. Along the panhandle westward to Alabama, salt marshes occur only in protected bays behind barrier islands.

Salt marsh plants have adapted to several environmental stresses including wide tidal fluctuations, low soil oxygen levels, and drought conditions induced by the salty environment. Vegetation is usually found in a zoned arrangement. Beginning from open water one encounters bands of cord grass and needle rush interspersed with salt flats or pannes containing saltwort, glasswort, and torpedograss. Salt marshes provide essential nursery habitat for a variety of fish and invertebrates, many of which are important bird foods.

Birds to be looked for in salt marshes are Clapper Rails, Marsh Wrens, Seaside and Sharp-tailed Sparrows, herons, egrets, ibises, Northern Harriers, and, in the numerous creek distributaries and oyster bars, Red-breasted Mergansers, oystercatchers, terns, and various shorebird species.

Mangrove

Florida is one of the few places in the world where a transition zone between salt marsh and mangrove habitat occurs. Generally, mangroves range from St. Johns County on the east and Levy County on the west southward into the Caribbean. Red mangrove is perhaps the most conspicuous of the four species of mangrove found in Florida. It is unique in preferring edges of tidal creeks and canals, in its bizarre arrangement of stiltlike prop roots, and its habit of producing large, fleshy seeds that germinate while still on the parent plant. Black mangrove can often be found growing in a zone behind red mangrove and can be distinguished by its emergent, pencillike root extensions known as pneumatophores. It is more cold-tolerant than the other mangrove species and is the species that pioneers north of the subtropical zone. White mangrove and buttonwood are less conspicuous than the other two mangrove species and are restricted to areas of less significant tidal action. Dwarf mangroves may occur when tidal influence is infrequent and salt concentrations are high or substrates are shallow. Periodic hard freezes kill back mangroves along the central Florida coasts.

High nutrient levels in waters supporting mangroves make these forests an important starting point for many estuarine and marine organisms. Mangroves also are important in stabilizing marine sediments and shoreline soils. Retaining mangrove systems near human developments should be encouraged to maintain this natural sea-land buffer zone.

Birds associated with mangrove include most wading birds—HERONS, EGRETS, IBISES, SPOONBILLS, and STORKS—as well as CLAPPER RAILS, BROWN PELICANS, CORMORANTS, and, in winter, several species of DUCKS and SHOREBIRDS. In summer, the MANGROVE CUCKOO, GRAY KINGBIRD, BLACK-WHISKERED VIREO, and PRAIRIE WARBLER breed in mangroves.

Wet Prairies and Freshwater Marshes

Wet prairies and freshwater marshes are treeless expanses of herbaceous (nonwoody) vegetation. They are unusual in requiring both the regular influence of changing water levels and fire to maintain their unique structure and species composition. Marshes and wet prairies include a number of varieties such as the much reduced but still extensive saw grass everglades of south Florida to highly variable cattail marshes throughout the state. Other types include pickerel weed ponds, alligator flag and duck potato marshes, and needle rush, maidencane, and sedge grass prairies. The exclusion of fire or a permanent drop in water level allows the invasion of woody species such as persimmon and wax myrtle. Good examples of a variety of these vegetation types can be found in Payne's Prairie State Preserve near Gainesville.

Highly fertile soils are often associated with these habitat types, and abundant invertebrate populations may support a number of wildlife species from crayfish and leopard frogs to Sandhill Cranes and round-tailed muskrats. Like other wetland habitats, wet prairies and freshwater marshes are threatened by drainage and agricultural expansion. Typical bird species found here include most of the long-legged waders—HERONS, EGRETS, IBISES, STORKS—as well as DUCKS, LIMPKINS, SNAIL KITES, RED-SHOULDERED HAWKS, SANDHILL CRANES and ANHINGAS.

Dry Prairie

Much of the grassland and cattle pasture surrounding the north and west sides of Lake Okeechobee today was once an extensive band of dry prairies. Commonly found between pine flatwoods or other wooded habitats and permanently wet sites, dry prairies depend upon fire to maintain their simple treeless structure. Saw palmetto often dominates a blanket of wiregrass and broomsedge, while gallberry, fetterbush, and wax myrtle are occasionally abundant.

A number of bird species including the BURROWING OWL, CRESTED CARACARA, and FLORIDA GRASSHOPPER SPARROW find their greatest abundance in this habitat type. These are populations of birds native to the prairie region of the western U.S. This prairie once extended around the edge of the Gulf of Mexico when sea level was much lower during glacial times. Hence, these "Western" species, now isolated by distance and time, are considered "relict" populations. The conversion of dry prairie vegetation to improved pasture or citrus groves may threaten the existence of a number of wildlife species.

Sand Pine Scrub

One of the better known and more widely distributed habitats in Florida is sand pine scrub, which occurs abundantly in the Ocala National Forest of central Florida. White, nutrient-poor sandy soils usually support a thick canopy made up entirely of sand pine. Understory plants (i.e., plants living under the sand pine canopy) include several scrub oaks, scrub hickory, saw palmetto, rosemary, staggerbush, and scrub holly. Unlike most Florida pine communities, fires are infrequent yet still essential in maintaining the structure and species composition typical of the habitat. Although the infrequent fires burn hot and devastate standing vegetation, this prepares the site for vigorous reproduction which ultimately returns to a sand pine dominated community. The Scrub Jay is a Florida specialty typical of the early successional stages of sand pine scrub. Other birds found here include a variety of WOODPECKERS, WHITE-EYED VIREOS, GNATCATCHERS, WRENS, and PINE WARBLERS. During spring and fall a number of migrant WARBLERS and other SONGBIRDS travel through scrub habitats.

Longleaf Pine/Turkey Oak Sandhill

Florida's sandhill vegetation, like many upland vegetation communities, is much reduced in its present statewide distribution. The well-drained soils and often scenic landscapes have made these habitats a prime target for development. Like sand pine scrub vegetation, sandhills depend upon fire to maintain their structure and species composition. Sandhill fires occur more frequently, however, and the structure of vegetation reflects this increased disturbance. The dominant species, longleaf pine and turkey oak, are thick-barked trees that can withstand ground fires occurring once every four or five years. Other species such as bluejack oak, post oak, wiregrass, and gopher apple also are adapted to withstand the influence of periodic burning. In sandhills where burning still occurs on a regular basis, vegetation is patchy and the understory is typically open and easily walked through. The burrows of gopher tortoises and pocket gophers are often conspicuous, and may also provide shelter from heat, cold, and fire for numerous other sandhill residents such as diamond-back rattlesnakes, opossums, indigo snakes, and gopher frogs. Tufted Titmice, Carolina Chickadees, Screech Owls, Mourning Doves, Bachman's Sparrows, and a number of other songbirds reside in sandhills.

Mesic Hammocks

Mixed broadleaf forests or mesic (moist, but not wet or flooded) hammocks exhibit the highest diversity and most complex structure of any vegetation community in Florida. Fire is much less an influence in this high-moisture habitat, resulting in the dominance of fire-intolerant trees such as southern magnolia, laurel oak, swamp chestnut oak, basswood, musclewood, and flowering dogwood. Vines and epiphytes such as resurrection fern and green fly orchid also may be conspicuous. A few coniferous species are typical in some areas and may include Atlantic white cedar, red cedar, loblolly pine, and spruce pine.

An important characteristic of hardwood-dominated hammocks is an abundance of hollow trees and limbs. Cavities caused by decay of old branches, lightning, and wind damage provide nesting and roosting habitat for a variety of wildlife species from flying squirrels to Carolina Chickadees and Barred Owls.

Mesic hammocks include live oak/cabbage palm/red cedar forests in coastal, island, and lake margin situations. Plant species diversity is typically lower here than in mixed broadleaf forests. A unique hardwood community is the tropical hammock of south Florida. The Caribbean influence in this extreme southeastern extension of the North American continent is evident in the predominance of a variety of tropical plant species. Trees such as wild tamarind, poisonwood, pigeon plum, Spanish stopper, mahogany, gumbo limbo, and strangler fig create a landscape more typical of the tropics. Warmer temperatures also allow a profusion of tree-blanketing orchids and bromeliads (air plants). The colorful and variable tree snail, *Ligulus*, is an eye-catching jewel in these verdant jungles. Unfortunately, the vast majority of tropical communities has disappeared in south Florida. Expanding urbanization, increasingly intensive agriculture, and rampant plant- and snail-collecting have taken their toll on the distribution and diversity of these Florida habitats.

Bird species to be expected in mesic hammocks include BLUE JAY, TUFTED TITMOUSE, RED-BELLIED WOODPECKER, DOWNY WOODPECKER, BLUE-GRAY GNATCATCHER, CAROLINA CHICKADEE, and RED-EYED VIREO. Typical species in subtropical hammocks include WHITE-CROWNED PIGEON, MANGROVE CUCKOO, BLACK-WHISKERED VIREO, AND NORTHERN CARDINAL.

Mixed Pine/Hardwood Forests

In Florida, many typically northern plant species find their southern range limit in the high clay soils of northwest Florida. Higher levels of soil moisture and nutrients combine with a cooler climate to permit trees such as American beech, Southern magnolia, mockernut hickory, tulip poplar, and a variety of oak species to thrive. A well-developed understory is usually present and may include musclewood, dogwood, redbud, and several azalea species. Shortleaf pine, spruce pine, and loblolly pine occur throughout this habitat type in varying amounts.

The feature that sets the mixed pine/hardwood community apart from all other Florida habitats is topographic diversity. While not comparable to mountainous terrain, the more rugged nature of northwest Florida provides many more life-style opportunities for plants and animals alike. The distribution of plants is particularly affected by percent slope and aspect (north- or south-facing); drier site species require higher, south-facing slopes, while species requiring greater moisture dominate lower, north-facing slopes. Typical birds include the NORTHERN CARDINAL, RED-EYED VIREO, NORTHERN PARULA, SUMMER TANAGER, INDIGO BUNTING, YELLOW-THROATED VIREO, and CHUCK-WILL'S-WIDOW.

Cypress Forests

Cypress-dominated habitats provide some of the most picturesque scenery in all of the South. The old sentinel trees festooned with Spanish moss and bromeliads seem to be an unofficial symbol of interior Florida.

Cypress swamps are not often extensive and may be interspersed within larger systems such as pine flatwoods and freshwater marshes. Subtle changes in drainage patterns and topography may explain the distribution of this plant community. Cypress is a deciduous conifer, losing its leaves in autumn. Other unique characteristics include trunk butressing and the development of "knees." Knees are knoblike extensions of the root system that protrude above the water surface. It has been suggested that these structures aid the plant in respiration and stability in waterlogged soils. Cypress can be found bordering lakes and streams, in meandering strands, or in isolated depressions where they form "domes"—a result of the older, taller trees growing in the center surrounded by younger or smaller trees. Cypress also may grow with a variety of other water-tolerant tree species. Wherever it occurs, though, naturally growing cypress is a sure sign of at least poorly drained if not frequently flooded sites.

Most of the large cypress trees in Florida were logged out during the last century. The disappearance of these often hollow giants meant the disappearance of denning and feeding habitat for a number of swamp-dwelling species including the black bear, and the now extinct Carolina Parakeet and Ivory-billed Woodpecker. Today, expect to see Barred Owls, Swallow-tailed Kites, Prothonotary Warblers, Wood Ducks, and White-eyed Vireos among other songbirds.

Hardwood Swamps

With the exception of the Fakahatchee strand in Collier County, Florida's hardwood swamps are only found north of Lake Okeechobee. The deciduous trees characteristic of this habitat are restricted to lake margins and river basins that experience floods or other significant water level fluctuations. Hardwood swamps contain some of the tallest and largest diameter trees (on the average) of any forested landscape in Florida. Other characteristics include a high tree density, a very open understory, and fewer tree species than occur in other hardwood habitats. Some of the typical tree species include bald cypress, cabbage palm, water oak, red maple, Florida elm, sweet bay, loblolly bay, red bay, and sweetgum. Swamp tupelo, another common swamp tree, may develop an above-ground convoluted root system that resembles the knees of cypress and may also aid the tree in gas exchange and stability.

The Fakahatchee strand, east of Naples, represents an extensive south Florida example of hardwood swamp. The tropical influence in this habitat is evident in trees festooned with epiphytic bromeliads, ferns, and a myriad of Caribbean and South American orchids. Scattered pond apple sloughs in this swamp system are home to the spectacular and bizarre leafless ghost orchid and also are part of the last stronghold of the endangered Florida panther.

The annual fluctuations in water level permit the existence of these intriguing plant communities. Rising and falling water levels are essential in maintaining soil nutrients and oxygen levels to which these plants are adapted. Channelization and drainage operations pose a serious threat to swamp vegetation and associated wildlife. Typical bird species include Pileated Woodpeckers, Wood Ducks, Blue-gray Gnatcatchers, White Ibis, Yellow-throated Warblers, and Carolina Wrens.

Pine Flatwoods

Half of Florida is virtually covered with pine flatwoods. And, to be expected in such a vast area, much variation occurs within this habitat type. Flatwoods are characterized by relatively level sandy soils underlain by an impermeable layer (hardpan) that maintains a "perched" water table during the rainy season. Flatwoods may be dominated by pond pine, longleaf pine, or most commonly today, slash pine. Pond and longleaf pine flatwoods probably accounted for most of this extensive habitat type before the advent of modern timber practices. With the recognition that slash pine provided higher economic returns in planted situations, most of the other pine flatwoods were converted to this species.

Fire played an important role in the original distribution of these three pine species. Longleaf is most fire-tolerant, prefers drier flatwoods, and was probably the most abundant of the three. Pond pine tolerates wet conditions best, and is least fire-tolerant, yet needs fire to open its cones. Slash pine is intermediate between the other two species and was probably restricted to swamp margins and sites intermediate in drainage characteristics. The south Florida variety of slash pine is commonly found in extensive open flatwoods south of Lake Okeechobee. Here, the understory shrub species are commonly of tropical origin.

Naturally occurring summer fires kept pine flatwoods appearing rather open and parklike. Scattered understory species include saw palmetto, gallberry, low bush blueberry, wax myrtle, runner oak, and fetterbush. Cypress-gum swamps, bayheads, and titi swamps (in north Florida) are often interspersed within the extensive flatwoods landscape. Intensively managed sites tend to have dense tree canopies and poorly developed understories. As a consequence, the value to wildlife is much reduced in many commercial pine flatwoods today. Good examples of old-fashioned (natural) flatwoods can still be found in the Apalachicola and Osceola National Forests. Management of pine flatwoods for shorter rotation harvests has reduced considerably the habitat for the endangered Red-cockaded Woodpecker. The decline in numbers of older pines infected with heart-rot has reduced the availability of nest sites to the point that the RED-COCKADED WOODPECKER now is in serious trouble throughout its range. Other species commonly found in pine flatwoods are RUFOUS-SIDED TOWHEE, BACHMAN'S SPARROW, BROWN-HEADED NUTHATCH, CAROLINA WREN, NORTHERN CARDINAL, PINE WARBLER, RED-BELLIED WOOD-PECKER, and GREAT HORNED OWL. The variety and number of bird species depend on the openness of the flatwoods and presence or absence of hardwood trees and shrubs in the understory.

Urban Environments

Florida's growing cities and suburbs are making significant impacts on the state's birdlife. Nearly 8000 new residents move to Florida each week with most locating primarily near Orlando, Tampa, and Miami. Over half of Florida's population soon will be located in these large urban centers.

To the naturalist, the most obvious impact of urban sprawl is the loss of natural plant and animal communities. This is especially true in coastal counties that will experience nearly 80% of Florida's growth and will be home for nearly 80% of the state's human population. Most native birds cannot survive in these highly altered, asphalt and concrete environments.

It seems incredible, then, that some of the most interesting bird watching can be enjoyed in megalopolized Florida. South Florida's large urban areas have become home for nearly 30 species of breeding exotic (nonnative) birds. Numerous other exotic species, though they may not yet breed in south Florida, survive as the result of the warm climate and food obtained at feeders and from introduced fruit-producing plants. Most of these birds are released cage birds or escapees from private bird collections and wildlife exhibits.

In the less altered and more vegetated suburbs, a number of native species—NORTHERN MOCKINGBIRD, BLUE JAY, NORTHERN CARDINAL,

MOURNING DOVE, and COMMON GRACKLE—do quite well. This becomes apparent in winter when a variety of migrants and residents make regular use of backyard feeders.

Few generalizations can be made about Florida's urban birdlife because these areas are influenced by variation in climate, vegetation, rainfall, and urban characteristics such as architecture, human population size, landscaping (greenspace), and building density. Many urban birds, however, share one characteristic: they are habitat generalists capable of tolerating or taking advantage of a wide variety of habitats and food. In most cases this also includes a tolerance if not dependence upon people. For example, MOCKINGBIRDS, MOURNING DOVES, BLUE JAYS, CARDINALS, and CAROLINA WRENS occur both in wild areas and in close proximity to people, while ROCK DOVES (feral pigeons), EUROPEAN STARLINGS, HOUSE SPARROWS, and BUDGERIGARS are exotics largely dependent upon humans and man-made structures for food and nesting sites. Birds such as Bald Eagles, Wild Turkeys, Red-cockaded Woodpeckers, Prothonotary Warblers, and many other species all are essentially wilderness species and are not expected to live or nest close to human developments. The preservation of many of Florida's unique native bird species is in no small part related to the control of urban sprawl.

In addition to the species already mentioned above, numerous other species occur in our cities where trees, shrubs, and lawns abound. Some of these are the AMERICAN ROBIN, NORTHERN FLICKER, RED-BELLIED WOODPECKER, EASTERN SCREECH-OWL, TUFTED TITMOUSE, CAROLINA CHICKADEE, and BROWN THRASHER.

Agricultural Environments

Agriculture is another intensive land use that has had significant impacts on Florida's birdlife. Our warm climate has permitted the establishment of a diverse array of crops most of which are destined for produce departments in northern supermarkets. Beef production on extensive cattle ranches is also an important Florida industry. These land uses have damaging impacts on many Florida birds but at the same time have created new habitats for others.

Our once extensive scrublands have been much reduced due to the spread of the citrus industry. Muck farms, major producers of winter vegetables in central and south Florida, have eliminated large tracts of productive wetlands. Other large farming operations have eliminated tropical hammocks in south Florida and other forest lands throughout the state. Improved pasture associated with cattle ranching is a dominant land use in parts of central and south Florida and has been created by draining and clearing large forests and prairies.

Florida's agricultural areas are similar in having greatly reduced plant diversity (i.e., reduced number of species). Indeed, many of these land uses can be considered as monocultures. Habitats composed of or dominated by a single cultivated plant species are usually unproductive wildlife habitats. Because of this, citrus groves are seldom visited by bird watchers even though a few MOCKINGBIRDS or CATTLE EGRETS may make regular visits there. On the other hand, where crop lands are seasonally flooded and then drained, spectacular gatherings of migrant SHOREBIRDS and resident WATERFOWL occur. Fertile soils and fluctuating water levels stimulate the growth and increase of aquatic invertebrates such as snails, worms, and copepods. The muckland farming areas around Lake Apopka in central Florida and Lake Okeechobee in south Florida are good examples of this phenomenon.

Finally, some habitats associated with phosphate mining in north and central Florida are extremely attractive to many birds. Nearly 200 species of birds have been found in or around these highly altered mined lands. Large freshwater impoundments, spoil piles, sand dunes, and willow swamps are characteristic of phosphate mines and provide nesting and feeding habitat for a variety of residents and migrants. A number of unusual birds, primarily WATERFOWL, have turned up in these unnatural landscapes. Unfortunately, many of these attractive habitats are only temporary while the losses of natural habitats are permanent. Old mines reclaimed to pasture or housing subdivisions are unsatisfactory replacements for the lost habitats where many of our native species evolved.

As Florida becomes more important in producing agricultural products, we will need to become increasingly diligent in preserving the state's unique birdlife. A balance in land uses must be reached to ensure a high quality of life that includes healthy, natural bird communities for Florida's future generations.

FLORIDA'S BIRDS

Order Gaviiformes: Loons

These are large-bodied water birds with webbed front toes and straight pointed bills. Their legs are inserted far back on the body, making them excellent surface divers and underwater swimmers, but making it difficult to walk on land.

Family Gaviidae: Loons

Red-throated Loon *(Gavia stellata)* L 17"

Jan	Feb	Mar	Apr	May	June	July	Aug	Sep	Oct	Nov	Dec

This rare wintering loon is smaller (24-27 inches) than the Common Loon (28-36 inches), with a thinner, slightly upturned bill, and in winter plumage it shows a more defined line between the dark head and white of face and neck. It generally inhabits inlets along the Atlantic and Gulf coasts off the northern half of the state between November and April. Its diet consists primarily of fish.

Common Loon *(Gavia immer)* p. 96

Floridians seldom see this large diving bird in its distinctive black and white breeding plumage nor hear its distinctive call of the summer north woods. Wintering Common Loons have a light-colored, heavy, sharply pointed bill, are white underneath and drab gray-brown above. In Florida, Common Loons chiefly inhabit the Atlantic Ocean and Gulf of Mexico, but also large bays and lagoons. Rarely are more than one or two seen at a time. They are less commonly seen on inland lakes and ponds. A nighttime migrant, the Common Loon rarely is seen flying but occasionally may alight on land after mistaking slick pavement for water. In such cases, the loon is helpless without human assistance. Because their feet are located so far back on their bodies, loons and grebes cannot walk on land, or take flight from land, but require a water surface to become airborne. In January and February when loons molt their flight feathers they are unable to fly.

Generally, Common Loons reside in Florida from November through March and occasionally into May when, rarely, a bird may be seen in full breeding plumage. Foods consist chiefly of small fish, but invertebrates and other aquatic life also are taken.

Order Podicipediformes: Grebes

Small diving birds with lobed toes, pointed bills, and legs placed far back on the body.

Family Podicipedidae: Grebes

Pied-billed Grebe *(Podilymbus podiceps)* p. 96

Other names: Didapper

This resident of Florida's freshwater lakes and ponds is one of our most widespread water birds. In breeding plumage, Pied-billed Grebes sport a white bill with a central, vertical black band and a black chin and throat. This contrasts with an overall drab brown-gray plumage outside of the breeding season. Three to 10 light-brown eggs are laid in a floating nest. Pied-bills occasionally utter an unusual chortling call that has a ventriloqual quality. This bird may be seen floating buoyantly, swimming partly submerged, or actively diving and resurfacing while feeding on aquatic invertebrates and small fish. In Florida it has a long breeding season that extends from March to December. Pied-bills become much more numerous in winter with an influx of northern migrants.

Horned Grebe *(Podiceps auritus)* p. 96

Horned Grebes can be found in very small numbers along the Gulf coast, in protected bays and inlets of the east coast, and occasionally on large inland lakes and ponds from October through April. This small grebe has a rather drab winter plumage that is white below and gray-brown above. A good field mark is a white cheek patch that extends behind the head. It shows more white and has a more slender bill than does the Pied-billed Grebe.

Order Pelicaniformes: Boobies, Pelicans, Cormorants, Anhingas

Large fish-eating birds with short legs and large wings. All members have all four toes joined in a web.

Family Phaethontidae: Tropicbirds

White-tailed Tropicbird *(Phaethon lepturus)* p. 98

Other names: Yellow-billed Tropicbird, Bos'un Bird, Longtail

Considered one of Florida's most spectacular specialties, the White-tailed Tropicbird is seldom seen anywhere else in North America. This graceful relative of the pelican nests nearby in the Bahamas. Occasionally swept to south Florida waters following tropical storms, White-tailed Tropicbirds are seen with relative regularity from April to June only in the Dry Tortugas (Ft. Jefferson National Monument), which can be accessed by boat or float plane. Tropicbirds seem to frequent the old military garrison in the early morning, providing an eye-catching contrast to the Civil War–era brick fort. This tropicbird is mostly white with a yellow bill, black eye stripe, black primary feathers, black streaking on the back, and a white tail with two long streaming tail feathers. Immature birds lack the long tail feathers. A similar species, the Red-billed Tropicbird (*Phaethon aethereus*), is rarely seen along Florida's east coast. It can be told from the White-tailed by its red bill, all black primaries and mottled back in adult plumages. Tropicbirds feed on marine invertebrates and fish.

Family Sulidae: Boobies and Gannets

Masked Booby *(Sula dactylatra)*   p. 98
Other names: Atlantic Blue-faced Booby

At first glance the Masked Booby can be mistaken for the closely related Northern Gannet. But yellowish bill and feet, and black tail, secondaries, and facial mask set this large seabird apart. Immatures are whiter underneath than are gannets or Brown Boobies while having similar brown upperparts. Nesting colonies of Masked Boobies are as near as the West Indies, but the Masked Booby occurs regularly in Florida only in the Dry Tortugas where it can be seen loafing on shifting sand bars and buoys. One pair of Masked Boobies attempted nesting (unsuccessfully) on Middle Key near Ft. Jefferson in 1984, and a pair successfully raised a young bird on Hospital Key in 1988, a first for North America. The nest is simply a scrape where one or two eggs are laid usually during spring. Like its relatives, the Masked Booby feeds mostly on fish.

Brown Booby *(Sula leucogaster)*   p. 98
Other names: White-bellied Booby

According to John James Audubon, the Brown Booby once nested in the Dry Tortugas. Although no longer breeding in Florida, Brown Boobies still can be seen in spring and summer in the vicinity of these distant islands. They occasionally are seen along Florida's east coast and in the Gulf of Mexico far from shore where they like to perch on buoys and channel markers. Brown boobies are dark brown above with contrasting white underbelly and wing linings. Immatures have light brown underparts. This bird's feeding methods are similar to those of the Northern Gannet, relying on fish taken from dives.

Northern Gannet *(Morus bassanus)*   p. 98
The Northern Gannet is an impressive winter visitor from its northern breeding grounds. These large white seabirds have wingspans reaching 6 feet and can be observed from shore skimming wave tops and making spectacular dives for fish. Adult wingtips and elegant facial highlights are black and the head is washed with a creamy buff. Immature gannets are mostly gray-brown; the second-year birds display increasing amounts of white on wings and head. Gannets nest in huge colonies, but are seen individually or in small groups most often offshore along Florida's east coast and occasionally off the Gulf coast from December to April or May.

Family Pelecanidae: Pelicans

American White Pelican *(Pelecanus erythrorhynchos)*   **p. 96**

With a wingspread of nearly 3 meters (10 feet), distinctive black wingtips and white plumage, the American White Pelican is one of Florida's most spectacular winter visitors. It is seen occasionally in north Florida freshwater lakes and coastal areas, but is more common in central and south Florida localities such as lakes of the upper St. Johns River, Merritt Island National Wildlife Refuge, Lake Okeechobee, and Florida Bay. In fall and spring huge migrating flocks may be seen circling high overhead along the Gulf coast. The White Pelican is a cooperative feeder, forming groups on the water surface and "herding" fish into a concentrated mass. Finding refuge from their north central U.S. and central Canada breeding grounds, White Pelicans are regularly seen in Florida from December to March. In recent years, numbers of nonbreeding birds have remained on some lakes and marshes during summer months.

Brown Pelican *(Pelecanus occidentalis)*   **p. 96**

The Brown Pelican is, perhaps, Florida's most distinctive and widely recognized bird. Captured in photographs, paintings, sculpture, and poetry (not to mention fisherman's lines), its image shows up everywhere from license plates to bank lobbies. Brown Pelicans dive, from 20- to 30-feet heights, for fish, and can be seen flying to and from feeding grounds in loose V-formations. Breeding pairs build bulky, flimsy-looking nests where usually 3 white eggs are laid. Colonies, most often on coastal mangrove islands, usually contain several hundred birds. In the past as many as 3000 pairs nested on Pelican Island in the Indian River opposite Sebastian. Four plumages are typically seen including the drab first-year juvenile plumage: dark above with white underparts; second-year plumage: dark breast and belly, with head and neck a dull brown; breeding adult: dark body feathers, dark redddish-brown on sides and back of neck, and white and yellow on the top of the head; and post-nuptial adult: white feathers replace the rich brown neck feathers of courting birds. Adults are silent; only young of the year make any sounds. Brown Pelicans are common along all of Florida's coastline and have not suffered the insecticide-related population declines experienced in other southeastern states and California. In recent years a few birds have been seen using central Florida phosphate mines.

Family Phalacrocoracidae: Cormorants

Double-crested Cormorant *(Phalacrocorax auritus)*   **p. 100**

Other names: Shag, Nigger-Goose

Florida supports a resident, breeding population of Doubled-crested Cormorants and, in winter, numerous cormorants from northern climes. This large, heavy-bodied relative of the pelican is an inhabitant of large bodies of open water, both fresh and salt, where it procures its diet of fish. Double-crested Cormorants are dark overall with an orange throat patch. First-year birds appear tawny underneath and dark brown above. Cormorants often swim with neck and head above water but can be told from Anhingas by their heavier, hooked bills. Three to 4 powder-blue to whitish eggs are laid in a flimsy stick nest often in the company of hundreds of other nesting cormorants and herons. Colonies appear in stands of cypress, mangrove, Australian pine, or other large trees along the coast as well as in the interior. Large colonies also occur in some phosphate mine impoundments where dead trees remain standing. Nesting may occur year-round but is concentrated from March through August. A larger species, the Great Cormorant (*Phalacrocorax carbo*), is occasionally seen during winter near east coast inlets. It is told from the similar Double-crested Cormorant by its heavier bill, larger size, yellow throat patch and the bright white belly of the immature.

Family Anhingidae: Anhingas

Anhinga *(Anhinga anhinga)*   p. 100
Other names: Snakebird, Water Turkey, Darter

The Anhinga symbolizes the mysterious, Spanish moss-draped interior wetlands of the deep South and Florida. As if standing sentinel over swampland haunts, these graceful birds perch with wings outspread over tannin-stained waters. Because their feather structure is designed to become waterlogged to facilitate diving and movement under water, Anhingas must spread their wings to dry when they emerge from the water. They skewer their fish prey with sharp, needlelike bills. The head and neck of the male is black, females exhibit a tan neck, while immatures appear mostly brown. The primary nesting season is March to June when 3 to 6 white to light bluish eggs are laid in the company of other nesting Anhingas, herons, or ibises. Equally at home in water and air the Anhinga is an extremely strong flier, and is often seen soaring vulturelike high over lakes and swamps. The extremely long neck and turkeylike tail distinguish this bird in flight.

Family Fregatidae: Frigatebirds

Magnificent Frigatebird *(Fregata magnificens)*   p. 98
Other names: Man-o'-war Bird, Hurricane Bird

Frigatebirds are distinctive coastal residents with huge wingspans (7.5 feet) and deeply forked tails. These elegant scavengers glean food scraps from the water's surface or harass other seabirds to give up their catch (even known to rob the baskets of South American fishermen). Primarily an inhabitant of tropical seas, the only known breeding sites in North America occur in mangroves, on Florida's Marquesas Keys and on Bush and Long Keys in the Dry Tortugas. Magnificent Frigatebirds seldom are seen inland, unless blown by storms, but show up regularly along both coasts of Florida's mainland. Adult males are completely black with a bright red inflatable throat pouch. Females also are black with a white breast patch, while juvenile birds possess white heads and underparts. Breeding pairs lay one egg per nesting cycle, and young may not fledge until 6 months old. In Florida, Magnificent Frigatebirds are considered threatened in part because of their few nesting sites and because the Marquesas colony lies along the edge of a U.S. Navy gunnery range, making them susceptible to disturbance or destruction from misplaced ordnance.

Order Ciconiiformes: Bitterns, Herons, Ibises, Storks
Long-legged and usually long-necked wading birds.

Family Ardeidae: Bitterns and Herons

American Bittern *(Botaurus lentiginosus)*   p. 106
Other names: Stake Driver, Thunder Pump, Sun-gazer, Indian Hen
The American Bittern is a casual nester in Florida becoming noticeably more abundant during winter after northern birds arrive. An inhabitant of freshwater and saltwater marshes, this large bittern uses its concealing plumage and behavior to stay hidden in tall marsh grass. Shades of tawny-brown above, dark-tipped wings, creamy below with brown flecking, black stripe below each eye, greenish legs, and a habit of standing erect with head pointed upward combine to create an effective camouflage for this secretive marsh bird. A deep resonant voice *(oonk-a-lunk)* resembling a variety of hydraulic machines gave rise to some of this bird's local names. Nests are usually flattened tangles of marsh grass in which about 4 eggs are laid during spring and summer. Food items include frogs, fish, and a variety of invertebrates.

Least Bittern *(Ixobrychus exilis)*   p. 106
Our smallest heron, the Least Bittern is a denizen of Florida's freshwater and saltwater marshes and mangrove swamps. It also is our only heron in which the sexes have noticeably different plumages. Mostly brown above and light below, males exhibit greenish-black top of head, tail, and back. In females the back and wings are mostly a rusty-brown. Immatures appear browner overall, and more streaked below. A low, monotonous, ventriloqual *cluck* is often the only evidence of this secretive bird's presence. Least Bitterns are so inconspicuous that little is known of their life history. Apparently preferring freshwater marshes for breeding, they construct nests of twigs or marsh grass placed over water, usually in cattails. About 4 eggs are laid during spring or summer, and the young leave the nest in 6 to 10 days. Food consists of frogs, fish, insects, and other invertebrates. Wherever clumps of cattails occur on Florida lakes, whether in urban centers or in open country, one may expect to find this species.

Great Blue Heron *(Ardea herodias)*   p. 102
Other names: Blue Crane, Poor Joe, Ward's Heron, Pond Scoggin, Gray Gaulin, Arsnicker, Great White Heron
The Great Blue Heron is one of Florida's most widely distributed and easily observed species in this family of long-legged waders. It also is a heron that readily loses its fear of man and may be seen in wetlands along busy highways as well as in suburban backyards. Florida birds are somewhat paler than their northern relatives, and a white color phase or "morph," is common in south Florida throughout the Keys. Formerly it was considered a separate species, the Great White Heron—and it may again enjoy this status in the future. The large size of this heron, around 50 inches tall, distinguishes it from all others. Adult birds are blue-gray, with yellow bill, white head, black stripe above each eye, and neck streaked with black. Immature birds have black crowns, and appear less resplendent than adults. White morphs possess large yellow bills and yellow legs. Occasionally a dark-bodied heron with a

white head and neck—a "hybrid" form—may be seen in the Keys. Great blues usually nest in trees, and may form large, single-species colonies. Less commonly, they may nest as single pairs. The breeding season may last from November through July or August, and up to 4 light blue eggs are laid in a large, loosely-constructed stick nest. Food is obtained by "still-hunting" and includes many fish as well as frogs, lizards, snakes, small mammals, and occasionally, other birds. Foraging occurs at night, especially under bright moonlight, as well as during the day.

Great Egret *(Casmerodius albus)* p. 102
> Other names: American Egret, Common Egret, White Crane, Long-white, Plume Bird

This white heron is a methodical, stalking hunter, seeking its prey in shallow wetlands such as salt marshes and shallow lake margins. Great Egrets stand about 40 inches tall, with long black legs and yellow bill. Breeding birds possess striking green flesh parts around the eyes, and long flowing plumes, called aigrettes. Great Egrets usually nest with large numbers of other wading birds in thick swamps dominated by low bushes and/or large trees and on mangrove-covered coastal islands. The breeding season extends from January through June when 3 to 4 light blue eggs usually are laid in a shallow stick nest. Early in this century, the Great Egret was hunted nearly to extinction to supply the high-fashion millinery trade with this bird's elegant plumes. Through intensive conservation efforts, and a fortunate change in fashions, this stately bird is once again abundant and widespread in Florida. Now the chief threat to this species, and all other wading birds, is continued drainage of wetlands.

Snowy Egret *(Egretta thula)* p. 102
> Other names: Snowy Heron, Little Plume Bird, Little Snowy, Short White

The Snowy Egret is another of Florida's stately white herons that was nearly wiped out at the turn of the century. The prominent head, neck, and back plumes of breeding adults made it a prime target for plume hunters. Like its larger cousin, the Great Egret, the Snowy has made a remarkable comeback from drastically low numbers. All-white plumage, black legs with yellow feet, black bill, and yellow around the eyes distinguish this active wader. It is about one-half the size of the Great Egret. Snowy Egrets stride quickly through shallow wetlands while in pursuit of frogs, fish, worms, shrimp, crayfish, aquatic insects, and even small snakes. Snowies nest in multi-species colonies located in shrub-covered wetlands or islands in lakes and coastal lagoons. Nesting begins in March or April and continues until August. Two to 5 light blue eggs are laid in a loosely constructed stick nest.

Little Blue Heron *(Egretta caerulea)* p. 104
> Other names: Calico Crane, Blue Crane

This medium-sized heron is widely distributed in Florida and utilizes a variety of nesting and feeding habitats. Although many nesting colonies may occur on saltwater sites, Little Blues seem to prefer fresh water for feeding. Foods consist of small fish, frogs, and invertebrates obtained by slow stalking. Adults are slate-blue overall, the head appearing somewhat darker.

Breeding individuals develop long back plumes, purplish feathers, and plumes on the head, black legs, and cobalt bill with black tip. Little Blues are unusual in exhibiting white plumage in juvenile birds and a calico blue-and-white pattern during their first winter as blue feathers replace white feathers. All nonbreeding birds have lime-green to blue-green legs. Little Blue Herons nest throughout Florida between late February and August in single species or mixed colonies. Usually, 3 light blue eggs are laid on a stick platform. Infrequently, calico birds are seen as breeding individuals. The general population trend of this interesting species is downward. While certainly related to wetlands losses, some have speculated that competition with Cattle Egrets for nest sites also may contribute to this decline.

Tricolored Heron *(Egretta tricolor)* p. 104
Other names: Louisiana Heron, Blue Crane

This medium-sized heron is still abundant through much of peninsular Florida. However, as with other herons, Tricoloreds have declined due to wetlands habitat loss. White underparts contrast with dark dorsal plumage in adults and immatures. Adults have bluish head, neck and wings, maroon at base of neck, and buff feathers on lower back. Immature birds exhibit rufous-brown patches on wings and on sides and back of neck. Primarily a bird of salt marshes and estuaries, the Tricolored Heron is most abundant coastally in the peninsula; however, it occurs in inland freshwater marshes also. Tricolored Herons use a variety of methods from "still hunting" to rapidly running to procure their primarily fish diet. A shallow platform nest is placed in a mangrove or other dense-growing aquatic shrub. Blue eggs, usually 3 or 4, are laid between late February and July.

Reddish Egret *(Egretta rufescens)* p. 104
Apparently still suffering the effects of century-past plume hunting, the Reddish Egret is Florida's least common heron. The rate of recovery following protection has been much slower than for other species. Primarily a Gulf coast bird, Reddish Egrets nest from Florida Bay north to Tampa Bay. In the mid-1970s nesting Reddish Egrets were found near Vero Beach in the Indian River and Merritt Island National Wildlife Refuge, both east coast locations. Often associated with mangroves, this colorful heron is strictly a coastal species. Nonbreeding individuals have been seen as far north as Fernandina Beach on the east coast and St. Marks National Wildlife Refuge on the Gulf. Appearing either in all-white plumage or blue-gray with reddish-brown head and neck, both phases have similar soft part (skin) coloration. Breeding adults develop flowing back plumes, a maned appearance on head and neck, bright pink bill with black tip, purple around eyes, and cobalt legs. Immature dark phase birds are gray-brown overall without the two-toned bill. Reddish Egrets are extremely active feeders, using spread wings and rapid steps to secure their marine prey. Breeding can occur from December in south Florida through June at northern locations. Red mangrove appears to be a favored nest site, where 2 to 5 eggs are laid on a loosely constructed platform of sticks.

Cattle Egret *(Bubulcus ibis)* p. 102

Other names: Buff-backed Heron, Cowbird

The Cattle Egret represents an amazing feat in avian natural history. Originally an Old World species, often associated with large ungulates on the East African plains, the Cattle Egret now is perhaps the most common heron in Florida. Apparently reaching South America on its own in the 1930s, breeding individuals were found in Florida in 1953. The Cattle Egret now occupies most of the Western Hemisphere and continues its range expansion. A relatively short-legged heron, the Cattle Egret appears white most of the year. During courtship, adult birds lose the yellowish coloration on bill and dark legs and acquire orange to red flesh parts and red irises. Buff feathers on the back, head, and chest complete the courtship color changes. The breeding season lasts throughout the spring when these birds are found in the company of other native colonial nesting herons. Cattle Egrets frequently are observed near livestock and farm equipment waiting for grazing animals or tractors to flush insects. These highly social herons even have been observed perched on the backs of cattle, horses, and deer. They also forage along roadside swales. Food items include grasshoppers, flies, butterflies, caterpillars, damselflies, spiders, frogs, lizards, snakes, and small rodents. Only occasionally do Cattle Egrets feed in or near water, although they prefer to nest in shrubs or trees over water, or on tree-covered islands surrounded by water. Usually 4 light blue eggs are laid in a stick nest.

Green-backed Heron *(Butorides striatus)* p. 104

Other names: Green Heron, Skeow, Shietpoke, Little Green Heron

The Green-backed is a small, cryptically colored heron. Normally seen perched in a frozen repose near a pond or stream edge, these birds prefer the seclusion of a wooded canopy. Adults have a greenish-black crown, and white undersides that are streaked with brown. The upper wing surfaces, tail, and back appear slate-gray. Immatures are browner overall with heavy brown streaking on white undersides. Flesh parts are grayish-yellow, except during breeding, when males exhibit bright orange legs. Green-backed Herons are typically solitary birds, but may nest in large colonies with other Green-backed Herons and, occasionally, in mixed species colonies. Three to 4 pale blue eggs are laid in a frail stick platform between March and June. Primarily a predator of small fish, Greenbacks also take crustaceans, mollusks, and a variety of insects. Some Green-backed Herons have learned to fish with bait, dropping pieces of bread and insects in water to attract minnows. An explosive *skeow* call is given when disturbed.

Black-crowned Night-Heron *(Nycticorax nycticorax)* p. 106

Other names: Quock, Indian Pullet

This aptly named medium-sized heron is widely distributed throughout the U.S. as well as in Florida. Solid black crown and back, gray on sides of neck and wings, white undersides, and short yellowish legs distinguish the Black-crowned Night-Heron. Immatures are brown above with tawny-streaked undersides, and are told from Yellow-crowned Night-Herons by yellow eyes, longer, narrower bill, and shorter legs. Black-crowned Night-Herons frequent shrub-bordered lakes and stream margins in search of fish, amphibians, crustaceans, snakes, and insects, as well as small birds and mammals. Occasionally they will eat nestlings of other heron species in the colony. In flight, these nocturnal herons utter a deep-pitched *quawk*, which gave rise to a local name. In Florida, Blackcrowns often are found nesting in multi-species heron colonies throughout the state. Nesting can begin as early as December in south Florida and last until June or July in the north. Two to 5 pale blue eggs are laid in a bulky nest of sticks.

Yellow-crowned Night-Heron *(Nyctanassa violacea)*   p. 106

Other names: Crab-eater, Crabier, Grosbec, Gauldin, Arsenicker, Quock, Indian Pullet, Skwok.

Longer-legged than their black-crowned relative, Yellow-crowned Night-Herons also are less nocturnal than our other night-heron. Adults are gray above and below, and the black head is crowned with white and marked with white cheek patches. During the breeding season a brilliant yellow patch highlights the forehead. Immature birds resemble young Black-crowned Night-Herons, but have longer legs, shorter and thicker bills, and orange eyes. Yellowcrowns can be found in a variety of habitats from coastal mangroves (e.g., Tampa Bay) to interior hardwood swamps (e.g., Osceola National Forest). Food is primarily crustaceans such as fiddler crabs and crayfish, although a variety of other wetland prey is taken. Yellow-crowned Night-Herons may nest singly, with other Yellowcrowns, or in large mixed-species colonies. Nest sites range from mangrove to Australian pines and live oaks. Loosely constructed stick nests may be found with 3 to 4 pale blue eggs from March through June.

Family Threskiornithidae: Ibises and Spoonbills

White Ibis *(Eudocimus albus)*   p. 108

Other names: White Curlew, Brown Curlew, Spanish Curlew, Stone Curlew, Chokoloskee Chicken, Florida Curlew

Although distributed throughout the state, the White Ibis is characteristic of south Florida's wild wetlands. Striking white plumage, black wingtips, and bright red flesh parts distinguish adults. Females are somewhat smaller and have shorter, less down-curved bills. Immatures are mostly brown above with white underparts. White Ibises nest in large colonies throughout the state from March through May. Well-constructed stick nests usually contain 3 to 4 white or light green eggs splotched with brown, tan, and purple. Interbreeding with Scarlet Ibises, introduced in Greynold's Park, Miami, from South America in the 1960s, has resulted in pink-colored hybrids. Such individuals have been seen infrequently as far north as Gainesville. White Ibises may be seen singly or in large impressive flocks on their way to or from feeding areas. Preferred habitats are freshwater marshes, shallow lakes, and estuaries, where crayfish, aquatic insects, grasshoppers, crabs, grass shrimp, and small snakes are consumed. The Florida population of this species has experienced drastic declines and fluctuations since the early 1900s, but the White Ibis is probably still the most abundant wading bird south of Lake Okeechobee. Human development and disturbance are apparently responsible for the White Ibis's decline.

Glossy Ibis *(Plegadis falcinellus)* p. 108

Other names: Black Curlew, Bronze Curlew

Until recently, the Glossy Ibis was never an abundant Florida resident. Over the last half of this century, this ibis has greatly increased its range, which now extends throughout Florida, through coastal Louisiana, and on the east coast to Maine. The long, decurved bill distinguishes this bird as an ibis. Appearing mostly dark overall, in good light Glossies exhibit a reddish plumage with a green and purple iridescence. Immature birds appear browner especially on head and neck. Glossy Ibises nest in large colonies with other wading birds. Colonies have been found in wooded wetlands from the Everglades through north Florida. Spring and summer constitute the breeding season when 3 or 4 eggs are laid in a stick platform nest. Glossy Ibises seem to prefer fresh water, where crayfish are an important food. Other foods include fish, snakes, grasshoppers, and other insects.

Roseate Spoonbill *(Ajaia ajaja)* p. 108

Other names: Pink Curlew, Pink

An unmistakable bird of south Florida's mangroves and freshwater estuaries, the Roseate Spoonbill is on the increase. Nearly extirpated by the middle of this century, Spoonbills now nest in several large Florida Bay colonies and recently have returned as breeding species to Tampa Bay and Merritt Island. The light pink wings and backs of immature birds deepen gradually over three years when adults take on a much brighter pink, highlighted by an orange tail, bright red rump, shoulders, and chest patch, and black skin on sides and back of neck. The broad, flattened bill is distinctive in all ages. Spoonbills build deep, well-constructed stick nests usually in association with heron and ibis colonies located in mangroves. In Florida Bay 3 eggs are usually laid during November or December. Farther northward breeding occurs in April. Feeding is accomplished by moving the bill side to side underwater or through shallow mud in search of small fish, insects, or crustaceans. Although population trends of this attractive wader are up, feeding habitat for spoonbills is being lost at an increasing rate. The survival of this species depends upon maintaining its shallow feeding grounds.

Family Ciconiidae: Storks

Wood Stork *(Mycteria americana)* p. 108

Other names: Flinthead, Gourdhead, Ironhead, Gannet, Preacher, Spanish Buzzard, Wood Ibis

The Wood Stork is an inhabitant of some of Florida's most pristine swamplands, often nesting in the thousands. A large, white-bodied wader, the Wood Stork exhibits a black tail, black on wingtips and trailing edges, black legs with pink feet, and a dark, featherless head capped with a lighter horny plate. Immatures have a more completely feathered neck and yellowish bill. Wood Storks are much reduced in numbers, totalling less than 20% of their 1930s population of 75,000, and are now on federal and state endangered lists. Degradation of nesting and feeding habitat certainly has contributed to this decline, yet Wood Stork colonies are still scattered widely throughout Florida. The largest colonies are in south Florida, at National Audubon's Corkscrew Swamp Sanctuary, and Everglades National Park. Wood Storks require concentrations of fish in shallow water where they "grope-feed" with bill partly open until prey contact is made. High water or extended droughts in feeding areas may reduce nesting success. Two to 4 white eggs are laid in bulky stick nests in cypress trees or mangroves from November in the south to April or May in north Florida.

Order Phoenicopteriformes: Flamingos
Large waders with long legs and bent bills.

Family Phoenicopteridae: Flamingos

Greater Flamingo (Phoenicopterus ruber) p. 108
Perhaps one of the world's most elegant animals, flamingos primarily are associated with the tropics. Apparently once common in extreme south Florida and occasionally north to Tampa Bay and Indian River, Greater Flamingos are no more than accidental today. Most individuals observed in the Miami area are the result of escaped zoo animals, although birds visiting in Florida Bay may be wild birds from the Bahamas. Except for black primaries and bill tip, Greater Flamingos are entirely pink. Extremely long legs and neck, extended in flight, further characterize this bird. This species may have once nested in the Everglades, but no evidence supports this belief. Most observations were of birds present in winter. Unfortunately, no confirmed evidence of eggs, young, or their unusually constructed raised nests of mud and muck now exists in Florida except in captive flocks. Food consists primarily of small shellfish.

Order Anseriformes: Swans, Geese, Ducks
Waterbirds with short legs, webbed front toes, and a naillike hook at the tip of the bill.

Family Anatidae: Swans, Geese, Ducks

Fulvous Whistling-Duck (Dendrocygna bicolor) p. 110
Other names: Fulvous Tree Duck, Mexican Squealer
Despite its name, the Fulvous Whistling-Duck is probably a closer relative to swans and geese than to typical ducks. Considered an accidental through the middle of this century, this duck is now an established breeder in south Florida. Long legs which extend beyond the black tail in flight, long neck, rufous-brown undersides, black back barred with brown, white band on rump, and black wings distinguish this species. A high-pitched whistle may be given in flight. This bird is most evident in and around agricultural land in central and south Florida. The expansion of large-scale vegetable farms where they find abundant food may explain the establishment of Fulvous Whistling-Ducks in Florida. A similar species, the Black-bellied Whistling-Duck (Dendrocygna autumnalis), has recently been found breeding in south Florida, possibly the result of escaped birds. Several large flocks have wintered near Sarasota in recent years. Red-orange bill, pink feet, brown back, and large white wing patches separate this whistling-duck from the Fulvous.

Tundra Swan *(Cygnus columbianus)* p. 100
Other names: Whistling Swan

One of the largest winter visitors to Florida is the Arctic-nesting Tundra Swan. These graceful white birds with black bills are seen only rarely in north Florida wetlands feeding on submerged plants and animals. Immature birds appear buff-gray overall. Their occurrence in Florida may be expected from November through March. Foods consist of a variety of grains, seeds, tubers, and invertebrates. A similar bird, the Mute Swan *(Cygnus olor)*, native to the Old World, is becoming increasingly common in residential areas. It is not yet established as a feral breeding species in Florida. The Mute Swan differs from the Tundra Swan in having a bright orange bill with a black knob at its base. Wings may be held in an arch over the back.

Snow Goose *(Chen caerulescens)* p. 100
Other names: Blue Goose

This large goose appears in two color phases: an all-white phase with black primaries, and a dark, or blue phase with a white head. The bill of adults is pink, the grayish (white phase) or brown (dark phase) immatures have a black bill. It is an uncommon wintering bird, chiefly in north Florida, most often seen at St. Marks National Wildlife Refuge, but several occasionally winter in south Florida. Food is primarily vegetation.

Brant *(Branta bernicla)* L 17″

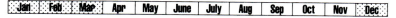

Jan	Feb	Mar	Apr	May	June	July	Aug	Sep	Oct	Nov	Dec

This small dark goose is a rare visitor to Florida, with only one or two sightings each winter in recent years. It may show up anywhere in the state. Its head, neck, and upper breast are black, with small white streaks on each side of the throat. Wings and back are dark brown and underparts are gray, fading to white on the belly and under the tail. White upper and under tail coverts hide a black tail. Its diet consists primarily of aquatic vegetation.

Canada Goose *(Branta canadensis)* p. 100
With flocks numbering over 30,000 birds, Canada Geese were one of Florida's most conspicuous wintering waterbirds. An expanding midwestern corn and grain belt has "short-stopped" these southward migrants, eliminating the need to travel to the unfrozen south. Nonetheless, Canada Geese still are regularly observed in north Florida, albeit in greatly reduced numbers. Efforts to establish a nonmigratory flock have been unsuccessful, although some nesting occurs. The large size, white cheek patches, black head and neck, and grayish bodies make the Canada Goose unmistakable. They are seen irregularly during winter in north Florida.

Muscovy Duck *(Cairina moschata)*   p. 114

Other names: Royal Duck

The wild form of this widely distributed exotic occurs in Central and South America. About the size of a large domesticated Mallard, Moscovies are commonly seen in urban parks where they can be quite prolific. Nests often are made in root tangles at the bases of trees, under yard shrubbery, and sometimes on condominium balconies. Trees also provide night roosts. A wide variety of color patterns are encountered in Florida, ranging from all white to a dark, lustrous green-black (similar to the wild form), with intermediate pied forms. Large patches of bumpy flesh encircle the eyes and base of the bill, especially in males. This large, aggressive duck is considered a pest by many. It is reputed to harbor diseases and parasites that may adversely affect native waterfowl in common habitats. The continued release and encouragement of this exotic should be discouraged.

Wood Duck *(Aix sponsa)*   p. 110

Other names: Summer Duck, Woodie, Squealer, Swamp Duck, Acorn Duck

A characteristic bird of Florida's wooded wetlands, the Wood Duck once was on the verge of extinction due to over-hunting. With stricter hunting regulations, Wood Ducks today are found wherever large tracts of swamp-lands and adjacent woodlands provide adequate cavities for nest sites and acorns, their principal fall food. Certainly our most colorful duck, males exhibit iridescent back and head plumage, red eye and base of bill, tan sides, white throat, and white-spotted, maroon chest. Both sexes exhibit head crests. Females are less resplendent with grayish plumage above, white undersides, white eye ring and eye line, and a light blue speculum (wing patch). During fall, Wood Ducks may form large flocks in areas with abundant food. Shallow, flooded oak woods are favored feeding grounds. Florida's breeding population of Woodies is resident and nonmigratory but interacts with a large number of northern Wood Ducks during fall and winter. The nest cavity may be located in a tree far from water. The female lays up to 20 eggs, one each day until her clutch is complete, then incubates 30 days. Within a day after hatching, she leaves the cavity and calls the nestlings from the ground, and they come tumbling out, dropping many feet to the ground, unhurt, and follow their mother to the nearest pond or river. Wood Ducks readily use man-made nest boxes and will even nest in highly urbanized locations, as long as both lakes and trees are abundant nearby.

Green-winged Teal *(Anas crecca)*   p. 110

Other names: Greenwing, Common Teal

One of many migrant ducks, the Green-winged Teal is a common visitor after early fall, with 4000-5000 birds overwintering in Florida. Greenwings migrate in large flocks usually at night. This is our smallest dabbling duck. Males exhibit russet head and broad green eye stripe; back and sides are vermiculated gray, and a white stripe divides flanks and chest. Females are mottled brown, with a black line through the eye. In both sexes a green speculum is visible in flight. Greenwings are fond of shallow fresh water and often may be seen feeding on exposed mudflats where small seeds of marsh vegetation are eaten. Flooded pastures and prairies also are used by foraging birds.

American Black Duck *(Anas rubripes)* p. 110
Other names: Black Mallard, Red Leg

Resembling the hen Mallard in size and coloration, Black Ducks are somewhat darker, exhibit a contrast between buff-colored head and darker body, and lack a white border on speculum and tail feathers. Once a common wintering bird in Florida's freshwater and coastal marshes, Black Ducks are seen infrequently today. Small groups and individuals can be seen occasionally from early October to April throughout north Florida. They are much less common in central and south Florida. Black Ducks are habitat generalists and have a diverse diet. Important foods include a variety of wetlands grasses and sedges as well as snails, insects, and mussels.

Mottled Duck *(Anas fulvigula)* p. 110
Other names: Florida Duck, Summer Mallard, Summer Duck

The Mottled Duck is a year-round resident through most of peninsular Florida. Both sexes exhibit fuscous-brown plumage which is lighter than the Black Duck yet darker than the hen Mallard. Females have dull orange bills flecked with black, while males have bright yellow bills with a black spot at the base. The speculum is blue, often with a greenish cast. Primarily associated with freshwater and brackish marshes, more than half of Florida's Mottled Duck population occurs in Charlotte, Glades, Hendry, and Lee counties. A large population also occurs in the St. Johns River marshes and Merritt Island National Wildlife Refuge in Brevard County. Nests are constructed near water in dense grass and/or in the cover of dense shrubs. In agricultural lands, nests even have been found in tomato fields. Most nesting activity occurs between early March and mid-April but may extend into September when about 10 eggs are laid. Food habits vary geographically but Mottled Ducks primarily are vegetarian. Animal foods such as insects and snails account for one-third of the diet in summer. Mottled Ducks are an important game species in Florida with over 13,000 harvested each year.

Mallard *(Anas platyrhynchos)* p. 110
Other names: Greenhead (drake), Gray Mallard (hen), Susie (hen)

Because of the drake's brilliant coloration and its popularity as a domestic, Mallards are probably the most widely recognized duck. Males have a metallic green head with white collar, yellow bill, chestnut breast, and curled tail feathers. Females are a lighter brown color than Mottled Ducks and have an orange bill marked with black. Both sexes exhibit a metallic blue speculum bordered front and back with white. Mallards are the most vocal of our ducks and are heard frequently during fall when other species are silent. Mallards are fairly common winter visitors from late September to early March in north Florida, where they can be seen feeding ("tipping up") in shallow fresh water. Aquatic vegetation makes up the bulk of its food. Although not a significant part of the waterfowl harvest in Florida, Mallards are considered an important game duck in North America. True wild Mallards do not breed in Florida. The breeding Mallards, chiefly seen on urban lakes and ponds, are of semi-domesticated stock, and some now breed in the wild.

Northern Pintail *(Anas acuta)* p. 110

Other names: Sprig, Sprigtail, Spike, Spiketail

A large, distinctive duck, pintails are common winter residents, especially on north Florida marshes and lakes. White on chest extending up the side of the neck, vermiculated gray body, chocolate-brown head, and long central tail feathers distinguish the male. Females are mottled brown with bluish bill and long tail (although shorter than the males'). Both sexes have relatively long, slender necks and exhibit a greenish speculum bordered with white. Some birds pass through Florida on their way to Cuba and the Caribbean in winter, but some winter residents can be seen here from mid-October to late March. Large ponds, freshwater marshes, and grain fields seem attractive to this handsome duck. A variety of vegetation including rice, panicum grasses, and sedges is eaten by Northern Pintails.

Blue-winged Teal *(Anas discors)* p. 112

Other names: Bluewing, Summer Teal, White-faced Teal

The Blue-winged Teal is our most abundant and widely distributed winter duck, arriving as early as late July and August, and remaining until April or May. This small duck is a regular although uncommon breeder in Florida, preferring shallow lakes and ponds and freshwater marshes for feeding and nesting activities. The breeding male has a gray head with a prominent white crescent in front of each eye. Through most of the fall, however, males resemble females, which are a mottled brown overall. Both sexes exhibit a green speculum (brighter in the male), and a large, light blue wing patch. Hen Bluewings occasionally may be heard "quacking" like Mallards. Foods include a variety of insects, seeds, and other vegetation.

Northern Shoveler *(Anas clypeata)* p. 112

Other names: Spoonbill, Spoon-billed Wigeon

The large, spatulate bill is the most diagnostic feature of this wintering marsh bird. Males exhibit a green head, black bill, white chest, and brown sides. Females resemble Blue-winged Teal hens but are considerably larger, and possess the spatulate bill. Northern Shovelers arrive in Florida during late September and may remain through April. Large flocks may be encountered throughout the state, feeding with other dabblers in deep or shallow freshwater lakes and marshes. Shovelers feed on surface plankton, small clams, aquatic insects, and a variety of aquatic vegetation.

Gadwall *(Anas strepera)* p. 112

Other names: Gray Duck, Gray Mallard

The Gadwall is a rather nondescript medium-sized duck that occurs in modest numbers throughout north and central Florida during winter. Males have light gray vermiculated sides, gray mottled chest, white belly, and brown head and back. Females are mottled brown above, with buff head and neck and white underparts. Both sexes have a white speculum (smaller in the female), and show a white patch of inner secondaries while swimming or at rest. Gadwalls usually arrive in Florida during late October and remain through early March, when they may be observed on large freshwater impoundments, lakes, and marshes. Their predominantly vegetable diet consists of stems of pondweeds as well as filamentous algae and other succulent plant growth.

American Wigeon *(Anas americana)*   **p. 112**
Other names: Baldpate, Gray Duck

A distinctive white crown and metallic green eye stripe sets the male American Wigeon apart from other waterfowl species. The female has a grayish head and a brown mottled body. In flight a white wing patch is evident in front of a black/green speculum in the male and a dark speculum in the female. Many thousands of Wigeons winter each year throughout Florida. Migrants arrive here in early October and may remain until mid-April. These handsome ducks may be seen in coastal estuaries and interior lakes or ponds feeding on leaves and stems of succulent vegetation. Occasionally Wigeons are observed robbing Coots, Redheads, and other diving ducks of their food. Vegetation accounts for over 90% of their fare. One of the best places to see this species close-up is Wakulla Springs State Park, south of Tallahassee. Each winter one or more Eurasian Wigeons *(Anas penelope)* occur in Florida, usually in a flock of American Wigeons. The male has gray sides and back, a rusty red head, and a cream-colored hood stripe. The female is very similar to American Wigeon females but may exhibit a rusty head.

Canvasback *(Aythya valisineria)*   **p. 112**
Other names: Can

One of our handsomest ducks, the Canvasback is distinguished from Redheads by its "ski slope" head and bill, and white back and flanks. In the male, chestnut head and neck are sharply demarcated from black chest, with sides and back a light gray (shows white from a distance). Females exhibit similar proportions but have brown heads and buff-gray backs and sides. Canvasbacks are not abundant throughout Florida but can be seen regularly in small flocks from early November to early March on large Florida lakes and estuaries such as Tampa Bay and St. Marks National Wildlife Refuge. Their numbers have declined considerably during this century due, in part, to a decline in their major food, wild celery. While vegetation accounts for at least 80% of the diet; animal foods such as mollusks and aquatic insects also are eaten.

Redhead *(Aythya americana)*   **p. 112**
Other names: Pochard

A large diving duck, the Redhead is similar to the Canvasback in overall coloration. The male's bluish bill has a white-bordered black tip, and the back and flanks are grayish (in contrast to the white back and sides of the Canvasback). Like Canvasbacks, Redheads have declined in the last 30 years, but Florida remains an important wintering ground. From early November to early March, these birds can be seen in large numbers along the east coast, especially Merritt Island, and on the Gulf coast from Apalachicola Bay to Tampa Bay. Redheads are expert divers but also may be seen "tipping up" to feed in shallow water. Plants such as shoalgrass, coontail, and pondweeds account for about 90% of its diet.

Ring-necked Duck (*Aythya collaris*)   p. 114

Other names: Ringbill, Ring-billed Duck, Blackjack, Blackhead

The Ring-necked Duck is one of Florida's most abundant wintering waterfowl and a very rare breeder. Although found frequently on salt water, Ring-necks seem to prefer inland fresh water such as Lake Okeechobee and even phosphate mine settling impoundments, and are often the most abundant duck on urban lakes and ponds. These medium-sized divers arrive in late October and may remain into early April, feeding in flocks on a variety of seeds, snails, clams, and aquatic insects. Although a brown necklace on breeding males is detectable at very close range, the first two alternate names probably are more descriptive for this bird. A gray bill ending with terminal bands of white and black are visible even from a distance. The purplish-black head is slightly peaked, and a white triangle in front of the wings and a black back distinguish it from the Lesser Scaup. Females are mostly brown, with dark crown, white eye ring, eye stripe, and facial mottling.

Lesser Scaup (*Aythya affinis*)   p. 114

Other names: Bluebill, Bullhead, Raft Duck, Little Bluebill, Blackhead

Similar in size and color to the Ring-necked Duck, Lesser Scaup males have a purplish "peaked" head, grayish-blue bill, and light gray back. Females are mostly brown but exhibit a distinct white facial crescent between bill and eye. Over 250,000 scaup winter throughout Florida using many types of open water from small lakes in urban settings to the Indian River Lagoon, Tampa Bay, and Lake Okeechobee where very large flocks are common. Lesser Scaups arrive here in late October and may linger through April. Occasionally, this species breeds in Florida. Lesser Scaup feed in relatively deep water (10-25 ft.), primarily on aquatic invertebrates such as clams, snails, crabs, shrimp, and a variety of insects. The Greater Scaup (*Aythya marila*) is very similar to but much less common than the Lesser Scaup. Fewer than 10% of all scaup harvested by hunters in Florida are Greaters. A larger bird, the Greater Scaup exhibits a smoothly rounded, greenish-black head. Females are similar to Lesser Scaup but have larger bills and may have darker heads. Feeding habits are similar. In flight, (or whenever wings are outstretched), the Lesser shows a distinct white stripe on the secondary feathers only, while this stripe on the Greater extends well out onto the primaries.

Oldsquaw (*Clangula hyemalis*)   p. 116

Other names: Long-tailed Duck, Sea Pintail, Cockertail, Coween Kakawi, Oldwife

This distinctive white sea duck is highlighted with dark on chest, cheeks, and back. Males exhibit a long upturned tail plume. Considered a rare winter visitor in Florida, an Oldsquaw may be seen occasionally along both coasts. Recently, inland-freshwater sightings have become more common in north-central Florida. Food, obtained by diving, consists of mollusks, shrimp, crustaceans, insects, seaweed, and small fishes.

Black Scoter *(Melanitta nigra)* p. 116
Other names: American Scoter, Common Scoter, Coot, Black Coot, Sea Coot, Black Duck
Primarily a bird of cold coastal waters, the Black Scoter is occasionally seen along the extreme north of Florida's Atlantic coast, and, in recent years, upper Gulf coast. Except for the yellow swelling at the base of the bill, males are entirely black. Females are dark gray with a light facial patch extending from the base of the bill to the throat. Mollusks form the bulk of the Black Scoter's diet.

Surf Scoter *(Melanitta perspicillata)* p. 116
Other names: Skunkhead, Coot, Sea Coot
The Surf Scoter is a regular wanderer to Florida, primarily reported along the east coast near Jacksonville and in the Gulf south of Tallahassee. They are seen infrequently inland. The male is black overall with white patches on the forehead and nape of neck. The bill is large and brightly patterned in orange, white, and black. Females are dull gray with a white patch behind the eyes and in front of and below the eye. The front white patch is more vertically oriented than in the female White-winged Scoter. As with the other scoter species, the diet is comprised chiefly of mollusks and crustaceans.

White-winged Scoter *(Melanitta fusca)* p. 116
Other names: Whitewing, Coot, Sea Coot
Our largest Scoter, the White-winged is another unusual winter visitor in Florida. White eye rings, white wing patches, and an orange bill with a basal knob distinguish the male. The dull gray female also exhibits a small white wing patch as well as white, elliptical patches in front of and behind the eyes. Because of the prominent white patches on this large sea duck, it is perhaps the easiest scoter to identify. It primarily is a bird of open salt water, and in Florida is seen very infrequently inland. White-winged Scoters feed mostly on mollusks, as well as crustaceans and insects.

Common Goldeneye *(Bucephala clangula)* p. 116
Other names: Whistler
The Common Goldeneye is a regular but uncommon winter visitor in north Florida, especially along the coasts. A black, knobby head, with a white patch in front of the eye and a black back spotted with white distinguishes the male from mergansers and the Bufflehead. Females and immatures have more rounded brown heads that contrast with mottled-gray flanks and back. A visitor from mid-December through early March, Common Goldeneyes feed by diving for crabs, crayfish, insect larvae, mollusks, seeds, and tubers.

Bufflehead *(Bucephala albeola)* p. 116
Other names: Butterball, Dipper, Spirit Duck
The Bufflehead is a small wintering duck that is most commonly encountered along the northern Gulf coast but also occurs on inland streams and lakes in peninsular Florida. Approximately 1000 spend the winter in Florida. The

male is distinguished by a metallic-green head with a large white patch extending from behind the eye to the top of the head, and white chest and flanks. Females are grayish-brown with white chest and a smaller, horizontal white patch behind the eye. Buffleheads are diving ducks, subsisting on fish, insect larvae, and plant seeds. These attractive birds may be seen from December through February.

Hooded Merganser *(Mergus cucullatus)*   p. 114
Other names: Sawbill, Fish Duck, Hairy-head

The striking black and white crest of the male Hooded Merganser is a conspicuous field mark. A white breast with a diagonal black back, white wing stripe, and tawny-vermiculated flanks further characterize the male. The female is mostly light brown with a rufous crest and dark back. In both sexes the crest can be quickly erected and relaxed. Migrants arrive in late November and may remain through April. Primarily a winter resident in Florida, Hooded Mergansers increasingly have been found nesting throughout the state. These cavity-nesters are frequent residents in Wood Duck boxes where about 10 white eggs are laid in late winter or early spring. Mixed-species clutches have been reported where Hoodeds have "dumped" eggs in Wood Duck nests. Hoodeds are inhabitants of lakes and ponds, wooded stream courses, hardwood swamps, and coastal salt marsh creeks. Small fish, crustaceans, and aquatic insects provide the bulk of their diet.

Red-breasted Merganser *(Mergus serrator)*   p. 114
Other names: Sawbill, Fish Duck, Hairy-head

Our most abundant large merganser, the Red-breasted Merganser is a common winter visitor in Florida. The green, tufted head of the male and the shaggy-headed female give this species one of its other common names. Adult males (which are rarely seen in Florida) exhibit a white throat, brown chest band, black back and gray, vermiculated flanks. Females and immatures are grayer overall with contrasting white and black showing on the folded wings. Both sexes have a long, narrow, serrated bill. Red-breasted Mergansers are particularly common along Florida's Atlantic and Gulf coasts, but are seen regularly on large inland lakes and impoundments. Migrants arrive in Florida in late October and may remain throughout winter and spring. Red-breasted Mergansers are entirely carnivorous, feeding primarily on small fish as well as shrimp and crabs. The much less abundant Common Merganser (*Mergus merganser*) is a larger duck that prefers freshwater habitats. Males are untufted with more white on the flanks, while females have a distinct contrast between the slightly tufted head and throat. Each winter one or more Common Mergansers are reported in north Florida, rarely as far south as Tampa Bay or Cape Canaveral.

Ruddy Duck *(Oxyura jamaicensis)*   p. 117
Other names: Butterball, Bull-necked Teal, Spiketail, Winetail, Sleeper, Dip-tail Diver, Fool Duck, Broadbill Dipper, Dumb Bird, Bumblebee Coot, Hardhead

The Ruddy Duck has a stout appearance, with short wings, thick neck, and an erect, fan-shaped tail. Black on top of the head, white cheeks, and rust-brown body and wings distinguish the male. Females and immatures are grayer overall with a light gray cheek patch. Florida is an important wintering location for this widely nicknamed duck. Most birds arrive in October and remain through April. Recently, however, Ruddy Ducks have been found breeding in north Florida phosphate mine impoundments and other artificial wetlands near Tampa. Ruddies may be seen on both coasts, brackish estuaries, as well as in a variety of inland freshwater habitats. Ruddy ducks primarily are vegetarians feeding on a variety of seeds, tubers, and grasses. Animal food consists of midge larvae and amphipods. A similar species, the **Masked Duck** (*Oxyura dominica*) is seen infrequently in Florida. This tropical bird exhibits white wing patches in flight, and during winter has distinct buff and dark brown stripes on the head. Breeding males have dark brown heads and reddish-brown mottled bodies. Nesting of the Masked Duck has been suspected to occur in Lake Okeechobee.

Masked Duck

Order Falconiformes: Birds of Prey
Birds of prey, usually with powerful talons and hooked bill.

Family Cathartidae: American Vultures

Black Vulture *(Coragyps atratus)*   p. 118
Other names: Black Buzzard

Black Vultures differ from Turkey Vultures in several subtle ways. Shorter wings and tail, black head, and light primaries distinguish this smaller vulture. In flight, Black Vultures hold their wings flat, flap more often than do Turkey Vultures, and their feet usually extend beyond the tail. Feeding habits are similar to those of Turkey Vultures; however Black Vultures are more aggressive around carcasses, often dominating the kill. Black Vultures are less adept at locating carrion due to their less sensitive sense of smell and often take advantage of food found by Turkey Vultures. Nesting habits also are similar to those of Turkey Vultures, but extend from January to August. A preferred nest site is often a bare patch of ground in a dense saw palmetto thicket.

Turkey Vulture *(Cathartes aura)*   p. 118
Other names: Turkey Buzzard

Turkey Vultures can scarcely be overlooked on warm summer afternoons, soaring effortlessly on thermal updrafts in search of fresh "road kills" or other carrion. There is virtually no place in Florida where this species cannot be observed. Bare red head, light primaries and secondaries when seen from underneath, relatively long tail, and wings held in a nearly flat "V" (dihedral) —all are characteristic of this most widespread of Florida's vultures. Immatures lack the red head of the adult. Turkey Vultures nest on the ground in the protection of dense vegetation, hollow log, or other cavity. The nesting season extends from March through July when usually 2 eggs are laid. During winter there is an influx of vultures from northern states. Occasionally vulture roosts containing several thousand individuals have been observed in south Florida. An extremely sensitive sense of smell allows this bird to detect rotting flesh from great distances.

Family Accipitridae: Kites, Eagles, Hawks

Osprey *(Pandion haliaetus)* p. 124
Other names: Fish Hawk

Ospreys are widely distributed in Florida due to the abundance of productive open-water habitats. A fish-catching specialist, the Osprey can be observed over many of our inland lakes and coastlines hovering at great heights (50-200 ft.) and plunging into the water feet first. At first glance these birds may be confused with the Bald Eagle but can be recognized by a black streak behind the eye, light streaking on the white belly, barring on secondaries, primaries, and tail, and crooked wings in flight. The Osprey is considered a threatened species in Florida due to concern over habitat loss and environmental contaminants. These factors were responsible for the drastic declines in Osprey populations throughout the rest of North America in the 1950s and 60s. The banning of chlorinated hydrocarbon pesticides has helped the northern population to recover. Three eggs are usually laid in large, bulky nests, built in dead or live trees near abundant food supplies. In particularly good areas, nests appear clustered, or colonial. The birds will nest readily on tall man-made platforms and other structures. The nesting season occurs from late spring through early summer. An influx of northern birds occurs in fall and early spring as birds travel to and from wintering grounds in tropical America.

American Swallow-tailed Kite *(Elanoides forficatus)* p. 120
When seen in flight, the Swallow-tailed Kite is undoubtedly one of the world's most beautiful birds. The deeply forked tail, contrasting black and white plumage, and graceful, often acrobatic flight set this bird apart from all others. In proper lighting conditions the upper wing and back reflect a metallic green-blue surface. Swallow-tails are still fairly abundant in peninsular Florida, nesting in bottomland hardwoods, or in flatwoods in tall pines or cypress trees. The nesting season extends from late March through June when 2 eggs are laid in a substantial nest placed near the top of the tree. A variety of prey from grasshoppers to lizards are deftly snatched from leaves and branches, and occasionally a snake can be seen dangling from a kite's talons as it returns to its nest. These birds reside in Florida from late February through September. The Swallow-tailed Kite is a symbol of the deep South, although it once nested as far north as Minnesota. Protection of hardwood bottomlands from development and conversion to pine plantations is essential in maintaining healthy populations of this elegant raptor.

Black-shouldered Kite *(Elanus caeruleus)* L 16"
Other names: White-tailed Kite

Jan	Feb	Mar	Apr	May	June	July	Aug	Sep	Oct	Nov	Dec

This gull-like kite has only recently (1986) returned to Florida as a breeding bird after an absence of over 80 years. Black shoulders, white underparts, and mostly white tail separate this kite from the similar Mississippi Kite. Immatures have a brown cinnamon wash on head and breast. Nests are built in tops of isolated trees in wet prairies or on dikes near marshes in south Florida. Three or 4 white eggs with brown blotches are laid in March or April. Young are usually fledged by June. The diet is primarily made up of insects; however, small mammals, birds, and reptiles also are taken and at times may compose a large part of the diet.

Snail Kite *(Rostrhamus sociabilis)*   p. 120
Other names: Everglade Kite, Snail Hawk

Although common in the neotropics, the Snail Kite's distribution in North America is restricted to the freshwater marshlands of south Florida. Drastic population declines through the 1960s resulted in the bird's endangered classification. Apparently, the population has rebounded somewhat and is in less danger of extinction today. Although large numbers may die and no production may occur during severe drought years in south Florida, high reproduction in other years compensates for these losses. Hence, the population experiences a "boom or bust" cycle. Except for the sharply hooked bill, Snail Kites look like typical raptors. Males are slate-gray, and darker on head, tail, secondaries, and primaries. Females are generally brown overall with a white/brown streaked breast. Immatures have brown eyes, adults red. All ages and sexes exhibit a squared-off tail, white at the base with a light terminal band. This bird derives its name from its exclusive prey, the apple snail *Pomacea*. Snail Kites snatch their prey on the wing, then extract the animal with hooked bill while perched. Three to 5 light blue, brown-spotted eggs are laid in a loosely constructed nest in emergent marsh vegetation. Nesting usually occurs from February to June but may extend from January through November. Wetlands drainage and the exotic weed, water hyacinth, must be controlled to ensure the continued existence of this unusual Florida specialty.

Mississippi Kite *(Ictinia mississippiensis)*   p. 120

The Mississippi Kite is a denizen of north Florida's moist hardwood forests. In the last 20 years it has expanded its range from a strictly panhandle distribution to one that now extends south to Gainesville and Ocala. This beautifully marked kite exhibits a light gray head and secondaries and a nearly black tail and wingtips. In flight, these birds usually appear dark overall and have been described as large swallows. Mississippi Kites are early spring nesters. After their 2 eggs hatch, adult birds become quite busy supplying insects and small vertebrates to their young. Nests are made in tall pines or hardwoods and often are located near human habitations. Mississippi Kites depart Florida during fall and return usually by April.

Bald Eagle *(Haliaeetus leucocephalus)*   **p. 118**

The Bald Eagle has experienced population declines throughout most of its range due to habitat destruction and environmental contamination. Despite the loss of many of Florida's wetlands, Bald Eagles are still abundant here, with the largest resident population in the lower 48 states. Adult birds are unmistakable with white head and tail visible from great distances. First- and second-year eagles appear lighter in color due to a scattering of white feathers at the base of tail, secondaries, and wing lining. Bald Eagles soar with wings held rigidly flat. Nests usually are built in tall pine trees near lakes, marshes, or coastlines. Paired eagles will use the same site year after year, adding material each season until nests become quite huge. Sometimes an alternate nest may be maintained and occasionally used not far from the primary nest tree. Two, sometimes 3 eggs are laid during late fall or winter. Young eagles are fed by both parents a varying diet dominated by fish (which are sometimes stolen from Ospreys). Large wetlands birds such as American Coots, Pied-billed Grebes, and Cattle Egrets also are eaten. Despite Florida's large eagle population, our national symbol is under continuous pressure due to habitat loss and increased human disturbance. Only concerted efforts to protect wetlands and nest sites statewide will ensure the continued existence of this magnificent bird.

Northern Harrier *(Circus cyaneus)*   **p. 118**

Other names: Marsh Hawk

Abundant avian predators during winter in Florida, the first big influx of Northern Harriers can be expected with early fall cold fronts. Usually they are seen flying close to the ground, seldom flapping, while hunting for small vertebrate prey. Immature birds and females are predominately brown; while males are mostly gray. A good field mark for both sexes is a distinctive white rump patch which can be seen from a distance. Preferred habitats are open, treeless areas that may include old fields, pastures, and marshes.

Sharp-shinned Hawk *(Accipiter striatus)*   **p. 120**

Other names: Little Blue Darter

Like its larger relative, the Sharp-shinned Hawk is a bird-eating specialist. The general appearance is that of a two-thirds-sized Cooper's Hawk, although Sharpshins have a more squared-off tail and males have less contrast between back and crown. Sharp-shinned Hawks do not nest in Florida but are common winter residents, following migrating passerine birds to and from their wintering grounds. They can be seen throughout Florida from late October through May.

Cooper's Hawk *(Accipiter cooperii)*   **p. 120**

Other names: Big Blue Darter

The Cooper's Hawk is a medium-sized raptor that preys primarily on small birds. Stout rounded wings and a relatively long tail suit this bird to a life in the forest, using its speed and maneuverability to pursue avian prey. Adult males are grayish-blue above, with a black crown, banded tail, and a lightly-barred red and white breast. Females and immatures are generally brown with white-streaked head and breast. All Cooper's Hawks exhibit a distinctly rounded tail in flight. In Florida, these hawks are restricted in the nesting season (April-July) to the northern two-thirds of the state as far south as the Lake Placid area. Three to 4 eggs are laid in a loosely constructed nest. Nest sites are found in a variety of woodlands usually 20-50 feet high in a pine or hardwood tree.

Red-shouldered Hawk *(Buteo lineatus)* p. 122
Other names: Chicken Hawk

The Red-shouldered is a common woodland hawk with a permanent, resident population throughout the mainland and Keys. Reddish-barred undersides and rufous shoulders characterize adults. A light wing "window" is visible from below in flying birds. Adults exhibit a black tail with white bands, and white highlights on dark upper plumage. Immatures are heavily streaked below and show little if any rufous coloring. A paler, smaller form is distinctive in south Florida, where these birds easily can be observed perched on signs and fence posts. Red-shouldered Hawks are inhabitants of moist hardwood forests and mixed pine/broadleaf woodlands. Their voice, a distinctive *kee-ah* (often imitated by Blue Jays), is frequently heard near their nest site, often in the crotch of a well-foliaged forest tree. Two is the usual number of eggs laid during late winter. Prey consists of small mammals, lizards, snakes, frogs, crayfish, and insects.

Broad-winged Hawk *(Buteo platypterus)* p. 122
While never an abundant breeder in Florida, the distribution of breeding Broad-winged Hawks may be less today than at the turn of the century. Slightly smaller than the Red-shouldered Hawk, the adult has broad white and black tail bands, reddish-barred belly, and dark-outlined wings. Immatures have paler tails and streaked undersides. The call is often heard while in flight, and is similar to the Eastern Wood-Pewee's call. Breeding birds are most likely to be encountered in the panhandle and south to Gainesville between March and June. Broadwings are probably seen most often during migration when large flocks navigate the coastlines. Most birds are circum-Gulf migrants, although a few remain all winter in southern Florida. Nesting and feeding habits are similar to that of the Red-shouldered Hawk.

Short-tailed Hawk *(Buteo brachyurus)* p. 122
This uncommon Florida specialty is resident from central Florida south through the peninsula. A stocky-appearing bird, the Short-tailed Hawk displays black and white banding on the tail, secondaries, and primaries, and either white or dark undersides. Immatures exhibit buffy undersides in the light phase and dark mottling in the dark phase. Short-tails utilize a variety of woodland types as long as open grasslands or marshes are adjacent. The mixed woodland-savannahs of Glades and Highlands counties and the upper St. Johns River provide good nesting and feeding habitat for this hawk. One or more pairs nest in Everglades National Park, and in winter up to 8 to 10

individuals have been seen along the road to Flamingo. The Short-tailed Hawk employs an active pursuit technique in capturing its small bird prey, especially meadowlarks and Red-winged Blackbirds. While hunting, Short-tails will often soar to great heights, which may help make this species inconspicuous. Nests are located near the tops of tall, woodland edge trees, where 2 eggs are laid in early spring.

Red-tailed Hawk *(Buteo jamaicensis)* p. 122

Perhaps our most visible and widely distributed hawk, the Redtail is also Florida's largest. A propensity to perch on power lines bordering major highways makes this raptor particularly conspicuous. When seen in flight the adult's red tail is distinctive. A brownish band across the otherwise white belly also is a good field mark. Immatures have black and dark brown tail bands and are heavily streaked below. Habitat requirements are variable although open country seems preferred for hunting. Nests containing 2 eggs can be found in late winter and are located in cabbage palms, live oaks, pines, or a variety of other trees throughout the state. The food of this large hawk consists primarily of rodents, although rabbits, snakes, and insects also are taken.

Golden Eagle *(Aquila chrysaetos)* p. 118

Primarily a bird of the western U.S., Golden Eagles are a rarity in Florida. These large raptors are similar in overall proportions to our more common Bald Eagle, but are a much darker-appearing bird. White base of tail and white underwing patches distinguish the immature bird, while a slightly barred tail is the most recognizable adult field mark. Although unusual anywhere in Florida, stragglers are probably most likely to occur in the panhandle during winter. Foods include snakes, small mammals, and occasionally carrion.

Family Falconidae: Caracaras and Falcons

Crested Caracara *(Polyborus plancus)* p. 124

Other names: Mexican Eagle, Mexican Buzzard, Audubon's Caracara

The open grassland and palmetto country to the north and west of Lake Okeechobee makes up most of the Crested Caracara's range in eastern North America. The Caracara exhibits the appearance and behavior of both the falcons and vultures. It is often seen on the ground or perched along fence lines and fence posts in south Florida pasturelands. Caracaras have long legs, black crown and crest, red facial skin, white and black banded tail with a wide, dark terminal band, and have black and white barring at the base of primaries. Immature birds appear similar, but duller overall. Scant information exists on the life history of this curious raptor. Apparently, cabbage palms are preferred nest sites, 2 to 3 eggs are laid in late winter, and adults occupy a fixed home range. Food consists of reptiles, birds, mammals, and carrion (it often is seen feeding with or harassing vultures). The spread of improved pastures and citrus groves as well as indiscriminant killing have contributed to the Caracara's decline in Florida. With only about 250 pairs remaining, it was officially listed on the federal list of threatened species in August 1987.

American Kestrel *(Falco sparvarius)*   **p. 124**
Other names: Sparrow Hawk, Killy Hawk

The Kestrel is our smallest and most colorful falcon, typically about the size of a robin. Florida is inhabited by a smaller race (*F. s. paulus*), which has been threatened by loss of cavity trees and reduced habitat availability. Both sexes and immatures exhibit vertical black streaks behind and in front of the eye. Males have slate-blue crowns and wing coverts, rusty tail with black terminal band, and rufous back. Undersides exhibit black spots on a buff background. Females are browner overall with more heavily marked back, tail, and undersides. Immatures resemble adults with more streaking below. Kestrels are found throughout Florida, usually nesting in abandoned woodpecker holes excavated in pine trees. A helpful tool for wildlife managers is the artifical nest box which these birds readily use. During spring (March-June) the female incubates 3 to 5 eggs while the male hunts for and feeds his mate. Insects make up the bulk of the diet although small mammals and reptiles frequently are taken. Florida experiences a large influx of northern Kestrels during winter. Like the Florida race, these birds often space themselves along telephone wires while hunting, but are distinguished by their larger size.

Merlin *(Falco columbarius)*   **p. 124**
Other names: Pigeon Hawk

Somewhat larger than Kestrels, Merlins are readily distinguished as falcons by their long, pointed wings. Males are blue-gray above while females are brown. White underparts are streaked with brown, and the tail has heavy black bands separated by white. These swift fliers have similar migration and wintering habits to their larger cousin the Peregrine Falcon. Behaviorally, the Merlin can be considered a miniature Peregrine. Usually, they take smaller birds, but their diet also includes small mammals and insects. Merlins are often seen along the coasts or inland in open landscapes from September through April.

Peregrine Falcon *(Falco peregrinus)*   **p. 124**
Other names: Duck Hawk

The Peregrine Falcon had a nearly worldwide distribution, but has suffered drastic population declines throughout its range. Florida represents an important wintering area, especially for the Arctic subspecies (*F. p. tundrius*). Migrant falcons can be seen in Florida after the first fall cold front and some remain all winter. Peregrine Falcons often are observed along Florida's coasts feeding on migrant shorebirds. Inland lakes and marshes, abundant with waterfowl, also attract these spectacular hunters. Peregrines take a wide variety of bird prey, specializing on wetlands species. Peregrines are the largest falcons found in Florida. Adults are slate-gray above with a distinct cheek/eye patch extending over the head. The breast is white with dark barring on the undersides. Immatures are brown above with brown streaking on breast and undersides. Pointed wings and strong, purposeful flight distinguish this spectacular bird overhead.

Order Galliformes: Gallinaceous Birds

Chickenlike birds with strong walking legs and short rounded wings.

Family Phasianidae: Turkeys and Quail

Wild Turkey *(Meleagris gallopavo)* p. 126

The Wild Turkey is our largest game bird, appearing much more slender than domesticated varieties. The mostly dark plumage occasionally exhibits colorful metallic hues in sunlight. Males are larger, have blue to pink facial skin, spurred heels, and a dark breast tuft (beard). Females and immatures are less ornate and dull in color. The Wild Turkey remains a widely distributed bird in Florida because of abundant forest cover. They have been reintroduced to many parts of their former range in the East and Midwest where adequate woodlands remain or have recovered. Wild Turkeys forage on the ground eating insects and a variety of seeds including tupelo fruits, acorns, and saw palmetto fruits. At night turkeys roost, usually in small groups, in trees. Females incubate about 10 eggs in a ground nest located at the base of a tree or in a palmetto thicket. The white eggs are laid between March and May. The characteristic gobble of the male can be heard during courtship from February through May.

Northern Bobwhite *(Colinus virginianus)* p. 126

Other names: Quail, Partridge

The call of the Northern Bobwhite is a characteristic summer sound of Florida's flatwoods, fields, and pastures. Associated primarily with agricultural land today, this diminutive game bird was common throughout Florida's once widespread longleaf pine flatwoods. It is still a popular game bird throughout the state. Two races occur in Florida, the peninsular bird exhibiting redder plumage than the northern race. White throat patch and eye stripe distinguish males, while female head plumage appears buff. All birds appear rusty with black and white highlights and lighter undersides. Ten to 15 eggs are laid in a ground nest during spring (February through June); second clutches may be attempted through July. Some nests containing more eggs may be the result of more than one females' efforts. Eggs and young often fall prey to a variety of predators including house cats, dogs, skunks, cotton rats, and opossums. Food consists primarily of a variety of grains, field seeds, and insects.

Order Gruiformes: Cranes, Rails, Limpkins

This order includes the tall long-legged cranes, the smaller coots and gallinules, and the secretive rails—most all of which are marsh inhabitants.

Family Rallidae: Rails, Gallinules, Coots

Black Rail *(Laterallus jamaicensis)* p. 128

Other names: Jamaican Crake, Little Black Crake

The Black Rail has been referred to as a "feathered mouse" due to its small size and extremely secretive habits. This is our smallest rail, about the size of a sparrow. The plumage is black with a rusty nape, white stripes underneath, a salt-and-pepper effect on the back, and a bright red eye. The Black Rail is probably much more common than its infrequent sightings indicate. During the breeding season (May-September) its distinctive call may be heard around dusk, *kick-key-do*. Black Rails apparently breed widely throughout Florida in extensive marshes, making their ground nests in a clump of grass. Six to 8 small white eggs, sprinkled with brown, are laid during summer. Food consists of insects and seeds.

Clapper Rail *(Rallus longirostris)* p. 128
Other names: Saltwater Marsh Hen, Mud Hen, Sedge Hen
   The Clapper Rail is similar in size and proportion to the King Rail. However, Clappers are duller-colored, exhibiting more gray than their fresh-water relative, and engage in a longer, less musical call. Strictly a coastal species, the Clapper Rail is a year-round resident in Florida, but northern birds migrate into north Florida marshes during winter. Nesting habits are similar to the King Rail with breeding activities extending from March to July. Foods consist of small crabs, shrimp, mollusks, and insects.

King Rail *(Rallus elegans)* p. 128
Other names: Freshwater Marsh Hen, Mud Hen
   The King Rail is a larger version of the Virginia Rail, but has less gray on the head. Its cinnamon-brown plumage is brighter than the similar Clapper Rail (which some authorities consider the same species). It is more often heard than seen. The loud, resonant notes of this primarily freshwater bird can sometimes be elicited by loud noises such as slamming car doors and hand-clapping. The King Rail is a permanent Florida resident and nests in dense marsh vegetation near the water's surface. Six to a dozen eggs are laid in late January to July. The black, downy chicks leave the nest immediately after hatching, following their parents in search of food such as aquatic insects, seeds, and succulent vegetation. Like most rails, King Rails rarely flush and prefer to escape danger on foot. Occasionally, both Clapper and King Rails may be found together in brackish water habitats.

Virginia Rail *(Rallus limicola)* p. 128
Other names: Marsh Hen
   The Virginia Rail is a common winter inhabitant of Florida's freshwater and saltwater marshes. Long legs, stout body, and slightly down-curved bill are used to advantage in muddy, inundated, and densely vegetated habitats. Rosy undersides with vertically striped (black and white) flanks, mottled brown upperparts, and short, pointed tail distinguish both sexes. Like most rails, the Virginia is a secretive bird, more often detected by its staccato notes than by sight. It is found in Florida usually from October through March. This very active feeder subsists on a variety of invertebrates as well as small fruits.

Sora *(Poranza carolina)* p. 128
Other names: Carolina Crake, Meadow Chicken, Ortolan
   This small, short-billed rail is a winter inhabitant of Florida's freshwater marshes. Although it is our most abundant rail it is more often heard than

seen. Its call, a descending staccato whistle, often can be elicited by hand-clapping near marsh borders. Soras are mostly gray, with black covering the face and throat, and vertically striped undersides. The bill and legs are yellow. Soras can be found in Florida from September through April. They feed primarily on marsh invertebrates and seeds.

Purple Gallinule *(Porphyrula martinica)* p. 130

Other names: Blue Peter, Mud Hen, Pond Chicken, Bonnet-walker

The Purple Gallinule is an extremely handsome bird of Florida's freshwater marshes and swamp borders. The adult's metallic green back and purple-blue head, neck, and undersides are unmistakable. The bill is similar to that of the Common Moorhen but has a white frontal shield. Immatures resemble young Moorhens but are more buff and lack white flanks. Extremely long toes are used to travel over floating marsh plants. The voice of the Purple Gallinule is similar to the closely related Common Moorhen. Loosely constructed nests are placed over water in marsh vegetation, usually cattails or sawgrass. Six eggs usually are laid in spring but nesting may last through summer. Purple Gallinules vacate the northern parts of Florida during winter but still are abundant in the warmer southern counties. One of the best places to see this species is Anhinga Trail in Everglades National Park. The diet consists of frogs, grasshoppers, spiders, other invertebrates, as well as a variety of marsh and aquatic vegetation.

Common Moorhen *(Gallinula chloropus)* p. 130

Other names: Common Gallinule, Florida Gallinule, Pond Chicken, Mud Hen, Pond Guinea

These very common wetland birds are not nearly as secretive as the closely related rails. Common Moorhens are widely distributed in Florida inhabiting inland freshwater lakes, ponds, canals, and marshes. These chickenlike birds can be seen scrambling through willows and cattails or swimming in open water. Adults are dark gray below and brownish above with a white lateral stripe on the flanks. The bright yellow-tipped, red bill and frontal shield are distinctive marks. Immatures are mostly gray with white flanks and lack brightly colored soft parts. Common Moorhens construct nests on floating tussocks, in cattails, or in woody vegetation such as willow and buttonbush trees. As many as a dozen eggs are laid between March and May. The precocial, black, downy young are capable of walking and swimming immediately following hatching. The voice is a variety of chickenlike clucks and noises that may be repeated monotonously. Food consists of a wide variety of marsh and aquatic vegetation, seeds, insects, and other aquatic invertebrates.

American Coot *(Fulica americana)* p. 130

Other names: Mud Hen, Pull-doo, Pond Crow, White-bill, Splatterer, Pelick

In winter the American Coot is Florida's most abundant wetland bird. Coots breed irregularly, but frequently in Florida, especially in the central lake region, but primarily are winter visitors with flocks numbering in the thousands in some areas. The general form of the American Coot is similar to that of Gallinules but it appears more ducklike on the water. The white bill and white rump contrast with the gray to black plumage. No other Florida bird has a white bill. The green legs end in widely lobed toes, which make the Coot a powerful swimmer, both above and under the surface. Nests are placed along wetland edges or on floating vegetation. Eight to 14 finely flecked buff eggs are laid in a loosely constructed nest during spring. Coots feed like grazing cattle on large mats of water hyacinth but also eat algae, aquatic insects, and a variety of other aquatic vegetation. The Caribbean Coot, *Fulica caribaea*, considered by some authorities to be a subspecies or color morph of the American Coot, is occasionally reported in Florida. It is characterized by a broader frontal shield that may be tinged with yellow.

Family Aramidae: Limpkins

Limpkin *(Aramus guarauna)* p. 126

Other names: Crying bird, Nigger Boy, Courlan

The range of this unusual species in North America is almost totally within Florida and thus it is another Sunshine State specialty. Combining character-istics of both cranes and rails, the Limpkin is a typical inhabitat of freshwater streams, swamps, and lake margins. Long, slightly down-curved bill, brown body with white flecking, buff-colored head, and long, dark olive legs distin-guish the Limpkin. Its unique call, a raucous *kurr-r-ee-ow, kurr-r-ee-ow, kr-ow, kr-ow*, is given mostly at night. The breeding season in Florida is apparently year-round and seems to depend upon food abundance. Four to 8 large eggs are laid in a nest made of matted aquatic vegetation placed near the water or up to 15 feet above in a tree. Limpkins, like Snail Kites, seem somewhat dependent upon the apple snail for food; however, a variety of other items are taken including frogs, worms, insects, crustaceans, and other mollusks. While feeding, Limpkins often twitch their tails, and walk with a limping gait. Flight is cranelike, with a slight hesitation in the upstroke.

Family Gruidae: Cranes

Sandhill Crane *(Grus canadensis)* p. 126

Other names: Whooper

The nonmigratory Florida Sandhill Crane is an inhabitant of the scattered marshes and wet prairies throughout the state. The Kissimmee Prairie and Payne's Prairie in south and north Florida, respectively, are both noted for their crane populations. Migrant cranes from the Midwest make Florida their home from late fall through winter. Adults are characterized by black legs, gray plumage (sometimes stained reddish brown), whitish cheeks and a red crown (sexes are similar). Immature birds have brown heads and necks. Nesting lasts from January through June. Large nests containing 2 eggs are located in thick patches of marsh vegetation such as pickerel weed and maidencane. Sandhills often are seen in improved pastures and open wood-lands feeding on a variety of plants and invertebrates. Their rattling, raucous call, usually given in flight, can be heard over long distances. A similar species, the Whooping Crane *(Grus americana)*, is larger than the Sandhill and nearly entirely white. Once on the verge of extinction, the Whooping Crane is now on the increase, but still extremely rare. Efforts are now underway to evaluate the potential of establishing a nonmigratory flock of Whooping Cranes in Florida.

Order Charadriiformes: Shorebirds, Gulls, Terns

This large, diverse order is made up of those species called shore-birds: plovers, sandpipers, gulls and terns—most of which have webbed front toes.

Family Charadriidae: Plovers

Black-bellied Plover *(Pluvialis squatarola)*   p. 132

Other names: Bull-head, Black-breasted Plover, Beetlehead

Black-bellied Plovers make coastal Florida their winter refuge from Arctic tundra breeding grounds. Fall migration begins in mid-July while spring migrants usually return in May. This is our largest plover and may be seen singly or with other shorebirds, feeding near the surf. Black-bellied Plovers occasionally may be seen inland along large lakeshores. A heavier bill and large black patches beneath the wings separate the Black-bellied from the Lesser Golden-Plover. While at least a few birds may be seen year-round in Florida, most are strictly winter residents. Small crabs, fish, and other marine invertebrates make up its diet.

Lesser Golden-Plover *(Pluvialis dominica)*   p. 132

Other names: American Golden Plover

The Lesser Golden-Plover is an unusual fall migrant in Florida, and even more uncommon during spring migration. These long-distance migrants usually fly non-stop from Labrador to the West Indies in fall and appear on Florida's coasts only under unusual weather conditions in spring. Lesser Golden-Plovers are only slightly smaller than the similar-appearing Black-bellied Plover and are best distinguished from their larger relative by the lack of black under the wings and a uniform gray beneath. Golden-Plovers may be seen feeding on insects and invertebrates between the high tide line and the surf, or in plowed fields.

Snowy Plover *(Charadrius alexandrinus)*   p. 132

Other names: Cuban Snowy Plover

This diminutive plover is a resident along Florida's Gulf coast. Slightly smaller and considerably paler than the Piping Plover, the Snowy Plover exhibits a dark crescent on the sides of the neck, dark legs, and a slender black bill. Immatures have gray-spotted backs. Snowy Plovers often are difficult to detect, especially when resting on beach sands with which they blend so well. Snowy Plovers nest from March through July on expansive, sandy beaches. Three eggs are usually laid in a slight depression on the open beach. Their food consists of worms, insects, and small crustaceans obtained from beaches and tidal flats. Because of extensive human disturbance on these sites, Snowy Plovers have declined and now are considered an endangered species on the Florida list. Preservation of extensive Gulf coast beaches and barrier islands will be necessary to preserve this specialized plover.

Wilson's Plover *(Charadrius wilsonia)*   p. 132

Other names: Ringneck, Thick-billed Plover

A wider single neck band, longer, heavier bill, and pinkish or flesh-colored legs distinguish the Wilson's Plover from the other "ringed" plovers. This permanent resident nests fairly commonly on both coasts. Usually 3 or 4 darkly marked, cream-colored eggs are laid in a slight depression, occasionally lined with shell fragments. Like the larger Killdeer, a Wilson's Plover will feign a broken wing upon disturbance near the nest. Nesting occurs from April through July. Foods consist of marine and beach invertebrates.

Semipalmated Plover *(Charadrius semipalmatus)* **p. 132**
Other names: Ringneck

Slightly larger than the Snowy Plover and smaller than Wilson's Plover, the Semipalmated Plover is a common winter visitor, especially on the coasts. In winter plumage the Semipalmated Plover has clear white undersides, dark brown upperparts, dark collar, dark band through the eye and yellowish legs. This small plover may be seen in great concentrations with other shorebirds on beaches and mudflats. Migrants arrive in Florida as early as July and may remain until May before returning to tundra nesting grounds. Crustaceans and other marine organisms along the coasts, and insects and other terrestrial invertebrates inland make up the diet.

Piping Plover *(Charadrius melodus)* **p. 132**
The Piping Plover is a rather nondescript, pale bird of seashore dunes and beaches. Strictly a winter visitor, this plover is white beneath, pale gray above (the color of "wet sand") with a black, incomplete neck band and yellowish legs. The flutelike call is two-noted and musical. Piping Plovers feed in a stop-and-go fashion searching beach sands and flotsam for invertebrate prey. This plover is on the federal list of threatened species.

Killdeer *(Charadrius vociferus)* **p. 132**
Other names: Killdee, Meadow Plover

The Killdeer is the familiar plover of suburbs, fields, and pastures. Our largest ringed plover, the Killdeer is a permanent resident, nesting throughout Florida. It is told from similar species by its large size, orange on upper tail, and double neck bands. Its call is a repetition of its name. Nesting occurs from March through July when 3 to 4 eggs, buff with dark markings, are laid in a simple depression. Killdeer numbers greatly increase during winter when northern migrants arrive. This conspicuous plover may be found close to human dwellings and also is fond of agricultural areas. Food consists mostly of insects and other invertebrates.

Family Haematopodidae: Oystercatchers

American Oystercatcher *(Haematopus palliatus)* **p. 130**
Other names: Mantled Oystercatcher, Brown-backed Oystercatcher

The American Oystercatcher is one of our most unmistakable shorebirds. Strictly a coastal species, this striking bird once was more abundant in Florida. Declining for many years, the American Oystercatcher seems to be maintaining relatively stable numbers on undisturbed Gulf coast beaches and islands, and on dredged material islands and shell bars along the Atlantic Intracoastal Waterway. Black head and dark brown upperparts contrast with white undersides. White at the base of the tail and white wing stripes are evident in flight. The long, heavy, red bill, yellow eyes rimmed in red, and pink legs are evident in adults. Two or 3 mottled eggs are deposited in modest nest scrapes directly on the sand between March and July. Oystercatchers are adept at snatching the soft tissues from slightly open oysters, but also feed on a variety of other mollusks, crustaceans, and other invertabrates.

Family Recurvirostridae: Stilts and Avocets

Black-necked Stilt *(Himantopus mexicanus)*   p. 130

Long, red legs are a distinctive field mark of this common inhabitant of shallow freshwater and saltwater wetlands. Black upperparts, and black, needlelike bill contrast the pure white undersides. These extremely vocal birds may nest singly or colonially, making shallow nest platforms. The large, brown-speckled, pointed eggs usually number 4 and are laid during spring and summer. Black-necked Stilts use a number of nesting sites from freshwater marshes to phosphate mine impoundments. Most stilts leave northern Florida during winter but some may remain all year south of Lake Okeechobee. Black-necked Stilts primarily feed on aquatic insects and other invertebrates.

American Avocet *(Recurvirostra americana)*   p. 130

The American Avocet primarily is a western species that regularly wanders through Florida especially in autumn and spring. Avocets appear in Florida in their paler winter plumage with cream-colored head and neck. No other shorebird exhibits such a long, upturned bill and long legs. Black upperparts with a white horizontal wing stripe contrast with light undersides. Avocets may be seen in small flocks feeding in flooded agricultural fields, marshes, and shallow ponds. They quickly sweep their bills back and forth under water and often submerge their heads and necks.

Family Scolopacidae: Sandpipers

Greater Yellowlegs *(Tringa melanoleuca)*   p. 134
Other names: Tell-tale Snipe

This active marsh and shallow lake shorebird is a common winter resident in Florida. As its name implies, this bird has long, yellow legs as well as a needlelike bill (whose length is 2 to 2.5 times the depth of the head behind the bill), white undersides barred with gray, and darker mottling above. Its voice is a clear, staccato ring, repeated 3 to 5 times. Migrants arrive in late August and may remain through May before returning to tundra breeding grounds. A variety of aquatic and terrestrial organisms are readily eaten.

Lesser Yellowlegs *(Tringa flavipes)*   p. 134
Other names: Tell-tale Snipe

Except for its smaller size, the Lesser Yellowlegs is nearly identical to the Greater Yellowlegs. These birds often may be seen together making their size differences a good field character. When seen singly or in single species flocks, Lesser Yellowlegs may be identified by a proportionally smaller bill (1.5 times the depth of the head behind the bill) and its call which is repeated only 1 to 3 times. Both birds utilize coastal as well as interior wetlands, where they feed often submerged to their bellies. The Lesser has similar food habits and migration pattern as the Greater Yellowlegs.

Solitary Sandpiper *(Tringa solitaria)* p. 136

Other names: Tip-up, Wood Sandpiper

The Solitary Sandpiper is a common migrant and wintering shorebird in Florida. As its name suggests these birds are most usually seen singly, or in very small groups. Solitary Sandpipers resemble miniature yellowlegs but with dark legs and darker upperparts. Stream banks, creeks, and edges of ponds and swamps are typical haunts of this bird. Tail bobbing is a characteristic behavior. Migrants arrive in mid-July and usually depart by mid-March. Food consists of freshwater insects, amphibians, and a variety of invertebrates.

Willet *(Catoptrophorus semipalmatus)* p. 136

Other names: Stone Curlew, Bill-willie, White-wing Curlew, Pill-willet

The Willet is a common sight on Florida's coasts, appearing quite plain when at rest or feeding, but displaying striking black and white wing patches or stripes when in flight. It is somewhat taller and stockier than a Greater Yellowlegs, with a stouter bill, blue-gray legs, and brown-streaked plumage. Willets nest in loose colonies from April to June in sparse to heavy vegetation, but sometimes on open bare ground, laying 4 large, heavily blotched eggs in a sandy or grass-lined scrape. In winter, plumage is grayer with less streaking. Northern birds swell the Florida population, while many Willets migrate through Florida to more southern wintering grounds in Central and South America. Marine invertebrates, crabs, grasshoppers, and other insects make up the diet.

Spotted Sandpiper *(Actitis macularia)* p. 136

Other names: Tip-up, Peet-weet, Teeter Snipe, Teeter Tail

Wintering Spotted Sandpipers in Florida are seen with clear white undersides instead of their bold-spotted breeding plumage which appears in late spring. Slightly smaller than the Solitary, Spotted Sandpipers constantly "teeter-totter" when walking. These common shorebirds may be seen singly or in pairs feeding on invertebrates along banks of streams, ponds, and swamp edges. In flight, the wings beat stiffly and rapidly. Migrants arrive in mid-July returning north as late as May.

Whimbrel *(Numenius phaeopus)* p. 134

Other names: Hudsonian Curlew

Smaller than the Long-billed Curlew, the Whimbrel has contrasting striping on the head, a shorter more sharply decurved bill, and mostly brown, mottled plumage. This large, common shorebird primarily is a fall and winter resident along the Atlantic and southern Gulf coasts. The Whimbrel uses its long, curved bill to probe the soft soils of marshes, mudflats, and beaches for shellfish, worms, and other marine invertebrates.

Long-billed Curlew *(Numenius americanus)* p. 134

Other names: Sickle-bill

This uncommon but regular winter resident in Florida was extremely rare early in this century. It now can be seen regularly at inlets along the northeast Atlantic coast and on some Gulf beaches probing for burrowing invertebrates with its long, down-curved bill. The unstreaked head and cinnamon wing linings are other good field characters. Long-billed Curlews occur in Florida from September to May.

Marbled Godwit *(Limosa fedoa)* p. 134

A once abundant winter resident, the Marbled Godwit is a less common Florida visitor today. It is a large shorebird with a very long, slightly upturned, two-toned bill, long legs, light brown barring beneath, and mottling above. The wing linings are a light cinnamon. The rare Black-tailed Godwit *(L. limosa)*, an Old World visitor, has a whitish belly and white wing linings. The rare Hudsonian Godwit *(L. haemastica)* is distinguished by its smaller size, black and white tail, and cinnamon undersides. The Marbled Godwit appears to prefer saltwater beaches and mud flats where it probes its long bill in search of small invertebrates and tubers. Godwits appear occasionally in late July and August on agricultural mucklands that are being drained for cultivation.

Ruddy Turnstone *(Arenaria interpres)* p. 138

Other names: Calico-back, Rock Plover, Brant Bird

This small, chunky shorebird is a common migrant and winter resident; however, a few nonbreeders remain through summer. They seem most abundant between July and April. While in Florida, Ruddy Turnstones appear brown above with a black bib and orange legs. Breeding birds develop bright, rusty back feathers and white head. Turnstones exhibit a pied (black and white) appearance in flight. Ruddy Turnstones primarily are inhabitants of coastal habitats and seem quite tolerant of humans and human acitivity. They are often seen on bridge railings, docks, and piers, feeding on fish remains. This active bird uses its slightly upturned bill to flip seaweed, shells, and other beach debris in search of invertebrate prey, hence its name "turnstone."

Red Knot *(Calidris canutus)* p. 138

Other names: Robin Snipe, Red-breasted Snipe, American Knot, Wah-quoit

The Red Knot is smaller than a dowitcher, has a short bill, lacks white tail feathers, and has rather short, greenish legs. During winter, it appears light gray with slight mottling. This gradually turns into its bright summer plumage with robinlike, rusty breast feathers. Red Knots are common migrants in fall beginning in August and spring as early as April when they are seen mostly along sandy beaches. Some birds remain through summer and, occasionally, a flock of wintering Knots is seen. The tiny shellfish, coquina, is its major food source.

Sanderling *(Calidris alba)* p. 140

Other names: Sand Snipe, Beach Bird, Whiting, Ruddy Plover, Peep

This is our most familiar coastal sandpiper. Sanderlings gather in small flocks and follow the advancing and receding surf as potential meals are exposed by wave action. In flight the Sanderling exposes a conspicuous white wing stripe and a light rump. In Florida most birds exhibit light gray plumage above, white below, and black at the bend in the wing. Sanderlings are common on the Gulf and Atlantic coasts from late summer through early spring. Food of the Sanderling is mostly marine invertebrates including the common sand flea and the shellfish, coquina.

Semipalmated Sandpiper *(Calidris pusilla)*   p. 140
Other names: Peep

The Semipalmated Sandpiper is one of the most abundant shorebirds in eastern North America. Black legs, short, stout bill, and gray back differentiate this peep from the similar Least and Western Sandpipers with which it is often found. Its most characteristic call is a low-pitched *churp*. It occurs in Florida during spring and fall migration, while a few individuals may overwinter in Florida Bay. Foods consist of marine and freshwater invertebrates found on sand and mud flats of beaches, inlets, and lakes.

Western Sandpiper *(Calidris mauri)*   p. 140
Other names: Peep

This sandpiper closely resembles the Semipalmated and Least, with which it may often be seen. The Western has a longer black bill with a slight droop at the end, and longer black legs; otherwise, in winter plumage it appears identical to the Semipalmated. In fresh breeding plumage, some of which is obtained prior to departing Florida, Westerns have bright tawny patches on the scapulars, back, and sides of the head. When together, Western Sandpipers tend to feed in deeper water than do Semipalmated Sandpipers. Western Sandpipers are abundant during winter and migration. They can be seen foraging for invertebrates on beaches and tidal flats from July through May. A few nonbreeders remain through the summer. Its call is a weak, high-pitched *peet*.

Least Sandpiper *(Calidris minutilla)*   p. 140
Other names: Peep

The Least Sandpiper is our smallest "peep" and may be abundant from July through May. It is distinguished from the other peep species chiefly by its yellowish leg color. The back is brown to gray in nonbreeding plumage. The breast is heavily streaked with brown or gray and the belly is white. In flight a narrow white wing stripe is obvious along with a black rump and tail stripe. It is easily confused with Semipalmated and Western Sandpipers with which it often associates. Its call is a high-pitched *wheet*. Least Sandpipers inhabit coastal as well as inland wetlands. They seem to prefer grassy flats at the edges of salt marshes and freshwater ponds, where they feed on insects, crustaceans, and small mollusks.

White-rumped Sandpiper *(Calidris fuscicollis)*   p. 140
Other names: Peep

This rather nondescript shorebird is a regular but not abundant spring and fall migrant in Florida. The White-rumped Sandpiper has dark legs, is gray above, white below, and has pale-gray mottling on the breast. The best field mark, however, is its clear white rump, seen when the bird flies. White-rumped Sandpipers are found along our coasts and inland and will allow a closer approach than many small shorebirds. Fall birds may be seen between July and September while spring migrants are present in Florida from May through June. Foods are mostly seeds and small aquatic invertebrates.

Pectoral Sandpiper *(Calidris melanotos)*   p. 138

Other names: Grass Snipe, Creaker

This robin-sized sandpiper is common in wet marshes, both fresh and salt, flooded fields, and heavily vegetated lake margins. Extensive floating water hyacinth mats occasionally attract large numbers of Pectorals. The streaked, dark breast contrasts with white belly. It has greenish legs and a slightly down-curved bill. Pectoral Sandpipers are most common during fall (July-November) in the newly drained mucklands around Lakes Apopka and Okeechobee, but may also be seen during spring migration. A variety of insects and invertebrates constitute its diet.

Purple Sandpiper *(Calidris maritima)*   p. 138

This small, dark shorebird is a rare, unpredictable winter visitor in Florida. Dark gray head and neck, yellow legs, and yellow base of bill are good field marks. Purple Sandpipers prefer rocky shores and may be seen on rock jetties and breakwaters anywhere along the Atlantic coast, rarely in the Gulf.

Dunlin *(Calidris alpina)*   p. 138

Other names: Red-backed Sandpiper, Sand-snipe

The rather long, slightly down-curved bill is a good field mark of this rather common winter resident. While in Florida, Dunlins usually are gray above and white below, with dark legs. Fall migrants appear in Florida during August and usually depart during May. In late spring some individuals may be seen coming into their distinctive rusty-backed, black-bellied breeding plumage. Dunlins are birds of coastal mudflats, lagoons, and beaches, but may occur inland as well. It is often seen in large flocks, and is probably our most abundant sandpiper. Foods primarily are marine and aquatic invertebrates.

Short-billed Dowitcher *(Limnodromus griseus)*   p. 136

Other names: Red-breasted Snipe

This common migrant and winter resident is found along both coasts but also may be seen regularly along freshwater lakes and marshes. Light-gray underparts, brown above, white rump and tail with dark barring, and very long bill distinguish the Short-billed Dowitcher. Individuals have been seen year-round in Florida with migrations usually peaking in mid-spring and in late summer. The Long-billed Dowitcher (*L. scolopaceus*) is very similar with a slightly longer bill. Both species have greenish-gray legs. While considered uncommon in Florida, this species' actual abundance is difficult to determine because of its close resemblence to the Shortbill. Both species obtain aquatic and marine invertebrates by probing sand and soft mud. In late spring both species have brilliant robin-redbreasts with heavy dark spotting in the neck and breast region of the Longbill, and little or no spotting on that of the Shortbill. The call of the Shortbill is a loud *tu-tu-tu*, repeated rapidly, while that of the Longbill is a high pitched *geek*, often repeated rapidly.

Common Snipe *(Gallinago gallinago)*   p. 136

Other names: Wilson's Snipe, Jack Snipe, English Snipe

The Common Snipe resembles a dowitcher with its long bill, but has heavier barring on the head, back, and neck, as well as a brown rump and orange tail. An erratic, zigzag flight when flushed is characteristic of this abundant shorebird. Snipes are marsh, wet prairie, and lake edge birds feeding on worms, insects, and other invertebrates. Migrants arrive in September and depart in April or May. This species apparently is less common in south Florida.

American Woodcock *(Scolopax minor)* p. 136
Other names: Timber Doodle

This odd-looking, cryptically colored, woodland bird sports a long bill, short legs, and high-set eyes that permit binocular vision. Florida primarily is a winter refuge for this species although Woodcocks breed regularly, but sparsely, throughout north and central Florida. Nests are small depressions on the forest floor usually containing 4 camouflaged eggs laid in February to June. The courtship flight of the male is quite spectacular. A nasal *peent* is uttered while the bird spirals upward nearly out of sight; then he plummets downward uttering a rapid chittering call before returning to his starting point. This pattern is repeated continuously over open fields or wet prairies. Food consists of worms, insects, and other invertebrates.

Family Laridae: Gulls, Terns, Skimmers

Laughing Gull *(Larus atricilla)* p. 142
Other names: Black-headed Gull

This is the largest of our black-headed gulls as well as our only nesting gull. During summer, the adult exhibits a black hood extending from the back of the head to the throat, red bill, reddish legs, and gray wings and back. The immature is dark brown above, with white rump and tail, black tail band, and dark bill and legs. The winter adult has a mottled gray head and dark bill and legs. Laughing Gulls primarily are coastal birds feeding on fish and other marine organisms. It may rob other sea birds of their prey. Nests are constructed of grass and other beach plants usually on a sandy barrier island. The nesting season peaks in late May when 3 to 4 dark colored, splotched eggs are laid.

Bonaparte's Gull *(Larus philadelphia)* p. 142
Other names: Surf Gull

This small gull is a common winter visitor along our coasts and occasionally inland. In winter plumage, the Bonaparte's Gull exhibits a white head, gray patch behind the eye, pink legs, dark bill, gray back, white tail and large white wedges at the ends of otherwise gray wings. Primaries are tipped in black. The immature has a narrow black tail band and incomplete white wedges on the wings. Bonaparte's Gulls are buoyant and ternlike in flight. Foods consist of insects, fish, snails, and other invertebrates. Migrants appear in early fall and may remain through May.

Ring-billed Gull *(Larus delawarensis)* p. 142
The Ring-billed is our most common gull in Florida. It may be seen on the coast and inland from October through May. Ring-billed Gulls are smaller than Herring Gulls, have a black band near the end of the bill, yellow legs,

and less streaking during winter than Herring Gulls. Immatures are paler overall than Herring Gulls and have a narrower, black tail band. This common gull may be seen in huge flocks near large bodies of water and on sanitary landfills. In addition, these birds seem particularly fond of shopping center parking lots, roosting on heat-retaining asphalt during cold spells. Foods consist of fish, insects, refuse, as well as vegetation such as cabbage palm seeds.

Herring Gull *(Larus argentatus)*   p. 142

The Herring Gull is perhaps the most familiar gull in North America. In Florida, this large bird is a common winter visitor especially along the coasts but also may be seen inland. Adults have light gray backs, black wingtips with white spots, pink legs and gray streaking on the head and neck. First-year birds exhibit dark tails and primaries, and mottled gray-brown upperparts; second-year birds have light gray backs, light head and rump, black-tipped pink bill, and gray-brown wings. Herring Gulls commonly feed on refuse in large garbage dumps as well as on fish, mollusks, carrion, and other debris along our coasts.

Lesser Black-backed Gull *(Larus fuscus)*   p. 142

Other names: Scandanavian Lesser Black-backed Gull

As the name suggests, Lesser Black-backed Gulls are smaller than the Greater Black-backed. Other field marks include a lighter back, yellow legs, thinner bill, and a long-winged appearance. This European visitor has been seen on both coasts of Florida with regularity in recent winters. While still uncommon, it is most likely to be found with other gulls along the Atlantic coast and around garbage dumps.

Great Black-backed Gull *(Larus marinus)*   p. 142

This aggressive, predatory bird is our largest "sea gull." In the U.S., the Great Black-backed Gull primarily is a bird of the northeast, but in recent years it has become increasingly common in winter along Florida's east and Gulf coasts. Adults are distinguished by dark black wings and back, and pink legs. First- and second-year birds have a narrower, dark tail band than other large, immature gulls. Like other gulls, the Great Black-backed eats a variety of fish, crustaceans, mollusks, birds, and beach debris.

Gull-billed Tern *(Sterna nilotica)*   p. 144

As its name suggests this tern has a stouter bill than its relatives. Gull-billed Terns also have a short, notched tail and pale upper parts. The head is black-capped in summer and white-gray in winter. Nests containing 2 to 3 tan eggs colored with black markings often are more elaborate than the nests of other terns and may contain vegetation and other debris in a shallow scrape. Nesting along both coasts and near inland freshwater lakes occurs from May through July. Gull-billed Terns commonly are seen over salt and freshwater marshes feeding on a wide variety of insects. Small fish and fiddler crabs also are eaten.

Caspian Tern *(Sterna caspia)*   p. 144

This is our largest tern, measuring even larger than the Ring-billed Gull. Nesting Caspian Terns (discovered in Florida in 1962) represent the southeastern breeding limit of the species in North America. Appearing more slender and darker underneath than the Royal Tern, Caspians have a large, blood-red bill and black crown. In winter the tip of the head appears gray or white and slightly crested. Nesting colonies are strictly coastal in Florida where spoil islands seem to be preferred. Caspian Terns feed on larger fish than their relatives do. Prey species include mullet and menhaden.

Royal Tern *(Sterna maxima)*   p. 144
Other names: Big Striker, Redbill, Cayenne Tern, Gannet Striker

These large terns are gray above, white below, have a yellow-orange bill, and a black, slightly crested cap. In winter the head is streaked with white and the crest is inconspicuous. Royal Terns nest on islands in the Banana River, Tampa Bay, Charlotte Harbor, on spoil islands near Yankeetown, and irregularly elsewhere along Florida's coasts. These colonial nesters lay one whitish egg covered with spots and blotches in an inconspicuous scrape. Nesting occurs during summer but birds are commonly seen throughout the year. Royal Terns plunge-feed, like most other terns, for a variety of small fish.

Sandwich Tern *(Sterna sandvicencis)*   p. 144
Other names: Cabot's Tern

This medium-sized tern is distinctive with a yellow-tipped black bill in all plumages. Breeding adults are black-capped with a short, shaggy crest. In winter they develop a white forehead. Sandwich Terns were a more common nester in Florida a century ago. Because of beach development and disturbance the only Florida colony is found on the Bird Islands in Nassau Sound (near Jacksonville). Usually, 2 eggs are laid in a shallow nest scrape above the high tide line during May or June in mixed colonies with Royal Terns. During winter, birds are frequently seen along both coasts usually from central to south Florida. Like most other terns, Sandwich Terns plunge for small fish.

Roseate Tern *(Sterna dougalli)*   p. 144
Roseate Terns have a black bill, are pale gray above, have a longer, more deeply forked tail and lighter wingtips than Common Terns. This medium-sized tern is uncommon as a migrant from its northeastern North American colonies but breeds regularly in the Dry Tortugas and at scattered locations through the Florida Keys. In Florida, 2 or 3 eggs are laid on the ground in shallow scrapes, on bare rock, or in beach debris. Nests are especially sensitive to storms and high tides, and in the Tortugas nesting success is generally poor. Less is known of Florida Keys colonies. Roseate Terns feed on fish close to shore.

Common Tern *(Sterna hirundo)*   p. 144
Other names: Mackerel Gull

Common Terns primarily are spring and fall migrants in Florida, with a few birds lingering through winter. Some nesting has occurred on the coast of the Florida panhandle. In winter plumage Common Terns have black on nape of neck, black flesh parts, dark wingtips, and forked tail. These birds usually migrate far offshore but occasionally may be seen coastally. Common Terns feed by diving for small fish.

Forster's Tern *(Sterna forsteri)*   p. 144

In winter plumage this abundant visitor is similar to the Common Tern but has a black mask extending behind the eye with less or no black on the nape. Some immature birds remain in Florida year-round but are most common during winter months. Forster's Terns can be seen over freshwater and saltwater marshes, inland lakes, and coastal beaches. The call is a grating *zaaap* note. Important foods are primarily insects and small fish.

Least Tern *(Sterna antillarum)*   p. 144

Other names: Sea Swallow, Kill-em Polly, Gaviota Chica, Pigeon de la Mer, Little Tern

This smallest North American tern is a familiar resident in Florida from March through September. Broad, short tail (swallowlike), black cap, white forehead, yellow bill with black tip and rapid wing beat distinguish the Least Tern. The immature is mottled above with tail more deeply forked than the adult. Historically, Least Terns nested on coastal beaches, dunes, and islands, creating shallow scrapes and laying 2 to 3 mottled eggs. Today, most nesting occurs on man-made habitats including dredged-material islands, construction sites, phosphate mines, and gravel roof tops from April through August. Their breeding range extends throughout Florida, both inland and on the coast. Least Terns feed by hovering and diving for small fish. Because of competition with humans for recreation and development space, Least Terns are considered a threatened species.

Bridled Tern *(Sterna anaethetus)*   p. 146

This seagoing tern closely resembles the Sooty Tern but is smaller, with white forehead patch extending behind the eye, and is lighter above with a light gray band separating the back and black-capped head. The Bridled Tern is a regular visitor off Florida's Atlantic coast during late summer and early fall. In 1987 two pairs nested in a colony of Roseate Terns in the Florida Keys, the first nesting record for the U.S.

Sooty Tern *(Sterna fuscata)*   p. 146

This Florida "specialty" finds its only regular U.S. breeding site in the Dry Tortugas. It is the only tern that is black above and white below. Immatures have dark heads, white-flecked upperparts, and shallowly forked tails. About 80,000 adults breed each year on Bush Key. One egg per nest is laid in a shallow scrape on open sand or under scattered shrubs during late February or early March. After the breeding season, which ends in August, Sooty Terns leave the Tortugas and become strictly pelagic (oceangoing). Sooties do not dive for fish but surface feed, capturing minnows, flying fish, squid, and other top-dwelling species.

Black Tern *(Chlidonias niger)*   p. 146

Migrating Black Terns may arrive in breeding plumage in Florida from northern nesting grounds as early as July. Black head and body, light rump, gray wings, and notched tail are distinctive. In winter, black plumage becomes mostly white with occasional black mottling. Black Terns may be seen over inland and coastal wetlands from April to June and late July to October, rarely in winter. Foods include insects and small fish.

Brown Noddy *(Anous stolidus)* p. 146

Other names: Noddy Tern, Common Noddy, Egg Bird, Booby, Lark
   In the U.S., the Brown Noddy nests only on Florida's remote Dry Tortugas. This medium-sized tern is dark brown overall with a light gray cap that fades toward the nape. Breeding begins in March and may last through summer. A single egg is laid in a nest that may be a simple stick platform or an elaborate mound of debris. Brown Noddies remain near their nesting grounds until October. Numbers of breeding birds have fluctuated greatly during the past century, but since the 1950s about 4,000 pairs have been present. Brown Noddies occasionally are scattered great distances by storms and have been observed in Florida as far away as Jacksonville. Feeding is accomplished by catching small, surface fish. **Black Noddies** *(Anous minutus)* appear most years in the nesting colony on Bush Key, although none has bred. It is almost three-fourths the size of the Brown Noddy, with darker plumage and a somewhat longer, more slender bill.

Black Skimmer *(Rynchops niger)* p. 146

Other names: Shearwater, Scissorbill, Sea-dog, Flood Gull, Razorbill
   Skimmers are unique among birds in having the lower half of the bill longer than the upper. This long-winged, ternlike bird has black upperparts, white cheeks and neck, red feet, and a red, black-tipped bill. Immatures are browner and more mottled above. Black Skimmers are found along all of the Florida coast, nesting in large colonies, often with other tern species. Four to 5 eggs are laid in a shallow scrape above the high tide line during June or July. Breeding activities may last until September. Skimmers feed by cutting the water's surface with the lower mandible and snatching their fish or shrimp prey with a quick downward snap. Several birds may be seen feeding together in this manner. Development of Florida's coastline has decreased the quantity and quality of nest sites for this unique shorebird. Spoil islands and even gravel rooftops, however, have begun to provide nest sites for Black Skimmers in Florida.

Order Columbiformes: Pigeons and Doves

Pigeonlike land birds with dense, easily shed plumage. Adults produce a milk in their crops to feed their young.

Family Columbidae

Rock Dove *(Columba livia)* p. 148

Other names: Pigeon
   This is the very familiar pigeon so common in cities, parks, farms, and industrial areas. Rock Doves were introduced into North America by early European settlers, and now are common in highly altered human environments. Many different color variations occur and may range from slate-gray to brown, white, or a number of combinations. Two black bars across the sides and back characterize the gray form. Rock Doves nest year-round on window ledges, under bridges, in barns or a variety of other structures. Large flocks may be seen circling feeding areas and roosts with upraised wings. Rock doves feed mainly on grains and seeds.

White-crowned Pigeon (*Columba leucocephala*)   p. 148
Other names: Baldpate, White-hooded Pigeon

Although this large pigeon is a sought-after Florida specialty, little is known of its life history. About the size of the Rock Dove, the White-crowned Pigeon is mostly dark, with an iridescent nape, and a white-crowned head. White-crowned Pigeons nest colonially in coastal mangroves in the Keys and Florida Bay. One or 2 eggs are laid in a stick nest usually in late spring. Some birds leave south Florida in late fall or winter, returning the following April or May. Occasionally, large winter roost flocks occur in Everglades National Park or the Keys. Whitecrowns are mostly inhabitants of dense coastal forests where they feed on a variety of fruits and seeds.

Eurasian Collared-Dove (*Streptopelia decaocto*)   p. 148
Other names: Collared Turtle-Dove

This Old World species is almost identical to the Ringed Turtle-Dove, except it is a darker tan, slightly larger, and its neck band is bordered with white. The primaries are distinctively darker than the rest of the wing. Its song is a series of *ca-coo-cuk*, with brief pauses between phrases. It also gives a Catbird-like mew in flight or upon landing. It first appeared in Florida in the early 1980s shortly after it was introduced into the Bahamas. It now numbers in the thousands and breeds from Miami to Key West, with scattered colonies in Pinellas and Pasco counties on the west coast and Okaloosa County in the panhandle. We predict it will spread throughout North America just as it spread throughout Europe from the Middle East in the 1940s. Nests containing 2 white eggs can be found in trees (especially palms) and shrubs mostly during spring. Food consists of grain and weed seeds.

Ringed Turtle-Dove (*Streptopelia 'risoria'*)   p. 148
Other names: Ringed Dove

The Ringed Turtle-Dove has been bred in captivity by many for hundreds of years. It and various white varieties of it are the doves used in research, by magicians, or sold as pets. Today, no natural wild populations are known to exist. However, escaped or released birds have successfully become established in St. Petersburg, Florida, and Los Angeles, California. The St. Petersburg population, established in the 1950s, appears to be holding its own and numbers between 500 and 1000 birds. Small numbers also occur in Tampa and Miami where people supplement their food supply. This feral species has now become so variable in appearance because of the variety of plumage types released by dove fanciers that it is probably best to refer to it as the Domestic Collared-Dove. The quotation marks around *"risoria"* suggest that it is not the name of a valid species. Ringed Turtle-Doves are about the size of Mourning Doves but have shorter, square tails, black at the base, and a lighter tan color overall. A narrow black band occurs around the back of the neck, except in immatures. The song is a distinctive *coo-ca-roo*. Flimsy nests of sticks are built in trees or shrubs during spring and 2 white eggs are laid. Eggs hatch in about 14 days and young fledge 14-15 days later. They primarily are grain feeders.

White-winged Dove *(Zenaida asiatica)*   **p. 148**
Other names: Eastern White-winged Dove

Early records of White-winged Doves in Florida were of birds shot by hunters in the Florida Keys. Band recoveries indicated these birds came from Texas. In the late 1950s numerous captive doves from Mexico being raised in Homestead were released and these now have spread throughout the Miami area. In the early 1970s the Florida Game and Fresh Water Fish Commission captured several hundred of these and released them at various locations as far north as Lake County. This species will probably continue to increase and spread in Florida. Large, white wing patches and long tail highlight an otherwise drab, grayish plumage. White-winged Doves behave similarly to the closely related Mourning Dove. The song is a distinctive *coo-cuk-ca-roo.* Foods primarily are grains and seeds.

Mourning Dove *(Zenaida macroura)*   **p. 148**
Other names: Turtle Dove, Carolina Dove, Wood Dove

The low, tranquil *coo* of the Mourning Dove is a common sound throughout suburban, rural, and wild Florida. While this bird is an abundant resident, Mourning Dove numbers increase dramatically in winter with the influx of northern migrants. Mourning Doves have an unusually long nesting season which may extend year-round, and, for individual pairs, include as many as 3 broods. Loosely constructed stick platforms serve as nests that usually contain 2 eggs. Young are fed a milky solution secreted from their parents' crops. Adults feed mostly on grains and weed seeds. Large flocks often are seen in winter grain fields, feeding on the ground or perched on fences or wires. Smaller than the Rock Dove, the Mourning Dove has a long, pointed tail with white-tipped feathers, black-spotted wings, grayish-brown above, a pinkish breast, and an iridescent patch on the sides of the neck. This patch is smaller in females than in males. Juveniles are much darker overall. The rapid whistling of the beating wings is distinctive when this bird takes flight. Mourning Doves are a very popular gamebird in Florida as well as the southeastern U.S.

Common Ground-Dove *(Columbina passerina)*   **p. 148**
Other names: Eastern Ground Dove

This is our smallest dove, found commonly in dry, open woodlands, old fields, and pastures. Perhaps even more prolific than the Mourning Dove, Ground-Doves may nest practically throughout the year laying as many as four clutches. Two eggs usually are laid in a loosely constructed nest on the ground, in a shrub, low tree branch, or the abandoned nest of another bird. This chunky bird is mostly gray above with a few black or purplish wing spots, a scalloped appearance on the head and neck, a short tail, and bright, chestnut primaries that are visible in flight. Ground-Doves seem to bob their heads continuously and often are seen in pairs. Foods consist of a variety of weed and grain seeds. This species may be locally abundant in some parts of Florida, but is becoming less common in much of the state.

Order Psittaciformes: Parrots and Parakeets

Family Psittacidae: Lories, Parakeets, Macaws, and Parrots

Subfamily Platycercinae: Australian Parakeets and Rosellas

Budgerigar *(Melopsittacus undulatus)*   p. 150

Other names: Budgey, Parakeet, Shell Parakeet

This colorful Australian native is a locally abundant breeding species along Florida's west coast from Tampa to Fort Myers and on the east coast from St. Lucie County southward. The typical plumage is light green underneath, yellow upperparts barred with black. Occasionally, blue-, white-, or yellow-colored individuals may be present in a colony, but the green color predominates. They are often seen in large flocks in urban settings. Budgerigars are cavity nesters and can compete with native species such as Purple Martins and Red-bellied Woodpeckers, or exotics like European Starlings and House Sparrows, for nest space. Budgies appear to be somewhat dependent upon supplemental feeding and may be sensitive to extremely low temperatures.

Subfamily Psittacinae: Typical Parrots

Birds with large heads, short necks, down-curved hooked bills with a prominent bulge or cere, and short grasping feet. No native species now exists in Florida, but numerous escaped or released species from elsewhere now live in the state. Four of the most widespread are described here.

Rose-ringed Parakeet *(Psittacula krameri)*   p. 150

This species is a native of Africa and India where it is a common inhabitant of lightly wooded areas, farmlands, and gardens around houses. Colonies of breeding Rose-rings occur in Miami and St. Augustine, while individuals have been seen in other Florida cities. The male is mostly green, with yellowish underparts, a black chin, a black stripe across the lower cheeks, and a rose-pink collar around the back of the neck. The nape and long central tail feathers are blue, and the top of the bill is red with a black tip. The female is plain green, lacks the distinctive markings of the male, and has a shorter tail. The call is a loud screeching *kee-ak*. Little is known about its breeding habits in Florida, but in the Old World it nests in tree cavities where it lays 2 to 6 eggs. Young fledge 6 or 7 weeks after hatching.

Subfamily Arinae: New World Parakeets, Macaws, Parrots

Monk Parakeet *(Myiopsitta monachus)*   p. 150

Other names: Quaker Parakeet

The Monk Parakeet is a South American native established in North America by accidental and intentional releases. It is larger than the Budgerigar, green above, with blue wings, light gray throat and chest, and yellow belly grading to a green rump. Monk Parakeets may be seen in urban and agricultural settings where their fruit-dominated diet makes them a potential pest. Bulky stick nests are built in treetops or other tall structures.

Canary-winged Parakeet *(Brotogeris versicolurus)*   p. 150

This small, mostly green parrot is highlighted with bright yellow wing patches appearing like windows in flight. Another South American native introduced as liberated cagebirds, Canary-winged Parakeets are regularly seen in southeast Florida, especially in and around Miami. This colorful parrot is most often found in small groups feeding on fruits and seeds or at evening roosts. They are commonest in suburban environments.

Order Cuculiformes: Cuckoos

Long-tailed birds with zygodactylous feet (two toes pointing forward, two toes backward).

Family Cuculidae: Cuckoos and Anis

Yellow-billed Cuckoo *(Coccyzus americanus)*   p. 152

Other names: Rain Crow

The Yellow-billed is the most common of Florida's cuckoos. This summer resident is a large secretive woodland bird about 12 inches long. Prominant white spots on the black undersides of the tail, yellow lower bill, white undersides, and chestnut-colored wings distinguish both sexes. Yellow-billed Cuckoos breed from Key West through mainland Florida. Loosely constructed stick nests are built during late spring usually in deciduous hardwoods. Three-6 eggs may be laid between May and August. Most individuals depart Florida by early October and return by early April. A variety of insects provide this cuckoo with most of its food. However, when tent caterpillars are particularly abundant, these defoliating insects dominate the diet. The ventriloqual, repeated clucking of the Yellow-billed Cuckoo is a characteristic sound of Florida's hardwood forests. The smaller, **Black-billed Cuckoo** (*C. erythropthalmus*) is an uncommon migrant in Florida during spring and fall.

Mangrove Cuckoo *(Coccyzus minor)*   p. 152

Other names: Black-eared Cuckoo, Rain Crow, Rain Bird

As its name implies, this cuckoo is an inhabitant of Florida's coastal mangrove forests. A year-round resident around Florida Bay and the Keys, Mangrove Cuckoos breed occasionally as far north as Tampa Bay. This Florida specialty is distinguished from similar species by its buff breast and black mask. The Mangrove Cuckoo is a late spring nester, laying 2 eggs in a loosely constructed twig platform. Like its relatives, the Mangrove Cuckoo is a caterpillar predator, consuming many bristled species that other birds avoid. These birds are quite secretive and prefer to remain well-hidden among dense growths of vegetation. Its characteristic call is a rapid *ga-ga-gaw*. Other vocalizations include a variety of gutteral clucks and notes as well as calls resembling those of the Yellow-billed Cuckoo.

Smooth-billed Ani *(Crotophaga ani)*   p. 152

Other names: Parrot Blackbird, Black Witch, Tickbird, Cuban Parrot

This unusual tropical cuckoo reaches its northern breeding limit at Cape Canaveral and Tampa Bay, where it is of rare to uncommon occurrence. A long "floppy" tail and ridged, black, parrotlike bill distinguish the Smooth-billed Ani from other "black" birds. This Florida specialty seems to be restricted to subtropical Florida. Nests are loosely constructed with twigs, leaves, and grass in shrubs, palms, or low tree branches. Anis have a long nesting season that may last from March to September. Apparently, several females may lay eggs in the same nest. Insects form the bulk of the diet. The distinctive call consists of a rising, questionlike note.

Groove-billed Ani (*Crotophaga sulcirostris*)   p. 152

Slightly smaller than the Smooth-billed, the Groove-billed Ani lacks the crest on upper bill, but the bill sometimes exhibits faint grooves. This southern Texas resident wanders widely in winter and is a regular but rare visitor in Florida. Individuals have been seen throughout the state from the panhandle to the Everglades.

Order Strigiformes: Owls

Usually nocturnal birds of prey with large eyes surrounded by a facial disk of feathers; short, hooked bill; strong legs and talons.

Family Tytonidae: Barn-Owls

Barn Owl (*Tyto alba*)   p. 154

Other names: Monkey-faced Owl, White Owl

This large nocturnal predator is not often seen in Florida, yet is a common bird throughout the state. The secretive Barn Owl is more strictly nocturnal than the other "typical" owls. When not hunting for small mammals or insects, Barn Owls retire to secluded tree cavities, abandoned buildings, or other dark recesses. At night this owl's presence is best confirmed by its eerie hissing or screechlike vocalizations. Barn Owls appear to nest throughout the year with a reduction of breeding activity only during July and August. As many as 9 rounded eggs are laid in a protected natural or man-made cavity or any flat surface in an attic, barn, shed, or similar structure. The presence of Barn Owls often is revealed by collections of "pellets" beneath a well-used roost. Pellets consist of the undigestible, regurgitated remains of insects, birds, and small mammals.

Family Strigidae: Typical Owls

Eastern Screech-Owl (*Otus asio*)   p. 154

Other names: Squinch Owl, Death Owl, Cat Owl, Shivering Owl, Mottled Owl

The Eastern Screech-Owl is Florida's smallest and perhaps best known owl. White undersides are heavily streaked and barred, eyes are yellow, and ear tufts are usually conspicuous. Most Florida birds exhibit brown plumage although red phases and gray phases are not unusual and all three color phases may occur in the same nest. Screech-Owls are more often heard than seen, uttering a trembling or quavering call that may sound deceptively distant. Habitat requirements are quite broad. Hollow cavities for nesting may be provided by a variety of forest types or man-made nest boxes. Roosting and hunting grounds may be found in hardwood swamps, pinelands, orange groves, or suburban back yards. Nesting occurs from March to June when about 4 white eggs are laid. While Screech-Owls consume a variety of small birds and mammals, the majority of their diet consists of insects.

Great Horned Owl *(Bubo virginianus)* p. 154
Other names: Cat Owl, Hoot Owl

The Great Horned is Florida's largest owl, reaching a wing span of nearly 5 feet. Prominent ear tufts, yellow eyes, white throat, heavily barred underparts, and dark back distinguish this nocturnal predator. The resonant hoots of this bird may carry a great distance; screamlike calls also are given, especially by juveniles. Great Horned Owls have broad habitat requirements including a variety of forest and prairie types. Nests are located in broad forks in trees such as live oaks, in abandoned Bald Eagle or other large raptor nests, and in other secluded sites. With adequate nest sites and food resources these owls may reside in close proximity to humans. Two rounded eggs usually are laid during winter. Foods consist of rodents, rabbits, skunks, opossums, domestic cats, ducks, and even other owls.

Burrowing Owl *(Athene cunicularia)* p. 154
Other names: Ground Owl, Howdy Owl

This small, long-legged, ground-dwelling owl is an inhabitant of open, well-drained landscapes. Florida and the Bahamas support the only eastern populations of this typical Great Plains species. Burrowing Owls are most common in the prairie region to the west and north of Lake Okeechobee. Scattered breeding locations, however, may be found from Jacksonville to Marathon. Many of these "outlying" individuals use the mowed strips between airport runways. Nests are located one to three feet underground where 3 to 7 eggs are laid between March and June. Several nesting pairs often are found in close proximity. Burrowing Owls are mostly nocturnal but also may be seen foraging in daylight. Foods consist primarily of insects, but rodents, amphibians, and small birds are eaten as well. Their name of "Howdy Owl" comes from their repeated bobbing or bowing motion.

Barred Owl *(Strix varia)* p. 154
Other names: Swamp Owl, Hoot Owl

Dark eyes and a rounded, uneared head distinguish the Barred Owl from the Great Horned Owl. Plumage is brown or grayish with dark scalloped throat feathers, dark streaks underneath, and mottled upperparts. The call is highly variable but a loud *who-cooks-for-you?* is most frequently heard. Found throughout mainland Florida, Barred Owls inhabit a variety of forest types but seem to prefer mixed hardwoods and swamps. They are cavity nesters, using natural holes in hardwoods or palms. Two or 3 eggs are laid between January and March. Barred Owls are predators of rodents such as cotton rats, flying squirrels, round-tailed muskrats, and deer mice. And, while Barred Owls eat birds and occasionally other owls, they in turn may fall prey to the larger and more powerful Great Horned Owl.

Order Caprimulgiformes: Goatsuckers
Nocturnal or crepuscular (i.e., active at dusk and dawn) species with long, pointed wings; small, weak feet; and large, gaping mouth.

Family Caprimulgidae: Goatsuckers

Common Nighthawk *(Chordeiles minor)* **p. 156**

Other names: Bull Bat

The Common Nighthawk is the most abundant and familiar of the goat-sucker family. A common summer resident throughout Florida, it can be seen in a variety of settings. They can be seen capturing insects at dusk and early morning over pastures, old fields, wetlands, and cities. Nighthawks also are cosmopolitan in their nesting requirements using open woodlands, pastures, beaches, disturbed ground, and even gravel rooftops. Between early April and late June, 2 eggs are laid in the open without protection of a nest. Although not secretive while feeding, Common Nighthawks are usually detected by their call, a repeated nasal *peent*. In their stiff-winged, buoyant flight a white stripe is visible beneath each wing. During courtship, males make spectacular dives toward the ground. The wings produce a deep growl or boom as the bird pulls out of its dive. Most birds arrive during late March and April and depart in September, although a few may remain until early November or, rarely, winter in south Florida.

Antillean Nighthawk *(Chordeiles gundlachii)* **p. 156**

Other names: Bull Bat, Cuban Nighthawk

In appearance, the Antillean Nighthawk is virtually indistinguishable from the Common Nighthawk. At close range it appears buffier, but is best told by its three-syllable call described as *pit-a-pit* or *kic-a-dic*. The Antillean Nighthawk breeds in the Florida Keys and may be seen during spring migration at Ft. Jefferson, Dry Tortugas. Feeding and nesting habits are similar to those of the Common Nighthawk.

Chuck-will's-widow *(Caprimulgus carolinensis)* **p. 156**

Other names: Dutch Whip-poor-will, Spanish Whip-poor-will

The Chuck-will's-widow is a typical spring and summer resident through-out most of Florida's woodlands. Cryptic coloration (mottled brown plumage) and nocturnal habits make this bird inconspicuous. A white throat band is the only obvious contrast to the Chuck-will's-widow's camouflage. Occasionally they are abundant along country roads and can be detected by the reddish glow of their eyes reflected from car headlights. The distinctly four-syllable call is an accurate imitation of its name with an emphasis on the "wid" of widow. These notes may be repeated incessantly throughout the night and into early morning. There is a brief period during spring when the Chuck-will's-widow and similar Whip-poor-will can be heard together. Although a few birds winter in south Florida, most return to Florida in early spring. Two eggs are laid on the ground in open woodlands from April to early June. Chuck-will's-widows roost along tree limbs which serve as good camouflage as well. Chucks have very small bills, but relatively enormous bristled mouths which are used for capturing a variety of flying nocturnal insects. Most birds leave Florida for Central and South America by late September.

Whip-poor-will *(Caprimulgus vociferus)* **p. 156**

Other names: Eastern Whip-poor-will

This rarely encountered winter visitor and transient is a smaller, northern version of our summer resident Chuck-will's-widow. Whip-poor-wills also appear grayer and have a black throat in contrast to the Chuck's buff throat. Whip-poor-wills arrrive in Florida in late September and some may remain through April using the same wooded habitats as its Florida relative. Most transients pass through the state in late February and March. The Whip-poor-will's call is more rapid and the accent is on the last of three syllables. It is behaviorally similar to the Chuck-will's-widow.

Order Apodiformes: Swifts and Hummingbirds

Two major groups make up this order—the swifts with long, pointed, stiff wings and tiny, weak feet, who spend most of their life in flight, and the hummingbirds, our smallest birds with the swiftest wingbeat and extraordinary ability to hover.

Family Apodidae: Swifts

Chimney Swift *(Chaetura pelagica)* **p. 156**

Other names: Chimney Swallow, Chimney Bat, Chimney Sweep

A "flying cigar" would be an appropriate description of this nearly tailless, dusky-colored swift. The rapid beat of its relatively long-pointed wings gives the Chimney Swift the appearance of constant motion. Its voice is a continuous staccato chattering that is made during flight. Chimney Swifts are cavity nesters using a variety of natural as well as man-made hollows such as wells and chimneys. Nests are plastered to vertical walls where 4 to 6 white eggs are laid between April and July. Roosting birds cling to these same surfaces with extremely small feet and the support of stiff tail bristles. Large numbers of swifts may inhabit a single smoke stack where they may appear wheeling around their roost like a cloud in early evening. Chimney Swifts return from South America in March and may remain in Florida until October. They are less frequently observed in south Florida, although they have extended their range southward in recent years to Palm Beach and Broward Counties. Food consists entirely of insects.

Family Trochilidae: Hummingbirds

Ruby-throated Hummingbird *(Archilochus colubris)* **p. 156**

The Ruby-throated Hummingbird is Florida's smallest bird. Males possess a metallic red throat, green upperparts, whitish undersides, and a dark, slightly forked tail. Females and immatures are green above, white below and have a white-tipped tail. Rubythroats return to Florida in early March when they can feed on nectar produced in early-blooming tubular flowers. While feeding, these tiny birds hover motionless or move adeptly back and forth. The wings beat so rapidly they are difficult to detect. Some birds remain in central or south Florida throughout the year while others depart in October for Central America. Nectar and small, nectar-eating insects form the diet of the Ruby-throated Hummingbird. The breeding season lasts from May through June when males exhibit an acrobatic, pendulous courtship flight. Its tiny lichen-covered nest, adhered to a small twig, usually contains 2 pea-sized, white eggs. Occasionally, other hummingbirds stray into Florida, especially in fall or winter. These include the Rufous Hummingbird (*Selasphorus rufus*), Black-chinned Hummingbird (*Archilochus alexandri*), Cuban Emerald (*Chlorostilbon ricordii*), and Bahama Woodstar (*Calliphlox evelynae*). In 1988 a Buff-bellied Hummingbird (*Amazilia yucatanensis*) spent a week near Destin, Florida.

Order Coraciiformes: Kingfishers

Birds of this group all have syndactylous toes, i.e., their front three toes are more or less joined along part of their length.

Family Alcedinidae: Kingfishers

Belted Kingfisher (*Ceryle alcyon*)   p. 156
Other names: Eastern Belted Kingfisher

The Belted Kingfisher is a chunky, slate-blue bird with large bill, crested head, and tiny feet. Females are distinguished by a red band across their white belly. They often are seen perched on telephone wires and power lines paralleling flooded roadside ditches. Kingfishers dive headfirst into rivers, lakes, swamps, impoundments, and other open water wetlands. Prey items include small fish such as shiners, killifish, and minnows as well as crayfish, frogs, and insects. Nests are made at the end of a 3'–15' tunnel, excavated into a cut-bank, bluff, or spoil pile. A few nests also have been found in hollow trees. Eggs, numbering around 4, are laid during April or May. Belted Kingfishers can be observed frequently year-round throughout Florida. They are not equally common, however, in all regions and seasons. Because they require sandy bluffs for burrowing, Kingfishers find the flat terrain of south Florida less suitable for nesting habitat. However, when winter brings numerous northern birds to Florida, Kingfishers become more common throughout the state.

Order Piciformes: Woodpeckers and Allies

All members of this order have zygodactulous feet (two toes forward, two backward), usually inhabit trees, and drill into wood for insects and nest cavities.

Family Picidae: Woodpeckers

Red-headed Woodpecker (*Melanerpes erythrocephalus*)   p. 160
Other names: White-wing, Redhead

The Red-headed Woodpecker is a conspicuous year-round inhabitant of open forests and suburban woodlands throughout most of Florida. Its distribution is patchy, being common in some localities, scarce or absent in others. The bright, entirely red head, white belly, rump and wing patches, and black wings and tail distinguish the adults. Immature birds have brown, mottled heads, darker brown backs, and light, mottled underparts. Hollow cavities in dead trees, limbs, fence posts and utility poles may be used for nest sites. Bluebird nest boxes occasionally are used. The long breeding season extends from May until August; 4 to 7 eggs are laid per clutch and two broods may be raised per season. Vegetation forms the bulk of the Red-headed Woodpecker's diet and may include acorns, berries, and a variety of grains. Insects also are taken. This colorful bird is often seen along suburban and country roads "hawking" for flying and crawling insects.

Red-bellied Woodpecker *(Melanerpes carolinus)* **p. 158**

Other names: Zebra Woodpecker, Cham-chack, Guinea Sapsucker, Orange Sapsucker, Ladderback

Although possessing a red cap from bill to nape, the Red-bellied Woodpecker is named for its often overlooked rosy belly patch. A black and white ladder-striped back is characteristic of both sexes. Females lack red on the forehead. The Red-bellied is probably our most widespread woodpecker. This highly adaptable species is found from suburban back yards to a variety of forest types throughout Florida. Cavities in dead and live trees such as cabbage palm, live oak, bald cypress, or slash pine serve as nest sites. They will also occupy bird houses. Breeding occurs from April through June when 4 to 6 eggs are laid. Red-bellied Woodpeckers are aggressive birds and may force other cavity nesters from established nest sites. They subsist on a variety of seeds and nuts as well as insects such as ants, grasshoppers, and beetle grubs.

Yellow-bellied Sapsucker *(Sphyrapicus varius)* **p. 160**

Yellow-bellied Sapsuckers are common winter residents throughout Florida. However, year-round reminders of their visits are evidenced in trees marked with concentric rings of holes. Flowing sap from these holes, and insects attracted to it, form a part of this colorful woodpecker's diet. An irregular black and white pattern marks the back. Both sexes exhibit a red crown, black and white facial stripes, white wing patches, black bib, and yellowish belly. Males have red throats. First-year birds may lack red coloring. Yellow-bellied sapsuckers can be expected in Florida woodlands from October through April.

Downy Woodpecker *(Picoides pubescens)* **p. 160**

Other names: Sapsucker

The Downy Woodpecker is a smaller version of the Hairy Woodpecker. A daintier, shorter bill (its length is one-half the depth of the head), black spots on outer tail feathers, and a faster, higher-pitched call distinguish the Downy from its close relative. Downies are more apt to utilize backyard feeders than are Hairy Woodpeckers. Nesting habits are similar to the Hairy's, although smaller trees and dead snags may be used. Downy Woodpeckers can be seen year-round throughout Florida. The diet consists of beetles, cockroaches, ants, and other insects. Vegetable matter makes up a small portion of the food intake.

Hairy Woodpecker *(Picoides villosus)* **p. 160**

Other names: Sapsucker

Although the Hairy Woodpecker can be found throughout Florida woodlands, it is not a common bird. Black wings and tail are contrasted against a white belly, neck, and back. The head is striped black and white, and white flecking occurs on the wings. The outer tail feathers usually are pure white (the very similar Downy Woodpecker shows black spots on these feathers). Hairies also have a heavier-appearing bill, whose length is equal to the depth of the head behind the bill. Males have a red nape patch. Nests are excavated in a variety of dead trees. Eggs, usually 3 or 4, are laid from April through

May. The call has been described as a louder version of the Downy's *peek*. Nuts, beetles, and bark-dwelling insects form the bulk of its diet.

Red-cockaded Woodpecker *(Picoides borealis)* p. 160

Other names: Sapsucker

Modern timber practices encouraging harvest of young, plantation-grown pines have created problems for the conservation of this species. Red-cockaded Woodpeckers require old-growth pine forests—usually longleaf pine—where nest cavities are excavated in living trees infected with red heart disease. Flowing resin wells are maintained around the nest entrance and may serve as a repellent to egg-eating snakes. The flowing resin often gives these cavity trees a white-washed appearance making them conspicous members of the forest. The red "cockades" of the males are rarely seen except when birds are in the hand. Red-cockaded Woodpeckers are best identified by black and white ladder-striped backs, and large, white cheek patches, and their distinctive calls. The Red-cockaded Woodpecker is a highly social bird and exists in small family groups known as clans. Nonbreeding individuals act as helpers during nesting activities. Three-5 eggs are laid from April through June. Foods consist of fruits, wood-boring beetles and other insects. The Apalachicola National Forest represents the largest concentration of Red-cockaded Woodpeckers in Florida; they also may be seen in scattered locations throughout the peninsula and panhandle where large expanses of old growth pines persist. However, numbers are declining throughout the state.

Northern Flicker *(Colaptes auratus)* p. 158

Other names: Yellowhammer, Highhole, Golden-winged Woodpecker

The Northern Flicker is a brightly colored, large woodpecker of open woods and suburbs. In flight, yellow underwings are conspicuous. Flickers are brown with black barring above, have a white rump, spotted underparts and black throat patch. Adult males exhibit a black cheek stripe extending from the base of the bill. Northern Flickers are found throughout the state, but are much less common in south Florida and the Keys. Nests usually are located in hollow cavities in palms, oaks, or pines at varying heights. About 6 white eggs are laid from late March to May. In suburban areas Flickers can become something of a nuisance due to their habit of "drumming" on a variety of surfaces from hollow trees to gutters, siding, and windows. Insects, especially ants, are the most important foods; hence, Flickers may often be seen foraging on the ground.

Pileated Woodpecker *(Dryocopus pileatus)* p. 158

Other names: Lord-god, Good-god, Logcock, Woodcock, Woodchuck, Wood-cady, Cock-o-the-woods.

The Pileated Woodpecker is one of the most distinctive birds of Florida's deep forests and swamps. But unlike its close relative, the Ivory-billed Woodpecker, the Pileated is very adaptable and often may be seen in close proximity to busy urban areas. This is our largest woodpecker. It has a red, crested head, white throat and white stripe from base of bill to the shoulders. The white wing linings, frontally located, are conspicuous in flight. The female's red plumage is restricted to a smaller portion of the crest. The raucous call, resembling a slower, louder flicker call, and methodical drumming may carry for long distances. Pileated Woodpeckers excavate rectangular cavities in soft or rotten wood. Eggs, usually 3 to 5, are laid between February and May. Carpenter ants and wood-boring beetles are important food items that are obtained by hammering apart rotten logs and stumps. During fall, a variety of fruits such as swamp tupelo, dogwood, and sugarberry also are eaten.

Ivory-billed Woodpecker *(Campephilus principalis)*   p. 158
Other names: Pait

It has been well over two decades since records of this largest North American woodpecker were verified. The Ivory-billed Woodpecker now is probably extinct on this continent; a few birds hang on in Cuba. The virgin cypress swamps throughout the southeast were the haunts of this impressive bird. The combination of widespread logging of our large cypress forests and the Ivorybill's inability to adapt to change spelled its demise. Ivorybills are larger than Pileated Woodpeckers. A heavy, whitish bill and large white wing patches are visible while perched. In flight, the undersides of the wings are bordered in white. Females lack a bright red crest.

Order Passeriformes: Passerine Birds
A large assemblage of birds, called perching birds, including well over half of all the living species. All have a foot with three toes forward, one backward, well adapted for gripping a perch.

Family Tyrannidae: Tyrant Flycatchers

Eastern Wood-Pewee *(Contopus virens)*   p. 162
A regular breeder in north Florida, the Eastern Wood-Pewee is often identified by its call, *pee-a-wee*, which closely resembles its name. It is less frequently seen in the open than other flycatchers, preferring the closed canopies of moist woodlands. The plumage is dark olive above, light below with grayish breast, white throat, black tail, and dark wings with pale wing bars. The cuplike nest is constructed of grasses and lichens and located on a tree branch. Three to 4 eggs usually are laid in May. Insects make up most of the diet, while small fruits occasionally are eaten. It departs Florida in September, returning the following April.

Yellow-bellied Flycatcher *(Empidonax flaviventris)* L 5"

Jan	Feb	Mar	Apr	May	June	July	Aug	Sep	Oct	Nov	Dec

With a greenish back, and distinctive wing bars, this migrant species is similar in appearance to the other Empidonax flycatchers but it has a yellow eye ring and a yellow wash over the throat and breast. Its song, never uttered in Florida, is an explosive *pse-ek* or a *pur-wee*. During fall some immature Acadian Flycatchers also possess a yellow breast; hence, care must be exercised in identifying these. It can be found in woody thickets or understories of hardwood swamps and other woodlands.

Acadian Flycatcher *(Empidonax virescens)* p. 162

Other names: Green Crested Flycatcher

Our smallest breeding flycatcher in Florida is the Acadian. Olive-green head and upperparts, dark wings with buff wing bars, buff eye ring, yellow lower abdomen, and grayish breast characterize the adult. Immatures show a more brown and mottled appearance above with no yellow underneath. The long, broad bill is dark above and yellowish below. The Acadian Flycatcher is an inhabitant of Spanish moss-festooned swamplands and moist woodlands from central Florida through the panhandle. A canoe trip down any central Florida river in spring will result in seeing or hearing this species. It may be seen from late April through September on its breeding grounds. The frail-looking nests usually are constructed of Spanish moss and hung from a forked branch of an understory tree. Eggs, numbering 2 to 4, are laid during May. The 2-syllabled call has been described as an explosive *wicky-up* or *peet-sit*. Foods are almost entirely insect.

Alder Flycatcher *(Empidonax alnorum)* L 5″
Willow Flycatcher *(Empidonax traillii)* L 5″

Jan	Feb	Mar	Apr	May	June	July	Aug	Sep	Oct	Nov	Dec

These two *Empidonax* flycatchers were once considered to be a single species, Traill's Flycatcher. Both are brown-olive above, with white throat and olive sides, two white wing bars on each wing, and a white eye ring. The only truly distinguishing feature is their songs, which, unfortunately, are rarely uttered in Florida. The Alder sings a distinctive *fee-bee-o*, and the Willow, a *fitz-bew*. Both occur during spring and fall migration, but are rarely identified other than as *Empidonax* or "Traill's" Flycatcher. They normally are seen in trees and shrubbery along rivers, swamps, and other wooded sites.

Least Flycatcher *(Empidonax minimus)* p. 162

This smallest North American flycatcher is seen only occasionally in Florida during migration to and from its north woods breeding grounds. However, in recent years several individuals have wintered in the south Dade County–West Palm Beach area. The Least Flycatcher is brown to olive-gray above, pale below with grayish breast and white throat, and has white wing bars and white eye rings. It looks similar to the other *Empidonax* flycatchers and is best distinguished from these by its call, a loud *che-bec*. Least Flycatchers are insect eaters and prefer open woodlands.

Eastern Phoebe *(Sayornis phoebe)* p. 162

Other names: Pee-wee, Tick Bird, Bridge Phoebe

Sitting on exposed perches, like most flycatchers, the Eastern Phoebe often is seen in silhouette only. But, its habit of rapidly pumping its tail readily identifies this bird even without visible field marks. The Eastern

Phoebe is rather nondescript with grayish-brown upperparts, light buff underparts, and black bill. Eastern Phoebes do not usually breed in Florida but are common residents from September through March. The first Florida nesting record occurred in May 1988 in northern Okaloosa County. Insects are preferred food but fruits from sugarberries, hollies, and other trees and shrubs also are eaten. This is a common roadside bird and perches frequently on utility lines and fences and may often be heard calling its name *phee-bee, phee-bee.*

Vermilion Flycatcher *(Pyrocephalus rubinus)* p. 162

This native of the southwestern U.S. and Mexico is seen sporadically in Florida during winter. Most birds have been observed in the panhandle but individuals have shown up throughout the state. The male is bright red with a black back and black eye stripe. The female is gray brown above with a white belly washed in light pink and streaked with brown. The Vermilion Flycatcher feeds primarily on flying insects and appears partial to perching in hardwood trees near lake shores. Arrivals and departures of the Vermilion are unpredictable but most have been seen between September and April.

Great Crested Flycatcher *(Myiarchus crinitus)* p. 162

Other names: Southern Crested Flycatcher, Crested Flycatcher, Freight-bird

About the size of the Eastern Kingbird, the Great Crested Flycatcher is one of our most familiar and vocal woodland birds in Florida. Olive-drab upperparts, ash-gray throat, yellow belly, chestnut tail, and barred wings distinguish this summer resident. Great Crested Flycatchers may be seen in mixed woodlands throughout the state from late March until early fall. Some birds remain in extreme south Florida year-round. This large flycatcher nests in cavities often excavated by woodpeckers and will nest in bird houses. The authors have observed single pairs occupying houses erected for Purple Martins. Nests contain from 4 to 6 streaked eggs laid from April through June. A common nest material is shed snake skin. In modern times, clear plastic material, which resembles snake skin has been used. A loud *weep* call is frequently made near nest sites. Great Crested Flycatchers choose exposed vantage points from which frequent sallies are made for grasshoppers, caterpillars, beetles, and other insects. Small fruits make up a small part of the Great Crested Flycatcher's diet. A similar species, the Brown-crested Flycatcher (*M. tyrannulus;* formerly Wied's Flycatcher) occasionally winters in extreme southern Florida (Everglades National Park). It is a duller brown color, with less reddish or chestnut colors in the tail, a paler (almost white) gray throat, and paler yellow underparts.

Western Kingbird *(Tyrannus verticalis)* p. 162

This regular winter visitor is seen annually although unpredictably throughout Florida. It appears at a time when most other large flycatchers are absent (September-April) and therefore should not be confused with our summer residents. They often are seen in open country on exposed perches. The Western Kingbird is gray above with bright yellow underparts, dark wings, and black tail. The red crown patch of the male is seldom observed. A variety of insects forms its diet.

Eastern Kingbird *(Tyrannus tyrannus)* p. 162
Other names: Bee Bird, Bee Martin

Black head, dark upperparts, white underparts, and a black tail with a white terminal band distinguish this common summer resident in Florida. The red patch behind the head is seldom seen. These birds often are conspicuous due to their habit of using exposed perches such as utility lines, telephone poles, treetops, and fences. From these vantage points frequent sallies are made for a variety of insects, many of which are agricultural pests. Nests may be placed in shrubs or trees that provide adequate protection from predators. These sites are frequently near water. Three to 4 eggs are usually laid during May. Eastern Kingbirds typically are seen in Florida from March until October. They do not breed in the Florida Keys.

Gray Kingbird *(Tyrannus dominicensis)* p. 162
Other names: Pipiry Flycatcher

This Florida specialty breeds in widely scattered localities along the Gulf and Atlantic coasts but seems to be more abundant near mangroves (i.e., southern Gulf coast and Keys). The Gray Kingbird is somewhat larger than the Eastern Kingbird, is lighter above with a slightly forked, unbanded tail, and has a larger, heavier bill. Like the Eastern Kingbird, Gray Kingbirds are resident from March through September. Loosely constructed nests often are placed in mangroves overhanging water. Eggs, numbering 2 or 3 are laid in May or early June. Gray Kingbirds feed on insects from exposed, elevated perches. They are quite tolerant of human activity provided there is ample feeding and nesting habitat. Gray Kingbirds are a common sight perched on power lines through the Keys.

Scissor-tailed Flycatcher *(Tyrannus forficatus)* p. 162
Few Florida birds are as unmistakable as the Scissor-tailed Flycatcher. This medium-sized flycatcher has a deeply forked tail that may be 12 inches long, pink wing linings, light gray head and neck, and dark upper wing and tail surfaces. Males have slightly longer tails than do females and the immatures' tails are about half the adult tail length. Scissor-taileds are summer residents in the south-central U.S. and usually reside in Central America during winter. A few birds, however, winter regularly in extreme south Florida and the Keys, and are occasionally seen in migration along the Gulf coast, rarely on the Atlantic coast. These distinctive birds are most often seen on exposed perches such as utility wires and tall, leafless trees. The diet consists mostly of insects. Birds wintering in Key West often feed on wild bees living in concrete utility poles.

Family Hirundinidae: Swallows

Purple Martin *(Progne subis)* p. 164
Other names: Black Martin, Gourd Martin, House Martin

Perhaps no other North American bird is so strongly sought as a tenant by landowners as the Purple Martin. This attractive gregarious swallow once relied on natural tree cavities for nest sites but because of extensive loss of forest land, it now relies on man-made Martin apartments. These range in design from dried gourds (originally used by Indians) to elaborate multifamily manufactured housing on poles. Martins also will occupy a wide range of other man-made structures ranging from commercial signs, street lamps, traffic lights to operating oil rigs. The most consistently utilized structures, regardless of design or purpose, are located not far from lakes or ponds. The Purple Martin is the largest swallow and the only one with readily distinguished sexes. Males are a dark metallic blue, while females and juveniles are blue-brown above, with a whitish belly. Females also exhibit a blue patch on the back of the head. Martins arrive in Florida during late January and early February. Nesting occurs from late March through early July when 4 to 6 white eggs are laid. Fall migration can begin as early as late June when flocks of several hundred to several thousand Martins may be seen gathering before their trans-Gulf flight to Brazil. Most of the Florida population leaves the state long before northern birds migrate through in late August and September. The diet is composed of a variety of insects, chiefly beetles and dragonflies.

Tree Swallow *(Tachycineta bicolor)* p. 164
Other names: White-bellied Swallow

From fall through spring these gregarious migrants may be observed in loose flocks or in wheeling clouds numbering in the thousands. Tree Swallows are glossy green (sometimes purple) above and white below. Their tails are slightly forked. Females are less colorful than males, and immatures are grayish above with an indistinct chest band. Insects make up the bulk of the Tree Swallow's diet; however, wax myrtle fruits are consumed in large quantities especially when cold temperatures reduce insect activity. Migrants may arrive in late August and linger through May.

Northern Rough-winged Swallow *(Stelgidopteryx serripennis)* p. 164
Other names: Sand Martin, Gully Martin, Bank Swallow, Gully Bird

This rather nondescript swallow is a moderately frequent migrant and nester in Florida. The Northern Rough-winged Swallow is brownish above, with a buff throat grading into a white belly. The tail is slightly notched. Roughwings are most frequently cavity nesters, burrowing into the sides of stream banks, canals, and spoil piles, but they will occasionally nest in drain pipes extending from bridges or buildings. Eggs, laid in May or June, number around 6 and are pure white. Nesting sites of this species are loosely scattered through north and central Florida. Its abundance is likely limited by suitable nest sites, a similar situation affecting the Belted Kingfisher. Roughwings are fairly common as migrants from fall through spring in south Florida with a few birds overwintering. Foods, as in other swallows, are nearly entirely insects.

Bank Swallow *(Riparia riparia)* p. 164
Other names: Sand Martin

The dull-colored Bank Swallow is a common Florida migrant. Brownish upperparts, dark wings, and white belly with contrasting brown chest band distinguish this small swallow from the similar Rough-winged Swallow. Like many other swallows the Bank Swallow is gregarious and may be seen in large flocks during migration. Insects are the mainstay of its diet fueling these birds to their South American wintering grounds. Spring migrants may be seen between March and May; fall migrants pass through between late August and early October.

Cliff Swallow *(Hirundo pyrrhonota)* p. 164

In Florida most Cliff Swallows are strictly migrants, occurring during spring and fall in variable, unpredictable numbers. A square tail, buff or rusty rump patch, dark reddish-brown throat and cream-colored forehead identify this bird. One colony of Cliff Swallows has been nesting under highway bridges at Port Mayaca on the northeast shore of Lake Okeechobee since the late 1960s. Nests are gourd-shaped and constructed of mud. Eggs, usually 4 to 5, are white with brown dots. The nesting season lasts from April through June. Cliff Swallows typically are seen foraging for flying insects over agricultural and other open landscapes. Spring migrants appear between late March and mid-May; fall birds pass through from mid-August through October.

Cave Swallow *(Hirundo fulva)* p. 164

Other names: Caribbean Cave Swallow

Like the similar Cliff Swallow this species has a square tail and buff rump patch, but differs by its buff throat and cinnamon forehead. Up until recently it had been considered an "accidental" in Florida with numerous sightings chiefly in spring. In 1987 sixteen pairs were found nesting under several Florida Turnpike bridges near Homestead, and this population now appears to be increasing. Nests are gourd-shaped mud structures built in early April. Elsewhere nests also are built under the eaves of buildings, concrete culverts, and rock walls. Eggs number 2 to 5 and are white with fine specks of brown. Food primarily is flying insects caught over waterways and fields.

Barn Swallow *(Hirundo rustica)* p. 164

This is probably our best known swallow, even though it primarily is a migrant in Florida. The Barn Swallow is distinguished by an extremely deeply forked tail, reddish undersides, pointed wings, and dark blue, metallic upperparts. Juveniles are lighter below and browner above. Most Barn Swallows are seen in Florida as they travel in flocks to wintering grounds in Central America (between July and November) or on their way north (between April and June). However, some birds remain in the state to nest usually during May-July. In recent years it has extended its range into the Florida Keys where it nests under highway bridges. Two to 6 eggs are laid in a nest constructed of mud, grass, and feathers and plastered underneath bridges, against houses, or in caves and hollow trees. The diet is mostly insects. Common prey, taken on the wing, includes flies, beetles, ants, and stink bugs.

Family Corvidae: Jays and Crows

Blue Jay *(Cyanocitta cristata)* p. 166

Other names: Jaybird, Florida Blue Jay

The Blue Jay is one of Florida's most widespread and recognized songbirds. This raucous, animated bird is as often heard as seen. Its calls vary from the typical *jay, jay,* and sometimes convincing Red-shouldered Hawk and Red-tailed Hawk imitations, to a wide range of clucks, rattles, and churrs. The Blue Jay also has a subdued musical whisper song, rarely heard. Blue Jays are crested, blue above, and whitish below. The face is masked in black while the wings are generously marked with blue, white, and black. The sexes are similar. It is a permanent Florida resident using a wide range of habitats from pine flatwoods and hardwood hammocks to urban environments. Blue Jays seem to have a fondness for acorns but will eat nearly anything smaller than themselves, including insects, rodents, lizards, and other birds. Nesting takes place between March and late July, and individual pairs may raise more than one brood each year. Nests are placed 10-40 feet above ground and are constructed of twigs, Spanish moss, pine needles, paper, and other debris. Eggs, usually numbering 3 or 4, are light green or brown and spotted with dark brown.

Scrub Jay *(Aphelocoma coerulescens)* p. 166
Other names: Florida Jay, Smooth-headed Jay

The Scrub Jay in eastern North America is found only in the dry oak scrublands of peninsular Florida. About the size of the Blue Jay, the Scrub Jay is crestless and paler in color. Sky blue upperparts and breast band, grayish back and light gray underparts distinguish both sexes. The Florida race can be separated from its western relatives by the light forehead and eyebrows. The Scrub Jay's calls are varied but less raucous than the Blue Jay's. In recent decades the range of this permanent Florida resident has been greatly reduced due to spreading urbanization and agriculture. Some of the more extensive patches of suitable habitat remain in the Ocala National Forest, Merritt Island National Wildlife Refuge, and in the uplands west and north of Lake Okeechobee. Florida Scrub Jays were officially designated as a threatened population by the U.S. Fish and Wildlife Service in July 1987. Scrub Jays seem dependent upon a variety of scrub oaks for nesting as well as food. Eggs are laid between late March and late May. Nests are constructed of twigs and lined with finer material. The average clutch has 3 greenish, brown-spotted eggs. Scrub Jays are gregarious and offspring of mated pairs often assist in subsequent nesting activities. Foods, other than acorns, include grasshoppers, beetles, ants, wasps, spiders, and a variety of berries and other fruits.

American Crow *(Corvus brachyrhynchos)* p. 166
Other names: Common Crow, Southern Crow, Florida Crow, Cawin' Crow, Corn Crow

The American Crow is our largest crow and the one most often found in and around large wooded uplands. This common, permanent resident is unmistakable; entirely black, large heavy bill, and familiar call—a repeated *caw*. Loosely constructed nests, occasionally abandoned by large birds of prey, usually are located high in a pine or tall hardwood tree. Eggs, averaging 4, usually are laid in early February to early April. Crows' habit of "mobbing" is often a good clue to finding otherwise secretive birds of prey, their raucous calls giving away both the crows' presence and that of the hawk or owl. American Crows have also earned a reputation as crop destroyers and remain a popular gamebird in some rural areas. The diet, however, is predominantly nonagricultural and includes a variety of insects, young rabbits, rodents, snakes, lizards, and the eggs and young of reptiles and birds.

Fish Crow *(Corvus ossifragus)* p. 166

Although the Fish Crow is smaller than the American Crow, identification by size alone is unreliable. The best single field character distinguishing the Fish Crow is its hoarse, nasal voice. The most frequent calls are the two-syllable *uh-oh* and a repetitive *ca*. Fish Crows are abundant in Florida especially near coastlines, rivers, lakes, and marshes. Nesting habits are similar to the American Crow but egg-laying may occur somewhat later in the spring. The diet is highly variable but includes a large proportion of wetland foods such as crabs, mollusks, crayfish, and the eggs and young of colonial nesting waterbirds such as Wood Storks, Anhingas, and herons.

Family Paridae: Titmice

Carolina Chickadee *(Parus carolinensis)* p. 168

Other names: Florida Chickadee

This tiny, energetic woodland bird is a common resident except in south Florida. Both sexes are gray above and white below with black cap and throat, and white cheek patch. The Carolina Chickadee is often detected by its voice: a distinctive *chick-a-dee-dee-dee*, or *fee-bee, fee-bay*. Carolina Chickadees use tree cavities and occasionally boxes for nest sites. Breeding occurs in April and May, when 5 to 7 white, brown-flecked eggs are laid. Chickadees tolerate close human contact and are residents in wooded suburbs. Foods are predominately insects but chickadees are frequent visitors at window and backyard feeding stations. Wild seeds and small fruits also are eaten.

Tufted Titmouse *(Parus bicolor)* p. 168

Other names: Peter Bird, Peto Bird, Tomtit

This close relative of the chickadee is slightly larger but similar in habits and distribution. The Tufted Titmouse is light gray above, with reddish or chestnut flanks and a prominent crest. Its call is a quickly-repeated *peter-peter-peter*. Titmice are residents of a variety of woodland types such as cypress swamps, hardwood hammocks, longleaf pine sandhills, and suburbs. They are absent from the Keys and the coastal belt south of Cape Canaveral/Tampa Bay. Natural cavities and boxes provide nest sites where 5 to 7 brown-flecked, white eggs are laid during April through June. Nests are composed of leaves, grass, bark, feathers, hair, and usually a snake skin or two. The absence of cavities may limit the distribution of this bird. Tufted Titmice are common visitors at feeding stations, especially during winter. Sunflower seeds are a favorite food. Wild foods include a variety of insects, seeds, berries, and acorns.

Family Sittidae: Nuthatches

Red-breasted Nuthatch *(Sitta canadensis)* p. 168

This typically northern species is considerably smaller than the White-breasted Nuthatch. Reddish underparts, smaller bill, and black eye stripe set the Red-breasted Nuthatch apart. Females and juveniles are a lighter buff underneath. The call is more nasal and does not carry as far as that of the White-breasted Nuthatch. Extreme north Florida provides the haunts for this bird, especially during harsh winters. However, it is never common in the state. Red-breasted Nuthatches can be looked for between November and January. It prefers pine woods where it can be seen extracting seeds from cones.

White-breasted Nuthatch *(Sitta carolinensis)* p. 168
Other names: Florida Nuthatch, Sapsucker

This is our largest nuthatch with blue-gray upperparts, black crown and upper neck, stout, needlelike bill, and black eye surrounded by white. Like most nuthatches, the White-breasted spends a considerable amount of time upside down foraging for insects along branches and tree trunks. It is often detected by its call, a nasal *yank-yank*. Formerly widespread in Florida, it has virtually disappeared as a breeding species, but still occurs in winter. White-breasted Nuthatches once bred in a variety of woodlands north of Lake Okeechobee. Nests are placed in tree cavities made by other birds or sometimes themselves. Eggs, numbering 4 to 6 are laid in March or April. Outside of the breeding season these nuthatches are occasionally seen in south Florida. During fall and winter the most important food is large mast such as acorns and hickory nuts. The meat of these large seeds is obtained by wedging the nut in a crevice and hammering away the outer covering. A variety of smaller seeds and fruits is also eaten. Insect food includes beetles, spiders, moths, ants, and other bark dwellers.

Brown-headed Nuthatch *(Sitta pusilla)* p. 168
Other names: Cha-cha, Gray-headed Nuthatch, "Squeeze-bird"

This inhabitant of Florida's open pine forests is our smallest nuthatch. A pale gray spot behind the neck separates the brown head from gray back. Underparts are white. The call is a rapid series of mechanical twitterings, which is an aid to locating feeding groups. Brown-headed Nuthatches are cavity nesters. They excavate their own holes or use abandoned woodpecker holes, fence posts, or boxes. A clutch consists of 4 to 6 white, brown-flecked eggs usually laid in March or April, but sometimes as early as February. The Brown-headed Nuthatch feeds on a variety of wood-boring and bark-inhabiting insects and other invertebrates as well as pine seeds. Its preferred flatwoods habitat is often the home of Red-cockaded Woodpeckers.

Family Certhiidae: Creepers

Brown Creeper *(Certhia americana)* p. 168
The mottled brown upper surfaces of the Brown Creeper blend with the rough bark surfaces on which it feeds. Stiff tail feathers assist the creeper in its circling ascent searching for bark-dwelling insects, spiders, and other arthropods. The undersides are white and the bill is narrow and down-curved. The call is a single, high-pitched *see*. The Brown Creeper is a winter resident of north Florida's woodlands from October through March. Because of its habits and coloration it probably is easily overlooked.

Common Loon *(Gavia immer)* L 32″   **p. 33**

Large, thick, straight bill.
Habitat: Open saltwater; open freshwater.

Jan	Feb	Mar	Apr	May	June	July	Aug	Sep	Oct	Nov	Dec

Horned Grebe *(Podiceps auritus)* L 14″   **p. 34**

White cheeks and throat (winter).
Habitat: Open saltwater; open freshwater.

Jan	Feb	Mar	Apr	May	June	July	Aug	Sep	Oct	Nov	Dec

Pied-billed Grebe *(Podilymbus podiceps)* L 13½″   **p. 34**

Short, stout, ringed bill and black throat (breeding) or white throat and plain
bill (nonbreeding).
Habitat: Open freshwater; wet prairies and marshes.

Jan	Feb	Mar	Apr	May	June	July	Aug	Sep	Oct	Nov	Dec

American White Pelican *(Pelecanus erythrorhynchos)* L 62″   **p. 36**

Large white body, black on wings.
Habitat: Open saltwater; open freshwater; wet prairies and marshes; mangroves.

Jan	Feb	Mar	Apr	May	June	July	Aug	Sep	Oct	Nov	Dec

Brown Pelican *(Pelecanus occidentalis)* L 48″   **p. 36**

Adult: Grayish-brown body; white head, neck.
Immature: All brown, or with whitish underparts.
Habitat: Coastal beaches; open saltwater; mangrove.

Jan	Feb	Mar	Apr	May	June	July	Aug	Sep	Oct	Nov	Dec

Present in Florida   Breeding in Florida

Common Loon

summer

winter

Horned Grebe

winter

Pied-billed Grebe

breeding

American White Pelican
nonbreeding

immature

breeding

nonbreeding

Brown Pelican

Karl E. Karalus

White-tailed Tropicbird *(Phaethon lepturus)* L 30″   **p. 34**

All white, black stripes on wing, yellow or orange bill, long white tail.
Habitat: Open saltwater.

Jan	Feb	Mar	Apr	May	June	July	Aug	Sep	Oct	Nov	Dec

Magnificent Frigatebird *(Fregata magnificens)* L 40″   **p. 37**

Long forked tail, long hooked bill.
Habitat: Open saltwater; mangrove.

Jan	Feb	Mar	Apr	May	June	July	Aug	Sep	Oct	Nov	Dec

Northern Gannet *(Morus bassanus)* L 37″   **p. 35**

Adult: White body; long, black-tipped wings.
Immature: Gray, or gray with white underparts.
Habitat: Open saltwater.

Jan	Feb	Mar	Apr	May	June	July	Aug	Sep	Oct	Nov	Dec

Brown Booby *(Sula leucogaster)* L 30″   **p. 35**

Adult: Dark brown head, breast, back; white belly.
Immature: All brown.
Habitat: Open saltwater; mangrove.

Jan	Feb	Mar	Apr	May	June	July	Aug	Sep	Oct	Nov	Dec

Masked Booby *(Sula dactylatra)* L 32″   **p. 35**

Adult: White body; black tail, wingtips, and trailing edge of wing.
Immature: Brown upperparts with white patches, white below.
Habitat: Open saltwater; coastal beaches.

Jan	Feb	Mar	Apr	May	June	July	Aug	Sep	Oct	Nov	Dec

    Present in Florida   Breeding in Florida

White-tailed Tropicbird

Magnificent Frigatebird

male

female

Brown Booby

immature

Northern Gannet

immature

adult

adult

Masked Booby

Double-crested Cormorant *(Phalacrocorax auritus)* L 32″   **p. 36**

Adult: All dark with orange throat patch, hooked bill.
Immature: Brown above, pale white below.
Habitat: Open saltwater; open freshwater; mangrove; cypress swamps; agricultural environments.

Jan	Feb	Mar	Apr	May	June	July	Aug	Sep	Oct	Nov	Dec

Anhinga *(Anhinga anhinga)* L 35″   **p. 37**

Long, snakelike neck, straight bill, long tail.
Habitat: Open freshwater; cypress swamps; wet prairies and marshes.

Jan	Feb	Mar	Apr	May	June	July	Aug	Sep	Oct	Nov	Dec

Canada Goose *(Branta canadensis)* L 40″   **p. 45**

Black head and neck, white chin strap.
Habitat: Salt marshes; open freshwater; wet prairies and marshes; agricultural environments.

Jan	Feb	Mar	Apr	May	June	July	Aug	Sep	Oct	Nov	Dec

Tundra Swan *(Cygnus columbianus)* L 52″   **p. 45**

Adult: Large white body, long neck.
Immature: Brownish or tan.
Habitat: Open freshwater; wet prairies and marshes; agricultural environments.

Jan	Feb	Mar	Apr	May	June	July	Aug	Sep	Oct	Nov	Dec

Snow Goose *(Chen caerulescens)* L 28″   **p. 45**

White phase: White with black primaries.
Blue phase: Gray with white head and neck.
Habitat: Salt marshes; open freshwater; wet prairies and marshes; agricultural environments.

Jan	Feb	Mar	Apr	May	June	July	Aug	Sep	Oct	Nov	Dec

⬚ Present in Florida   ▨ Breeding in Florida

Double-crested Cormorant

Anhinga

male

female

Canada Goose

Tundra Swan

Snow Goose

blue phase

white phase

Karl E. Karalus

Great Blue Heron *(Ardea herodias)* L 46″   **p. 38**

Gray-blue with heavy yellow bill.
White morph: All white with light yellow bill and legs.
Habitat: Coastal beaches; salt marshes; open freshwater; mangrove; hardwood swamps; cypress swamps; wet prairies and marshes; urban environments; agricultural environments.

Great Egret *(Casmerodius albus)* L 39″   **p. 39**

All white with black legs, bright yellow bill.
Habitat: Coastal beaches; salt marshes; open freshwater; mangrove; hardwood swamps; cypress swamps; wet prairies and marshes; urban environments; agricultural environments.

Cattle Egret *(Bubulcus ibis)* L 20″   **p. 41**

Breeding: White with buff on head, neck, breast, and back.
Nonbreeding: All white with short yellow bill, yellowish legs.
Habitat: Dry prairies; wet prairies and marshes; agricultural environments.

Snowy Egret *(Egretta thula)* L 24″   **p. 39**

All white with thin black bill, black legs, yellow feet.
Habitat: Coastal beaches; salt marshes; mangrove; hardwood swamps; cypress swamps; wet prairies and marshes; urban environments; agricultural environments.

    Present in Florida   Breeding in Florida

Great Blue Heron

white morph

Great Egret

Snowy Egret

Cattle Egret

breeding

immature

Karl E. Karalus

Reddish Egret *(Egretta rufescens)* L 30″   p. 40

Dark phase: Rufous head, neck; blue-gray body.
White phase: All white. Both phases have pink bill with black anterior half.
Habitat: Coastal beaches; mangrove.

Jan	Feb	Mar	Apr	May	June	July	Aug	Sep	Oct	Nov	Dec

Tricolored Heron *(Egretta tricolor)* L 26″   p. 40

Blue-gray upperparts, white neck and belly.
Habitat: Coastal beaches; salt marshes; mangrove; wet prairies and marshes;
agricultural environments.

Jan	Feb	Mar	Apr	May	June	July	Aug	Sep	Oct	Nov	Dec

Little Blue Heron *(Egretta caerulea)* L 24″   p. 39

Adult: Slate blue (reddish head, neck when breeding), greenish legs, gray bill.
Immature: White with dusky wingtips, greenish yellow legs, whitish bill.
Habitat: Coastal beaches; salt marshes; mangrove; hardwood swamps; cypress
swamps; wet prairies and marshes; agricultural environments.

Jan	Feb	Mar	Apr	May	June	July	Aug	Sep	Oct	Nov	Dec

Green-backed Heron *(Butorides striatus)* L 18″   p. 41

Small with dark crown, green-gray back, chestnut neck, yellow legs.
Habitat: Salt marshes; mangrove; hardwood swamps; cypress swamps; wet prairies
and marshes; urban environments; agricultural environments.

Jan	Feb	Mar	Apr	May	June	July	Aug	Sep	Oct	Nov	Dec

   Present in Florida   Breeding in Florida

Reddish Egret

white phase

dark phase

Tricolored Heron

Little Blue Heron

immature

molting

adult

Green-backed Heron

Karl E. Karalus

Black-crowned Night-Heron *(Nycticorax nycticorax)* L 25" p. 41

Adult: Stocky; black crown, back; white underparts.
Immature: Brown with white spotting.
Habitat: Salt marshes; mangrove; hardwood swamps; cypress swamps; wet prairies and marshes; agricultural environments.

Jan	Feb	Mar	Apr	May	June	July	Aug	Sep	Oct	Nov	Dec

Yellow-crowned Night-Heron *(Nyctanassa violacea)* L 24" p. 42

Adult: All gray, black head with buffy white crown, white ear patch.
Immature: Gray-brown with narrow white spots.
Habitat: Salt marshes; mangrove; hardwood swamps; cypress swamps.

Jan	Feb	Mar	Apr	May	June	July	Aug	Sep	Oct	Nov	Dec

American Bittern *(Botaurus lentiginosus)* L 28" p. 38

Brown with black neck stripes.
Habitat: Salt marshes; wet prairies and marshes.

Jan	Feb	Mar	Apr	May	June	July	Aug	Sep	Oct	Nov	Dec

Least Bittern *(Ixobrychus exilis)* L 13" p. 38

Black crown and back (brown in female), buffy wing patches, dark wingtips.
Habitat: Wet prairies and marshes; agricultural environments.

Jan	Feb	Mar	Apr	May	June	July	Aug	Sep	Oct	Nov	Dec

Present in Florida   Breeding in Florida

Black-crowned Night-Heron

adult

immature

Yellow-crowned Night-Heron

adult

immature

American Bittern

Least Bittern

Wood Stork *(Mycteria americana)* L 40″   **p. 43**

White with black primaries and tail, blackish head (naked in adult), heavy bill, pink feet.
Habitat: Salt marshes; cypress swamps; wet prairies and marshes; agricultural environments.

Jan	Feb	Mar	Apr	May	June	July	Aug	Sep	Oct	Nov	Dec

Greater Flamingo *(Phoenicopterus ruber)* L 46″   **p. 44**

Adult: Large; pink body, black primaries, short heavy bill.
Immature: Grayish white, with some pink.
Habitat: Salt marshes; wet prairies and marshes.

Jan	Feb	Mar	Apr	May	June	July	Aug	Sep	Oct	Nov	Dec

Roseate Spoonbill *(Ajaia ajaja)* L 32″   **p. 43**

Adult: Pink body with spatulate bill, bare greenish head, orange tail.
Immature: Paler, more white.
Habitat: Salt marshes; mangrove; wet prairies and marshes; agricultural environments.

Jan	Feb	Mar	Apr	May	June	July	Aug	Sep	Oct	Nov	Dec

White Ibis *(Eudocimus albus)* L 25″   **p. 42**

Adult: All white, black wingtips, red decurved bill and legs.
Immature: Brown with white underparts.
Habitat: Hardwood swamps; cypress swamps; wet prairies and marshes; agricultural environments.

Jan	Feb	Mar	Apr	May	June	July	Aug	Sep	Oct	Nov	Dec

Glossy Ibis *(Plegadis falcinellus)* L 23″   **p. 43**

Dark plumage, chestnut-bronze in some light, decurved brownish bill.
Habitat: Wet prairies and marshes; agricultural environments.

Jan	Feb	Mar	Apr	May	June	July	Aug	Sep	Oct	Nov	Dec

Present in Florida   Breeding in Florida

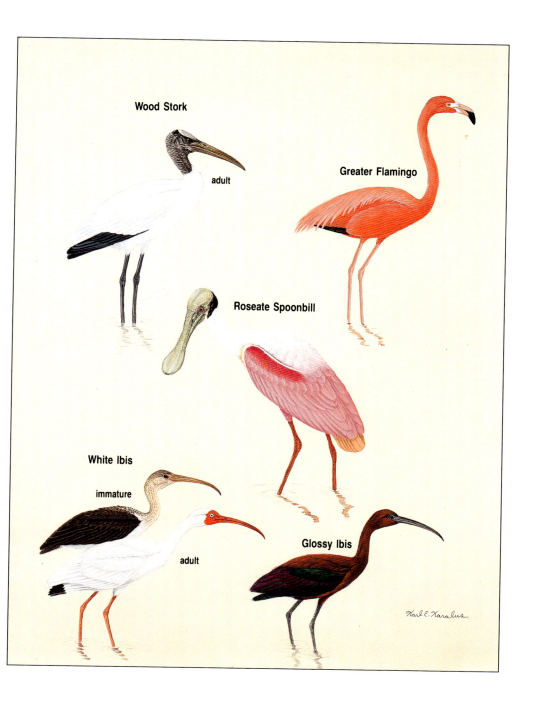

Wood Stork

adult

Greater Flamingo

Roseate Spoonbill

White Ibis

immature

adult

Glossy Ibis

Karl E. Karalus

Fulvous Whistling-Duck *(Dendrocygna bicolor)* L 20″   **p. 44**

Tawny color with dark back, long neck and legs, white rump.
Habitat: Wet prairies and marshes; agricultural environments.

Jan	Feb	Mar	Apr	May	June	July	Aug	Sep	Oct	Nov	Dec

Green-winged Teal *(Anas crecca)* L 14″   **p. 46**

Male: Chestnut head with green ear patch, gray flanks.
Female: Brown, white undertail coverts, small bill.
Habitat: Salt marshes; mangrove; wet prairies and marshes; agricultural environments.

Jan	Feb	Mar	Apr	May	June	July	Aug	Sep	Oct	Nov	Dec

Wood Duck *(Aix sponsa)* L 18″   **p. 46**

Male: Crested green head, white neck, red breast, red eye and base of bill.
Female: Dull brown, white teardrop eye patch.
Habitat: Hardwood swamps; cypress swamps; wet prairies and marshes; agricultural environments.

Jan	Feb	Mar	Apr	May	June	July	Aug	Sep	Oct	Nov	Dec

American Black Duck *(Anas rubripes)* L 23″   **p. 47**

Black-brown body, pale face and neck, yellow bill, violet speculum.
Habitat: Salt marshes; wet prairies and marshes; agricultural environments.

Jan	Feb	Mar	Apr	May	June	July	Aug	Sep	Oct	Nov	Dec

Mottled Duck *(Anas fulvigula)* L 22″   **p. 47**

Pale black-brown body, lighter head and neck, green speculum.
Habitat: Salt marshes; wet prairies and marshes; agricultural environments.

Jan	Feb	Mar	Apr	May	June	July	Aug	Sep	Oct	Nov	Dec

Mallard *(Anas platyrhynchos)* L 23″   **p. 47**

Male: Green head, chestnut breast, grayish white back and sides.
Female: Mottled brown body; orange bill with black markings.
Habitat: Wet prairies and marshes; agricultural environments.

Jan	Feb	Mar	Apr	May	June	July	Aug	Sep	Oct	Nov	Dec

Northern Pintail *(Anas acuta)* L 20-26″   **p. 48**

Male: Brown head, long white neck, white extends up back of neck, long central tail feathers.
Female: Mottled brown body; pale head and neck.
Habitat: Salt marshes; wet prairies and marshes; agricultural environments.

Jan	Feb	Mar	Apr	May	June	July	Aug	Sep	Oct	Nov	Dec

Present in Florida   Breeding in Florida

Fulvous Whistling-Duck

Green-winged Teal
female   male

Wood Duck
male   female

American Black Duck   Mottled Duck

Northern Pintail
male

female

Mallard
female

male   female

Blue-winged Teal *(Anas discors)* L 16″ — p. 48

Male: Gray head with white crescent on face.
Female: Mottled brown with spotted undertail coverts.
Habitat: Salt marshes; wet prairies and marshes; agricultural environments.

Jan	Feb	Mar	Apr	May	June	July	Aug	Sep	Oct	Nov	Dec

Northern Shoveler *(Anas clypeata)* L 19″ — p. 48

Large spatulate bill.
Habitat: Open freshwater; wet prairies and marshes; agricultural environments.

Jan	Feb	Mar	Apr	May	June	July	Aug	Sep	Oct	Nov	Dec

Gadwall *(Anas strepera)* L 20″ — p. 48

Male: Gray with white belly, black undertail coverts.
Female: Mottled brown body, lighter head, white belly.
Habitat: Open freshwater; wet prairies and marshes; agricultural environments.

Jan	Feb	Mar	Apr	May	June	July	Aug	Sep	Oct	Nov	Dec

American Wigeon *(Anas americana)* L 19″ — p. 49

Male: White forehead and cap, green ear patch.
Female: Grayish head.
Habitat: Salt marshes; open freshwater; wet prairies and marshes; agricultural environments.

Jan	Feb	Mar	Apr	May	June	July	Aug	Sep	Oct	Nov	Dec

Redhead *(Aythya americana)* L 19″ — p. 49

Male: Rounded red head, gray bill with white ring.
Female: Brown head.
Habitat: Salt marshes; open saltwater; open freshwater; wet prairies and marshes; agricultural environments.

Jan	Feb	Mar	Apr	May	June	July	Aug	Sep	Oct	Nov	Dec

Canvasback *(Aythya valisineria)* L 21″ — p. 49

Long sloping forehead and bill.
Male: Chestnut head, neck; white back.
Female: Brown head, neck; gray back.
Habitat: Salt marshes; open saltwater; open freshwater; wet prairies and marshes; agricultural environments.

Jan	Feb	Mar	Apr	May	June	July	Aug	Sep	Oct	Nov	Dec

Present in Florida   Breeding in Florida

Blue-winged Teal

male

female

Northern Shoveler

female

male

Gadwall

male

female

American Wigeon

male

female

female

Canvasback

female

male

Redhead

female

male

male

Ring-necked Duck *(Aythya collaris)* L 17″   **p. 50**

Male: Purplish head, white crescent between black breast and gray sides, white ring on bill.
Female: Brown.
Habitat: Salt marshes; open saltwater; open freshwater; wet prairies and marshes; urban environments; agricultural environments.

Jan	Feb	Mar	Apr	May	June	July	Aug	Sep	Oct	Nov	Dec

Muscovy Duck *(Carina moschata)* L 28″   **p. 46**

Both sexes variable: all black, or black and white, or all white. Male has red warty face.
Habitat: Urban environments; agricultural environments.

Jan	Feb	Mar	Apr	May	June	July	Aug	Sep	Oct	Nov	Dec

Lesser Scaup *(Aythya affinis)* L 17″   **p. 50**

Male: Peaked crown, purple gloss on head, dark back, white sides.
Female: Brown with white patch around base of bill.
Habitat: Salt marshes; open saltwater; open freshwater; wet prairies and marshes; agricultural environments.

Jan	Feb	Mar	Apr	May	June	July	Aug	Sep	Oct	Nov	Dec

Hooded Merganser *(Lophodytes cucullatus)* L 18″   **p. 52**

Male: Black crested head with white head patches.
Female: Reddish-brown crest with no white.
Habitat: Salt marshes; open freshwater; hardwood swamps; cypress swamps; wet prairies and marshes; urban environments; agricultural environments.

Jan	Feb	Mar	Apr	May	June	July	Aug	Sep	Oct	Nav	Dec

Red-breasted Merganser *(Mergus serrator)* L 23″   **p. 52**

Male: Green shaggy head, white collar, red-streaked breast.
Female: Brown shaggy head, pale throat and neck.
Habitat: Salt marshes; open saltwater; open freshwater; agricultural environments.

Jan	Feb	Mar	Apr	May	June	July	Aug	Sep	Oct	Nov	Dec

Ruddy Duck *(Oxyura jamaicensis)* L 15″   **p. 52**

Dark cap, white cheeks, long cocked tail. Cheek patch of females less distinct.
Habitat: Open saltwater; open freshwater; wet prairies and marshes; agricultural environments.

Jan	Feb	Mar	Apr	May	June	July	Aug	Sep	Oct	Nav	Dec

▢ Present in Florida   ▨ Breeding in Florida

Ring-necked Duck

female

male

Muscovy Duck

Lesser Scaup

female

male

female

Red-breasted Merganser

male

Hooded Merganser

female

male

Ruddy Duck

female

male

Karl E. Karalus

Black Scoter *(Melanitta nigra)* L 19″   p. 51

Male: All black, orange knob at base of bill.
Female: Brown with pale face and throat.
Habitat: Open saltwater.

Jan	Feb	Mar	Apr	May	June	July	Aug	Sep	Oct	Nov	Dec

White-winged Scoter *(Melanitta fusca)* L 21″   p. 51

Male: Black with white crescent below eye, white in wings, black knob at base of orange bill.
Female: Brown with indistinct facial patches.
Habitat: Open saltwater; open freshwater.

Jan	Feb	Mar	Apr	May	June	July	Aug	Sep	Oct	Nov	Dec

Surf Scoter *(Melanitta perspicillata)* L 20″   p. 51

Male: Black with white patches on forehead and nape; black, white, orange bill.
Female: Brown with two white patches on side of face.
Habitat: Open saltwater; open freshwater.

Jan	Feb	Mar	Apr	May	June	July	Aug	Sep	Oct	Nov	Dec

Bufflehead *(Bucephala albeola)* L 13″   p. 51

Male: Black above, white below, large white head patch.
Female: Dark head and back, all-white face patch.
Habitat: Open saltwater; open freshwater; agricultural environments.

Jan	Feb	Mar	Apr	May	June	July	Aug	Sep	Oct	Nov	Dec

Oldsquaw *(Clangula hyemalis)* L 22″   p. 50

Winter male: Mostly white, brown breast and back, long tail.
Female: Whitish head, dark wings.
Habitat: Open saltwater; open freshwater; agricultural environments.

Jan	Feb	Mar	Apr	May	June	July	Aug	Sep	Oct	Nov	Dec

Common Goldeneye *(Bucephala clangula)* L 18″   p. 51

Male: Green head, white face spot, yellow eye.
Female: Brown head, yellow eye.
Habitat: Open saltwater; open freshwater.

Jan	Feb	Mar	Apr	May	June	July	Aug	Sep	Oct	Nov	Dec

   Present in Florida   Breeding in Florida

Black Scoter

female

male

White-winged Scoter

female

male

Surf Scoter

male

female

Bufflehead

female

male

Oldsquaw

male

female

Common Goldeneye

male

female

Karl E. Karalus

Black Vulture *(Coragyps atratus)* L 25″ p. 53

Black head, white at base of primaries, short tail.
Habitat: Coastal beaches; salt marshes; pine scrub; mangrove; hardwood swamps; dry prairies; cypress swamps; mesic hammocks; mixed pine and hardwood forests; wet prairies and marshes; urban environments; pine flatwoods; sandhills; agricultural environments.

Jan	Feb	Mar	Apr	May	June	July	Aug	Sep	Oct	Nov	Dec

Turkey Vulture *(Cathartes aura)* L 27″ p. 53

Red head (black in immatures), long tail, underside of wings dark anteriorly, lighter posteriorly.
Habitat: Coastal beaches; salt marshes; pine scrub; mangrove; hardwood swamps; dry prairies; cypress swamps; mesic hammocks; mixed pine and hardwood forests; wet prairies and marshes; urban environments; pine flatwoods; sandhills; agricultural environments.

Jan	Feb	Mar	Apr	May	June	July	Aug	Sep	Oct	Nov	Dec

Northern Harrier *(Circus cyaneus)* L 20″ p. 56

Male: Gray upperparts, white rump.
Female: Brown upperparts, white rump.
Habitat: Salt marshes; dry prairies; wet prairies and marshes; agricultural environments.

Jan	Feb	Mar	Apr	May	June	July	Aug	Sep	Oct	Nov	Dec

Bald Eagle *(Haliaeetus leucocephalus)* L 31-37″ p. 56

Adult: White head and tail.
Immature: All dark, with variable white streaking below. Thigh feathers do not cover legs.
Habitat: Coastal beaches; salt marshes; dry prairies; mixed pine and hardwood forests; wet prairies and marshes; pine flatwoods; sandhills; agricultural environments.

Jan	Feb	Mar	Apr	May	June	July	Aug	Sep	Oct	Nov	Dec

Golden Eagle *(Aquila chrysaetos)* L 30-40″ p. 58

Adult: Brown with golden wash on head, neck; leg feathers reach to toes.
Habitat: Salt marshes; wet prairies and marshes; agricultural environments.

Jan	Feb	Mar	Apr	May	June	July	Aug	Sep	Oct	Nov	Dec

Present in Florida   Breeding in Florida

Black Vulture

Turkey Vulture

Bald Eagle

Northern Harrier

male

female

immature

adult

Golden Eagle

immature

adult

Mississippi Kite *(Ictinia mississippiensis)* L 14″   p. 55

Dark gray back, light gray head, long wings and tail.
Habitat: Mesic hammocks; mixed pine and hardwood forests; urban environments.

Jan	Feb	Mar	Apr	May	June	July	Aug	Sep	Oct	Nov	Dec

Snail Kite *(Rostrhamus sociabilis)* L 17″   p. 55

White at base of tail, red or orange eyes and facial skin.
Male: Slate blue.
Female and immature: Brown.
Habitat: Wet prairies and marshes.

Jan	Feb	Mar	Apr	May	June	July	Aug	Sep	Oct	Nov	Dec

Sharp-shinned Hawk *(Accipiter striatus)* L 10-14″   p. 56

Short, square tail and small head.
Habitat: Pine scrub; mesic hammocks; mixed pine and hardwood forests; pine flatwoods; sandhills; agricultural environments.

Jan	Feb	Mar	Apr	May	June	July	Aug	Sep	Oct	Nov	Dec

American Swallow-tailed Kite *(Elanoides forficatus)* L 23″   p. 54

Deeply forked tail; black and white pattern.
Habitat: Pine scrub; hardwood swamps; cypress swamps; mesic hammocks; mixed pine and hardwood forests; wet prairies and marshes; pine flatwoods; agricultural environments.

Jan	Feb	Mar	Apr	May	June	July	Aug	Sep	Oct	Nov	Dec

Cooper's Hawk *(Accipiter cooperii)* L 14-20″   p. 56

Long rounded tail, large head.
Habitat: Pine scrub; mesic hammocks; mixed pine and hardwood forests; pine flatwoods; sandhills; agricultural environments.

Jan	Feb	Mar	Apr	May	June	July	Aug	Sep	Oct	Nov	Dec

   Present in Florida   Breeding in Florida

Mississippi Kite

adult

immature

Snail Kite

female

male

American Swallow-tailed Kite

Sharp-shinned Hawk

male

female

Cooper's Hawk

female

male

Red-tailed Hawk *(Buteo jamaicensis)* L 22″   **p. 58**

Adult: Chestnut tail, dark belly band (most birds).
Immature: Finely banded brown tail.
Habitat: Pine scrub; hardwood swamps; dry prairies; cypress swamps; mesic hammocks; mixed pine and hardwood forests; wet prairies and marshes; urban environments; pine flatwoods; sandhills; agricultural environments.

| Jan | Feb | Mar | Apr | May | June | July | Aug | Sep | Oct | Nov | Dec |

Broad-winged Hawk *(Buteo platypterus)* L 16″   **p. 57**

Wide black and white bands on tail, light underwings with dark border.
Habitat: Mangrove; hardwood swamps; cypress swamps; mesic hammocks; mixed pine and hardwood forests; pine flatwoods; sandhills; agricultural environments.

| Jan | Feb | Mar | Apr | May | June | July | Aug | Sep | Oct | Nov | Dec |

Red-shouldered Hawk *(Buteo lineatus)* L 19″   **p. 57**

Adult: Reddish shoulders, tail with narrow white bands, whitish crescent at base of primaries.
Immature: Browner; little or no red on shoulders.
Habitat: Pine scrub; hardwood swamps; cypress swamps; mesic hammocks; mixed pine and hardwood forests; wet prairies and marshes; urban environments; pine flatwoods; sandhills; agricultural environments.

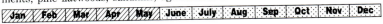

| Jan | Feb | Mar | Apr | May | June | July | Aug | Sep | Oct | Nov | Dec |

Short-tailed Hawk *(Buteo brachyurus)* L 16″   **p. 57**

Dark phase: Black above, black underparts.
Light phase: Black above, white underparts.
Habitat: Hardwood swamps; dry prairies; mesic hammocks; mixed pine and hardwood forests; wet prairies and marshes.

| Jan | Feb | Mar | Apr | May | June | July | Aug | Sep | Oct | Nov | Dec |

Present in Florida   Breeding in Florida

Red-tailed Hawk

adult

immature

Broad-winged Hawk

adult

immature

Red-shouldered Hawk

adult

immature

Short-tailed Hawk

dark phase

light phase

Karl E. Karalus

Crested Caracara *(Polyborus plancus)* L 23″   p. 58

Dark overall with white throat, neck, and barring on tail and wings, red-orange facial skin.
Habitat: Dry prairies; agricultural environments.

Jan	Feb	Mar	Apr	May	June	July	Aug	Sep	Oct	Nov	Dec

American Kestrel *(Falco sparvarius)* L 10″   p. 59

Small; russet back and tail, two black facial stripes.
Habitat: Pine scrub; dry prairies; mixed pine and hardwood forests; urban environments; pine flatwoods; sandhills; agricultural environments.

Jan	Feb	Mar	Apr	May	June	July	Aug	Sep	Oct	Nov	Dec

Osprey *(Pandion haliaetus)* L 24″   p. 54

Dark brown above, white below; dark eyestripe.
Habitat: Coastal beaches; salt marshes; open saltwater; open freshwater; mangrove; wet prairies and marshes; agricultural environments.

Jan	Feb	Mar	Apr	May	June	July	Aug	Sep	Oct	Nov	Dec

Merlin *(Falco columbarius)* L 12″   p. 59

Dark above, heavily barred tail, no distinct facial markings.
Habitat: Coastal beaches; salt marshes; dry prairies; wet prairies and marshes; agricultural environments.

Jan	Feb	Mar	Apr	May	June	July	Aug	Sep	Oct	Nov	Dec

Peregrine Falcon *(Falco peregrinus)* L 16-20″   p. 59

Dark crown and nape forming helmet.
Habitat: Coastal beaches; salt marshes; dry prairies; wet prairies and marshes; agricultural environments.

Jan	Feb	Mar	Apr	May	June	July	Aug	Sep	Oct	Nov	Dec

Present in Florida   Breeding in Florida

Crested Caracara
adult

American Kestrel

female

male

Osprey

female

Merlin

male

Peregrine Falcon
female

male

Karl E. Karalus

Wild Turkey *(Meleagris gallopavo)* L 45″   **p. 60**

Large; dark, iridescent body, naked head.
Habitat: Pine scrub; hardwood swamps; cypress swamps; mesic hammocks; mixed pine and hardwood forests; pine flatwoods; sandhills.

Jan	Feb	Mar	Apr	May	June	July	Aug	Sep	Oct	Nov	Dec

Northern Bobwhite *(Colinus virginianus)* L 9″   **p. 60**

Mottled reddish-brown with white (male) or buffy (female) throat and eyestripe.
Habitat: Pine scrub; dry prairies; mesic hammocks; mixed pine and hardwood forests; urban environments; pine flatwoods; sandhills; agricultural environments.

Jan	Feb	Mar	Apr	May	June	July	Aug	Sep	Oct	Nov	Dec

Limpkin *(Aramus guarauna)* L 26″   **p. 63**

Brown body, streaked with white; slightly decurved bill.
Habitat: Hardwood swamps; cypress swamps; wet prairies and marshes.

Jan	Feb	Mar	Apr	May	June	July	Aug	Sep	Oct	Nov	Dec

Sandhill Crane *(Grus canadensis)* L 40″   **p. 63**

Large gray or brown body; red crown and lores (adults only).
Habitat: Dry prairies; wet prairies and marshes; agricultural environments.

Jan	Feb	Mar	Apr	May	June	July	Aug	Sep	Oct	Nov	Dec

Present in Florida   Breeding in Florida

Wild Turkey

male

female

Northern Bobwhite

male

female

Limpkin

Sandhill Crane

King Rail *(Rallus elegans)* L 15″   **p. 61**

Mottled rufous-brown and black back, cinnamon underparts.
Habitat: Wet prairies and marshes; agricultural environments.

Jan	Feb	Mar	Apr	May	June	July	Aug	Sep	Oct	Nov	Dec

Clapper Rail *(Rallus longirostris)* L 14″   **p. 61**

Mottled gray-brown and black back, buff underparts.
Habitat: Salt marshes; mangrove.

Jan	Feb	Mar	Apr	May	June	July	Aug	Sep	Oct	Nov	Dec

Virginia Rail *(Rallus limicola)* L 9″   **p. 61**

Gray cheeks, chestnut wings.
Habitat: Wet prairies and marshes; agricultural environments.

Jan	Feb	Mar	Apr	May	June	July	Aug	Sep	Oct	Nov	Dec

Black Rail *(Laterallus jamaicensis)* L 6″   **p. 60**

Small; black or gray-black with white speckling.
Habitat: Salt marshes; wet prairies and marshes.

Jan	Feb	Mar	Apr	May	June	July	Aug	Sep	Oct	Nov	Dec

Sora *(Porzana carolina)* L 8″   **p. 61**

Small; short, thick yellow-green bill.
Habitat: Wet prairies and marshes; agricultural environments.

Jan	Feb	Mar	Apr	May	June	July	Aug	Sep	Oct	Nov	Dec

Present in Florida   Breeding in Florida

King Rail

Clapper Rail

Virginia Rail

Black Rail

Sora

Common Moorhen *(Gallinula chloropus)* L 14″   **p. 62**

Gray-black head and neck, red forehead shield (summer), duller or brown in winter and immature.
Habitat: Wet prairies and marshes; urban environments; agricultural environments.

| Jan | Feb | Mar | Apr | May | June | July | Aug | Sep | Oct | Nov | Dec |

American Coot *(Fulica americana)* L 15″   **p. 62**

Black body, white bill with dark band, small reddish-brown forehead shield.
Habitat: Salt marshes; open saltwater; open freshwater; wet prairies and marshes; agricultural environments.

| Jan | Feb | Mar | Apr | May | June | July | Aug | Sep | Oct | Nov | Dec |

Purple Gallinule *(Porphyrula martinica)* L 13″   **p. 62**

Adult: Purple-blue body, blue forehead shield.
Immature: Buffy yellow-brown underparts, greenish-blue or olive above.
Habitat: Wet prairies and marshes; agricultural environments.

| Jan | Feb | Mar | Apr | May | June | July | Aug | Sep | Oct | Nov | Dec |

American Avocet *(Recurvirostra americana)* L 18″   **p. 66**

Black and white wings, gray (winter) or rusty (spring) head and neck, thin upturned bill.
Habitat: Wet prairies and marshes; agricultural environments.

| Jan | Feb | Mar | Apr | May | June | July | Aug | Sep | Oct | Nov | Dec |

American Oystercatcher *(Haematopus palliatus)* L 18″   **p. 65**

Black hood, heavy red bill, white underparts, pink legs.
Habitat: Coastal beaches.

| Jan | Feb | Mar | Apr | May | June | July | Aug | Sep | Oct | Nov | Dec |

Black-necked Stilt *(Himantopus mexicanus)* L 14″   **p. 66**

Black upperparts, white below, long thin pink legs and black bill.
Habitat: Wet prairies and marshes; agricultural environments.

| Jan | Feb | Mar | Apr | May | June | July | Aug | Sep | Oct | Nov | Dec |

     Present in Florida   Breeding in Florida

Common Moorhen

immature

adult

American Coot

Purple Gallinule

adult

immature

American Avocet

winter

American Oystercatcher

Black-necked Stilt

Karl E. Karalus

Lesser Golden-Plover *(Pluvialis dominica)* L 10″ **p. 64**

Golden-yellow mottled upperparts, small bill, dark rump, gray wing linings.
Habitat: Coastal beaches; agricultural environments.

Jan	Feb	Mar	Apr	May	June	July	Aug	Sep	Oct	Nov	Dec

Semipalmated Plover *(Charadrius semipalmatus)* L 7″ **p. 65**

Brown upperparts, orange bill and legs (breeding) or dull yellow (nonbreeding).
Habitat: Coastal beaches; agricultural environments.

Jan	Feb	Mar	Apr	May	June	July	Aug	Sep	Oct	Nov	Dec

Black-bellied Plover *(Pluvialis squatarola)* L 11″ **p. 64**

White rump, black under wings, white wing stripe.
Habitat: Coastal beaches; agricultural environments.

Jan	Feb	Mar	Apr	May	June	July	Aug	Sep	Oct	Nov	Dec

Killdeer *(Charadrius vociferus)* L 10″ **p. 65**

Two black breast bands, rufous rump and upper tail.
Habitat: Coastal beaches; dry prairies; urban environments; agricultural environments.

Jan	Feb	Mar	Apr	May	June	July	Aug	Sep	Oct	Nov	Dec

Piping Plover *(Charadrius melodus)* L 7″ **p. 65**

Upperparts pale gray, orange legs, white rump.
Habitat: Coastal beaches.

Jan	Feb	Mar	Apr	May	June	July	Aug	Sep	Oct	Nov	Dec

Wilson's Plover *(Charadrius wilsonia)* L 8″ **p. 64**

Heavy black bill, pinkish legs, brown back.
Habitat: Coastal beaches.

Jan	Feb	Mar	Apr	May	June	July	Aug	Sep	Oct	Nov	Dec

Snowy Plover *(Charadrius alexandrinus)* L 6″ **p. 64**

Pale gray-brown upperparts, incomplete black breast band, gray legs.
Habitat: Coastal beaches.

Jan	Feb	Mar	Apr	May	June	July	Aug	Sep	Oct	Nov	Dec

Present in Florida   Breeding in Florida

Lesser Golden-Plover

winter

Semipalmated Plover

winter

Black-bellied Plover

breeding

winter

Kildeer

Piping Plover

breeding

winter

Wilson's Plover

female

male

Snowy Plover

breeding

Karl E. Karalus

Greater Yellowlegs *(Tringa melanoleuca)* L 14″   **p. 66**

Bill is 2-2½ times width of head. Call: 3-5 notes, *tew, tew, tew.*
Habitat: Coastal beaches; salt marshes; wet prairies and marshes; agricultural environments.

Jan	Feb	Mar	Apr	May	June	July	Aug	Sep	Oct	Nov	Dec

Lesser Yellowlegs *(Tringa flavipes)* L 10½″   **p. 66**

Bill is 1-1½ times width of head. Call: 1-2 notes, *tew-tew.*
Habitat: Coastal beaches; salt marshes; wet prairies and marshes; agricultural environments.

Jan	Feb	Mar	Apr	May	June	July	Aug	Sep	Oct	Nov	Dec

Whimbrel *(Numenius phaeopus)* L 17″   **p. 67**

Decurved bill, head stripes, grayish underparts.
Habitat: Coastal beaches; agricultural environments.

Jan	Feb	Mar	Apr	May	June	July	Aug	Sep	Oct	Nov	Dec

Long-billed Curlew *(Numenius americanus)* L 23″   **p. 67**

Very long decurved bill, no head stripes, buff underparts.
Habitat: Coastal beaches.

Jan	Feb	Mar	Apr	May	June	July	Aug	Sep	Oct	Nov	Dec

Marbled Godwit *(Limosa fedoa)* L 18″   **p. 68**

Cinnamon buff underparts, slightly upturned pink bill with dark tip.
Habitat: Coastal beaches; agricultural environments.

Jan	Feb	Mar	Apr	May	June	July	Aug	Sep	Oct	Nov	Dec

   Present in Florida   Breeding in Florida

Greater Yellowlegs

Lesser Yellowlegs

Whimbrel

Long-billed Curlew

Marbled Godwit

Solitary Sandpiper *(Tringa solitaria)* L 8½"   **p. 67**

White eye ring, dark upperparts speckled with white, greenish legs; bobbing motion.
Habitat: Hardwood swamps; wet prairies and marshes; agricultural environments.

Jan	Feb	Mar	Apr	May	June	July	Aug	Sep	Oct	Nov	Dec

Willet *(Catoptrophorus semipalmatus)* L 15"   **p. 67**

Long straight bill, gray or brown plumage, black and white wing pattern in flight.
Habitat: Coastal beaches.

Jan	Feb	Mar	Apr	May	June	July	Aug	Sep	Oct	Nov	Dec

Spotted Sandpiper *(Actitis macularia)* L 7½"   **p. 67**

White wing stripe, stiff-winged flight; teetering motion.
Habitat: Hardwood swamps; wet prairies and marshes; agricultural environments.

Jan	Feb	Mar	Apr	May	June	July	Aug	Sep	Oct	Nov	Dec

American Woodcock *(Scolopax minor)* L 11"   **p. 71**

Long pale bill, upperparts mottled with black, brown, gray, rust. Cinnamon tan below, black crown with buffy cross stripes.
Habitat: Mesic hammocks; mixed pine and hardwood forests; wet prairies and marshes; agricultural environments.

Jan	Feb	Mar	Apr	May	June	July	Aug	Sep	Oct	Nov	Dec

Common Snipe *(Gallinago gallinago)* L 10"   **p. 70**

Very long straight dark bill, buff stripes on heavily mottled upperparts, striped head, buffy streaked breast, zigzig flight.
Habitat: Wet prairies and marshes; agricultural environments.

Jan	Feb	Mar	Apr	May	June	July	Aug	Sep	Oct	Nov	Dec

Short-billed Dowitcher *(Limnodromus griseus)* L 11"   **p. 70**

Breeding: Russet underparts, barring on flanks, white belly and vent.
Winter: Gray upperparts. Identify by call: *tu-tu*, or *tu-tu-tu*.
Habitat: Coastal beaches; salt marshes; wet prairies and marshes; agricultural environments.

Jan	Feb	Mar	Apr	May	June	July	Aug	Sep	Oct	Nov	Dec

⬚ Present in Florida   ▨ Breeding in Florida

Solitary Sandpiper

Willet

breeding

American Woodcock

Spotted Sandpiper

summer

winter

Common Snipe

Short-billed Dowitcher

winter

Purple Sandpiper *(Calidris maritima)* L 9″   **p. 70**

Dark gray head, breast, back, white belly, dull orange legs, long drooped bill. Inhabits rock jetties.
Habitat: Coastal beaches.

Jan	Feb	Mar	Apr	May	June	July	Aug	Sep	Oct	Nov	Dec

Ruddy Turnstone *(Arenaria interpres)* L 9″   **p. 68**

Winter: Brown head and back, black breast, white belly, orange legs.
Breeding: Rusty upperparts, black and white head.
Habitat: Coastal beaches.

Jan	Feb	Mar	Apr	May	June	July	Aug	Sep	Oct	Nov	Dec

Pectoral Sandpiper *(Calidris melanotos)* L 9″   **p. 70**

Brown upperparts, heavily streaked breast sharply demarcated from white belly.
Habitat: Salt marshes; wet prairies and marshes; agricultural environments.

Jan	Feb	Mar	Apr	May	June	July	Aug	Sep	Oct	Nov	Dec

Red Knot *(Calidris canutus)* L 10″   **p. 68**

Winter: Dark gray above, white below, short tapered bill, greenish legs.
Breeding: Rufous face and underparts, brown back, mottled with black and white.
Habitat: Coastal beaches.

Jan	Feb	Mar	Apr	May	June	July	Aug	Sep	Oct	Nov	Dec

Dunlin *(Calidris alpina)* L 8½″   **p. 70**

Winter: Brownish gray above, lighter below, black bill drooped at tip.
Breeding: White underparts with black belly patch, chestnut back.
Habitat: Coastal beaches; salt marshes; agricultural environments.

Jan	Feb	Mar	Apr	May	June	July	Aug	Sep	Oct	Nov	Dec

Present in Florida   Breeding in Florida

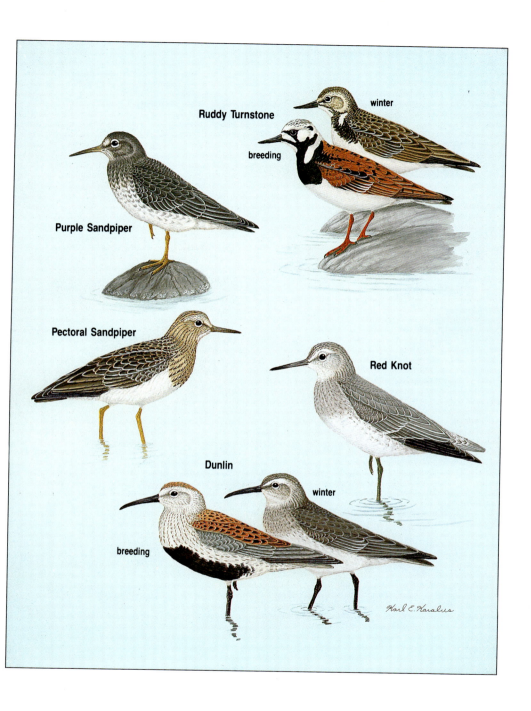

Ruddy Turnstone

winter

breeding

Purple Sandpiper

Pectoral Sandpiper

Red Knot

Dunlin

winter

breeding

Karl E. Karalus

White-rumped Sandpiper *(Calidris fuscicollis)* L 7½" p. 69

White rump, wings extend beyond tail.
Winter: Dusky gray head, breast, back; white eyebrow.
Breeding: Rust on head and ear coverts, dark streaks on white breast and sides.
Habitat: Coastal beaches; salt marshes; wet prairies and marshes; agricultural environments.

Jan	Feb	Mar	Apr	May	June	July	Aug	Sep	Oct	Nov	Dec

Least Sandpiper *(Calidris minutilla)* L 6" p. 69

Short thin black bill, dull yellow or greenish legs.
Winter: Brown head, back, breast; white belly.
Breeding: Brown, mottled above, dark streaked breast.
Habitat: Coastal beaches; salt marshes; wet prairies and marshes; agricultural environments.

Jan	Feb	Mar	Apr	May	June	July	Aug	Sep	Oct	Nov	Dec

Sanderling *(Calidris alba)* L 8" p. 68

Winter: Light gray above, white below, black along bend of wing.
Breeding: Rusty head, back, breast, spotted with black; white below.
Habitat: Coastal beaches.

Jan	Feb	Mar	Apr	May	June	July	Aug	Sep	Oct	Nov	Dec

Western Sandpiper *(Calidris mauri)* L 6½" p. 69

Slight droop at tip of black bill, black legs.
Winter: Similar to Semipalmated. Flight call: A high *zeep*.
Breeding: Rusty wash on crown, ears, back; V-shaped streakings on breasts to flanks.
Habitat: Coastal beaches; salt marshes; wet prairies and marshes; agricultural environments.

Jan	Feb	Mar	Apr	May	June	July	Aug	Sep	Oct	Nov	Dec

Semipalmated Sandpiper *(Calidris pusilla)* L 6¼" p. 69

Short stout bill, black legs.
Winter: Brown above, white below. Call: A coarse *cherk*.
Breeding: Rufous, buff mottled above, brown breast streaks, white belly.
Habitat: Coastal beaches; salt marshes; wet prairies and marshes; agricultural environments.

Jan	Feb	Mar	Apr	May	June	July	Aug	Sep	Oct	Nov	Dec

Present in Florida Breeding in Florida

White-rumped Sandpiper
winter

Least Sandpiper

Sanderling
winter

Western Sandpiper

Semipalmated Sandpiper

Karl E. Karalus

Great Black-backed Gull *(Larus marinus)* L 30″ p. 72

Large; black mantle, white head and body, heavy yellow bill, pink legs.
Immature: Brown or black mottled upperparts, light head.
Habitat: Coastal beaches; open saltwater.

Jan	Feb	Mar	Apr	May	June	July	Aug	Sep	Oct	Nov	Dec

Lesser Black-backed Gull *(Larus fuscus)* L 21″ p. 72

Adult: Dark gray mantle, yellow bill and legs, white head, underparts.
Immature: Similar to Herring Gull, but more white in head and rump, more black in wings.
Habitat: Coastal beaches; open saltwater.

Jan	Feb	Mar	Apr	May	June	July	Aug	Sep	Oct	Nov	Dec

Laughing Gull *(Larus atricilla)* L 16″ p. 71

Adult: Black head, dark gray mantle, dark red bill and legs.
Winter adult and immature: Mottled gray head, black bill and legs.
Juvenile: Brown.
Habitat: Coastal beaches; salt marshes; open saltwater; open freshwater; urban environments; agricultural environments.

Jan	Feb	Mar	Apr	May	June	July	Aug	Sep	Oct	Nov	Dec

Bonaparte's Gull *(Larus philadelphia)* L 13″ p. 71

Winter: Small; black bill, white head with black ear spot, gray mantle with a white wedge on outer wing.
Habitat: Coastal beaches; salt marshes; open saltwater; open freshwater; wet prairies and marshes; agricultural environments.

Jan	Feb	Mar	Apr	May	June	July	Aug	Sep	Oct	Nov	Dec

Herring Gull *(Larus argentatus)* L 25″ p. 72

Adult: Pale gray mantle, black wingtips, yellow bill, pink legs.
Immature: Gray-brown, streaked, black tail band, pink legs.
Habitat: Coastal beaches; salt marshes; open saltwater; open freshwater; urban environments; agricultural environments.

Jan	Feb	Mar	Apr	May	June	July	Aug	Sep	Oct	Nov	Dec

Ring-billed Gull *(Larus delawarensis)* L 17″ p. 71

Adult: Pale gray mantle, black wingtips, yellow bill with black band, yellow legs.
Immature: Pink bill with black tip, mottled gray-brown, narrow tail band.
Habitat: Coastal beaches; salt marshes; open saltwater; open freshwater; wet prairies and marshes; urban environments; agricultural environments.

Jan	Feb	Mar	Apr	May	June	July	Aug	Sep	Oct	Nov	Dec

Present in Florida   Breeding in Florida

Great Black-backed Gull

adult

immature

second winter

Laughing Gull

Lesser Black-backed Gull

Bonaparte's Gull

Herring Gull

first winter

Ring-billed Gull

first winter

adult

adult

Least Tern *(Sterna antillarum)* L 9″

p. 74

White forehead, black crown, yellow bill with black tip.
Immature: Brown back, black nape, black at bend of wing.
Habitat: Coastal beaches; salt marshes; open saltwater; open freshwater; wet prairies and marshes; agricultural environments.

Jan	Feb	Mar	Apr	May	June	July	Aug	Sep	Oct	Nov	Dec

Royal Tern *(Sterna maxima)* L 20″

p. 73

Black cap and crest, often with white forehead, orange-yellow bill.
Habitat: Coastal beaches; open saltwater.

Jan	Feb	Mar	Apr	May	June	July	Aug	Sep	Oct	Nov	Dec

Common Tern *(Sterna hirundo)* L 14″

p. 73

Winter: Dark nape, dark bar at bend of wing, black feet and bill.
Breeding: Black cap, gray back, black-tipped red bill and legs.
Habitat: Coastal beaches; salt marshes; open saltwater.

Jan	Feb	Mar	Apr	May	June	July	Aug	Sep	Oct	Nov	Dec

Caspian Tern *(Sterna caspia)* L 21″

p. 72

Black cap and forehead, heavy orange-red bill.
Habitat: Coastal beaches; open saltwater; open freshwater.

Jan	Feb	Mar	Apr	May	June	July	Aug	Sep	Oct	Nov	Dec

Roseate Tern *(Sterna dougallii)* L 15″

p. 73

Black cap and bill, orange-red feet. Winter: Similar to Common Tern.
Habitat: Coastal beaches; open saltwater.

Jan	Feb	Mar	Apr	May	June	July	Aug	Sep	Oct	Nov	Dec

Forster's Tern *(Sterna forsteri)* L 14″

p. 74

Winter: White head, black ear-eye patch, black bill, orange legs.
Breeding: Black-tipped orange bill and legs, primaries lighter than rest of wing and back.
Habitat: Coastal beaches; salt marshes; open saltwater; open freshwater; wet prairies and marshes; agricultural environments.

Jan	Feb	Mar	Apr	May	June	July	Aug	Sep	Oct	Nov	Dec

Gull-billed Tern *(Sterna nilotica)* L 14″

p. 72

Short, stout black bill, black legs and cap.
Habitat: Coastal beaches; salt marshes; wet prairies and marshes; agricultural environments.

Jan	Feb	Mar	Apr	May	June	July	Aug	Sep	Oct	Nov	Dec

Sandwich Tern *(Sterna sandvicencis)* L 15″

p. 73

Black head with crest, slender black bill with yellow tip, black legs.
Habitat: Coastal beaches; salt marshes; open saltwater.

Jan	Feb	Mar	Apr	May	June	July	Aug	Sep	Oct	Nov	Dec

 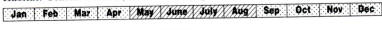 Present in Florida   Breeding in Florida

Least Tern

Royal Tern

nonbreeding

breeding

winter

Common Tern

breeding

Caspian Tern

adult

Roseate Tern

immature

Forster's Tern

winter

Gull-billed Tern

breeding

Sandwich Tern

winter

Karl E. Karalus

Black Tern *(Chlidonias niger)* L 10″   **p. 74**

Spring: Black head and body, gray wings and tail, white vent.
Fall: Dark cap and breast patches, gray mantle.
Habitat: Coastal beaches; salt marshes; open saltwater; open freshwater; wet prairies and marshes; agricultural environments.

Jan	Feb	Mar	Apr	May	June	July	Aug	Sep	Oct	Nov	Dec
▪	▪	▪				▪	▪	▪	▪	▪	▪

Bridled Tern *(Sterna anaethetus)* L 15″   **p. 74**

Gray upperparts, black cap with white forehead, whitish collar.
Habitat: Coastal beaches; open saltwater.

Jan	Feb	Mar	Apr	May	June	July	Aug	Sep	Oct	Nov	Dec
						▪	▪	▪	▪		

Sooty Tern *(Sterna fuscata)* L 16″   **p. 74**

All black above, except for white forehead, white below.
Habitat: Coastal beaches; open saltwater.

Jan	Feb	Mar	Apr	May	June	July	Aug	Sep	Oct	Nov	Dec
		▨	▨	▨	▨	▨	▨				

Black Noddy *(Anous minutus)* L 13″   **p. 75**

Smaller than Brown Noddy; dark brown body, sharply defined white cap, slender bill appears slightly decurved.
Habitat: Coastal beaches; open saltwater.

Jan	Feb	Mar	Apr	May	June	July	Aug	Sep	Oct	Nov	Dec
			▪	▪	▪						

Brown Noddy *(Anous stolidus)* L 16″   **p. 75**

All brown, with white cap.
Habitat: Coastal beaches; open saltwater.

Jan	Feb	Mar	Apr	May	June	July	Aug	Sep	Oct	Nov	Dec
		▨	▨	▨	▨	▨	▨	▪	▪		

Black Skimmer *(Rynchops niger)* L 18″   **p. 75**

Red and black bill, lower mandible longer than upper. Black upperparts, white forehead and underparts.
Habitat: Coastal beaches; salt marshes.

Jan	Feb	Mar	Apr	May	June	July	Aug	Sep	Oct	Nov	Dec
▪	▪	▪	▪	▨	▨	▨	▨	▪	▪	▪	▪

   ▪ Present in Florida   ▨ Breeding in Florida

Black Tern

spring

fall

Bridled Tern

Sooty Tern

Black Noddy

Brown Noddy

Black Skimmer

Karl E. Karalus

Common Ground-Dove *(Columbina passerina)* L 6″   **p. 77**

Small; gray-brown with purplish spots on wings. Outer half of wings bright rufous.
Habitat: Coastal beaches; pine scrub; dry prairies; mixed pine and hardwood forests; pine flatwoods; sandhills; agricultural environments.

Jan	Feb	Mar	Apr	May	June	July	Aug	Sep	Oct	Nov	Dec

White-crowned Pigeon *(Columba leucocephala)* L 13″   **p. 76**

Slate-blue overall with white cap. Immatures may lack white cap.
Habitat: Mangrove; mesic hammocks; urban environments.

Jan	Feb	Mar	Apr	May	June	July	Aug	Sep	Oct	Nov	Dec

Ringed Turtle-Dove *(Streptopelia risoria)* L 11″   **p. 76**

Light tan or cream to whitish body, white undertail coverts. Song: *Cook, ca-roo.*
Habitat: Urban environments; agricultural environments.

Jan	Feb	Mar	Apr	May	June	July	Aug	Sep	Oct	Nov	Dec

Rock Dove *(Columba livia)* L 12″   **p. 75**

Dark gray body, light gray mantle with black wing bars, white rump. Many variations of blacks, whites, reds, and grays.
Habitat: Urban environments; agricultural environments.

Jan	Feb	Mar	Apr	May	June	July	Aug	Sep	Oct	Nov	Dec

Eurasian Collared-Dove *(Streptopelia decaocto)* L 11½″   **p. 76**

Dark tan upperparts; buffy gray head, neck and underparts; gray primaries and undertail coverts. Song: *Ca-coo, cook.*
Habitat: Urban environments; agricultural environments.

Jan	Feb	Mar	Apr	May	June	July	Aug	Sep	Oct	Nov	Dec

White-winged Dove *(Zenaida asiatica)* L 11″   **p. 77**

Grayish-brown body; white in bend of wing, shows at rest.
Habitat: Urban environments; agricultural environments.

Jan	Feb	Mar	Apr	May	June	July	Aug	Sep	Oct	Nov	Dec

Mourning Dove *(Zenaida macroura)* L 12″   **p. 77**

Brown back, buff or tan head and underparts, long white-tipped tail.
Habitat: Pine scrub; dry prairies; mesic hammocks; mixed pine and hardwood forests; urban environments; pine flatwoods; sandhills; agricultural environments.

Jan	Feb	Mar	Apr	May	June	July	Aug	Sep	Oct	Nov	Dec

   Present in Florida   Breeding in Florida

Common Ground-Dove

White-crowned Pigeon

Ringed Turtle-Dove

Eurasian Collared-Dove

Rock Dove

Mourning Dove

White-winged Dove

Monk Parakeet *(Myiopsitta monachus)* L 11″   **p. 78**

Grayish throat and breast, yellow belly, green upperparts, blue primaries.
Habitat: Urban environments; agricultural environments.

Jan	Feb	Mar	Apr	May	June	July	Aug	Sep	Oct	Nov	Dec

Rose-ringed Parakeet *(Psittacula krameri)* L 16″   **p. 78**

Bright green with red bill and long tail; adult male has black chin, pink collar.
Habitat: Urban environments.

Jan	Feb	Mar	Apr	May	June	July	Aug	Sep	Oct	Nov	Dec

Yellow-headed Parrot *(Amazona oratrix)* L 14″   **p. 279**

Head and throat yellow, body green.
Habitat: Urban environments.
Permanent residents. Breeding season unknown.

Budgerigar *(Melopsittacus undulatus)* L 7″   **p. 78**

Usually, black and yellow barred head and upperparts, green below, long blue-green tail.
Habitat: Urban environments.

Jan	Feb	Mar	Apr	May	June	July	Aug	Sep	Oct	Nov	Dec

Red-crowned Parrot *(Amazona viridigenalis)* L 12½″   **p. 279**

Forehead and crown red, body green.
Habitat: Urban environments.
Permanent residents. Breeding season unknown.

Canary-winged Parakeet *(Brotogeris versicolurus)* L 9″   **p. 79**

All green with yellow in bend of wing at rest; extensive yellow and white in wings in flight.
Habitat: Urban environments.

Jan	Feb	Mar	Apr	May	June	July	Aug	Sep	Oct	Nov	Dec

Present in Florida   Breeding in Florida

Monk Parakeet

Rose-winged Parakeet

Yellow-headed Parrot

Budgerigar

Red-crowned Parrot

Canary-winged Parakeet

Karl E. Karalus

Mangrove Cuckoo *(Coccyzus minor)* L 12″   **p. 79**

Black ear patch, buffy belly, buff may extend onto breast.
Habitat: Mangrove; mesic hammocks.

Jan	Feb	Mar	Apr	May	June	July	Aug	Sep	Oct	Nov	Dec

Yellow-billed Cuckoo *(Coccyzus americanus)* L 12″   **p. 79**

Rufous primaries, large white spots under tail.
Habitat: Pine scrub; hardwood swamps; cypress swamps; mesic hammocks; mixed pine and hardwood forests; urban environments; pine flatwoods; sandhills.

Jan	Feb	Mar	Apr	May	June	July	Aug	Sep	Oct	Nov	Dec

Black-billed Cuckoo *(Coccyzus erythropthalmus)* L 12″   **p. 79**

Red eye ring, small spots under tail, all-black bill.
Habitat: Hardwood swamps; mixed pine and hardwood forests; urban environments.

Jan	Feb	Mar	Apr	May	June	July	Aug	Sep	Oct	Nov	Dec

Smooth-billed Ani *(Crotophaga ani)* L 14″   **p. 79**

All black with long floppy tail; high ridged, parrotlike bill.
Habitat: Dry prairies; wet prairies and marshes; urban environments; agricultural environments.

Jan	Feb	Mar	Apr	May	June	July	Aug	Sep	Oct	Nov	Dec

Groove-billed Ani *(Crotophaga sulcirostris)* L 13″   **p. 80**

All black with long floppy tail; grooves on parrotlike bill, no high ridge.
Habitat: Urban environments; agricultural environments.

Jan	Feb	Mar	Apr	May	June	July	Aug	Sep	Oct	Nov	Dec

   Present in Florida   Breeding in Florida

Mangrove Cuckoo

Yellow-billed Cuckoo

Black-billed Cuckoo

Smooth-billed Ani

Grove-billed Ani

Karl E. Karalus

Eastern Screech-Owl *(Otus asio)* L 8″   **p. 80**

Small; ear tufts; gray, red, or brown body streaked with brown and white.
Habitat: Pine scrub; hardwood swamps; cypress swamps; mesic hammocks; mixed pine and hardwood forests; urban environments; pine flatwoods; sandhills; agricultural environments.

Jan	Feb	Mar	Apr	May	June	July	Aug	Sep	Oct	Nov	Dec

Great Horned Owl *(Bubo virginianus)* L 21″   **p. 81**

Large with long ear tufts; gray-brown above; black, white, buff below.
Habitat: Hardwood swamps; dry prairies; mesic hammocks; mixed pine and hardwood forests; wet prairies and marshes; urban environments; pine flatwoods; sandhills; agricultural environments.

Jan	Feb	Mar	Apr	May	June	July	Aug	Sep	Oct	Nov	Dec

Barn Owl *(Tyto alba)* L 16″   **p. 80**

Heartshaped "monkey" face; cinnamon-brown above, white or buff below.
Habitat: Dry prairies; mesic hammocks; mixed pine and hardwood forests; wet prairies and marshes; urban environments; pine flatwoods; sandhills; agricultural environments.

Jan	Feb	Mar	Apr	May	June	July	Aug	Sep	Oct	Nov	Dec

Barred Owl *(Strix varia)* L 20″   **p. 81**

Rounded gray-brown head (no ear tufts), gray-brown back, lighter below with barring and streaking.
Habitat: Pine scrub; hardwood swamps; cypress swamps; mesic hammocks; mixed pine and hardwood forests; wet prairies and marshes; urban environments; pine flatwoods; sandhills; agricultural environments.

Jan	Feb	Mar	Apr	May	June	July	Aug	Sep	Oct	Nov	Dec

Burrowing Owl *(Athene cunicularia)* L 9″   **p. 81**

Brown overall with barring and spotting of white and brown, white or gray eyebrows, no ear tufts; usually on ground near burrow.
Habitat: Dry prairies; urban environments; agricultural environments.

Jan	Feb	Mar	Apr	May	June	July	Aug	Sep	Oct	Nov	Dec

      Present in Florida   Breeding in Florida

Eastern Screech-Owl

gray phase

red phase

brown phase

Great Horned Owl

Barn Owl

Barred Owl

Burrowing Owl

Karl E. Karalus

Chuck-will's-widow *(Caprimulgus carolinensis)* L 12″   **p. 82**

Brown mottled with black, gray, buff; lighter throat bordered by narrow white (male) or buff (female) collar.
Habitat: Pine scrub; mesic hammocks; mixed pine and hardwood forests; wet prairies and marshes; pine flatwoods; sandhills.

Jan	Feb	Mar	Apr	May	June	July	Aug	Sep	Oct	Nov	Dec

Whip-poor-will *(Caprimulgus vociferus)* L 10″   **p. 82**

Mottled gray-brown; black throat bordered by white (buff in female).
Habitat: Pine scrub; mesic hammocks; mixed pine and hardwood forests; wet prairies and marshes; pine flatwoods; sandhills.

Jan	Feb	Mar	Apr	May	June	July	Aug	Sep	Oct	Nov	Dec

Common Nighthawk *(Chordeiles minor)* L 9″   **p. 82**

Mostly black or gray with white throat, long pointed wings with white patch about ⅓ distance from tips. Call: A drawn-out *peeent*.
Habitat: Pine scrub; dry prairies; mesic hammocks; mixed pine and hardwood forests; wet prairies and marshes; urban environments; pine flatwoods; sandhills; agricultural environments.

Jan	Feb	Mar	Apr	May	June	July	Aug	Sep	Oct	Nov	Dec

Antillean Nighthawk *(Chordeiles gundlachii)* L 9″   **p. 82**

Similar to Common but with a buff or golden wash. Best identified by call: *Kitty-kay-dick.*
Habitat: Mesic hammocks; mixed pine and hardwood forests; urban environments; agricultural environments.

Jan	Feb	Mar	Apr	May	June	July	Aug	Sep	Oct	Nov	Dec

Belted Kingfisher *(Ceryle alcyon)* L 13″   **p. 84**

Blue-gray above, white below; blue breast band, large bill, crested head. Female also has a chestnut belly band.
Habitat: Salt marshes; hardwood swamps; cypress swamps; wet prairies and marshes; agricultural environments.

Jan	Feb	Mar	Apr	May	June	July	Aug	Sep	Oct	Nov	Dec

Chimney Swift *(Chaetura pelagica)* L 5″   **p. 83**

Brownish-black above; gray throat, breast; narrow, stiff bowed wings.
Habitat: Pine scrub; hardwood swamps; cypress swamps; mesic hammocks; mixed pine and hardwood forests; urban environments; pine flatwoods; sandhills.

Jan	Feb	Mar	Apr	May	June	July	Aug	Sep	Oct	Nov	Dec

Ruby-throated Hummingbird *(Archilochus colubris)* L 3½″   **p. 83**

Iridescent green upperparts, white below. Male has ruby red throat; female and immature have white throat.
Habitat: Pine scrub; mesic hammocks; mixed pine and hardwood forests; urban environments; pine flatwoods; sandhills; agricultural environments.

Jan	Feb	Mar	Apr	May	June	July	Aug	Sep	Oct	Nov	Dec

Present in Florida   Breeding in Florida

Chuck-will's-widow

Whip-poor-will

Common Nighthawk

Antillean Nighthawk

Belted Kingfisher

male

female

Chimney Swift

Ruby-throated Hummingbird

male

female

Karl E. Karalus

Pileated Woodpecker *(Dryocopus pileatus)* L 16″   p. 86

Large; black with large red crest (less red on female), red or black mustache, white throat, face, neck. No white shows on wing at rest.
Habitat: Pine scrub; hardwood swamps; cypress swamps; mesic hammocks; mixed pine and hardwood forests; urban environments; pine flatwoods; sandhills.

Jan	Feb	Mar	Apr	May	June	July	Aug	Sep	Oct	Nov	Dec

Ivory-billed Woodpecker *(Campephilus principalis)* L 20″   p. 87

Large white wing patch on wing at rest; black face, forehead, throat; ivory bill; white stripe from side of head to side of back.
Habitat: Cypress swamps.

Jan	Feb	Mar	Apr	May	June	July	Aug	Sep	Oct	Nov	Dec

Northern Flicker *(Colaptes auratus)* L 12″   p. 86

Brown barred with black upperparts, white rump, black-spotted tan below with broad black breast patch, small red spot on nape; male has a black mustache.
Habitat: Pine scrub; hardwood swamps; cypress swamps; mesic hammocks; mixed pine and hardwood forests; urban environments; pine flatwoods; sandhills; agricultural environments.

Jan	Feb	Mar	Apr	May	June	July	Aug	Sep	Oct	Nov	Dec

Red-bellied Woodpecker *(Melanerpes carolinus)* L 9″   p. 85

Black and white barring on back; tan or gray underparts; red on head extends from bill to back of neck in male, only on back of head in female.
Habitat: Pine scrub; hardwood swamps; cypress swamps; mesic hammocks; mixed pine and hardwood forests; urban environments; pine flatwoods; sandhills.

Jan	Feb	Mar	Apr	May	June	July	Aug	Sep	Oct	Nov	Dec

Present in Florida    Breeding in Florida

Pileated Woodpecker

female

male

Ivory-billed Woodpecker

Northern Flicker

male

female

Red-bellied Woodpecker

Yellow-bellied Sapsucker *(Sphyrapicus varius)* L 8½″   **p. 85**

White wing stripe on side; striped face; red forehead, crown, throat in male; red crown, white throat in female.

Habitat: Pine scrub; mangrove; hardwood swamps; cypress swamps; mesic hammocks; mixed pine and hardwood forests; urban environments; pine flatwoods; sandhills.

Jan	Feb	Mar	Apr	May	June	July	Aug	Sep	Oct	Nov	Dec

Red-cockaded Woodpecker *(Picoides borealis)* L 8″   **p. 86**

Overall black and white, barred back and wings, large white cheek patch.

Habitat: Pine flatwoods.

Jan	Feb	Mar	Apr	May	June	July	Aug	Sep	Oct	Nov	Dec

Red-headed Woodpecker *(Melanerpes erythrocephalus)* L 9″   **p. 84**

Entire head and neck is red, black tail and wings with white patches, white belly. Immature has brown head.

Habitat: Pine scrub; mixed pine and hardwood forests; urban environments; pine flatwoods; sandhills.

Jan	Feb	Mar	Apr	May	June	July	Aug	Sep	Oct	Nov	Dec

Hairy Woodpecker *(Picoides villosus)* L 9″   **p. 85**

Black and white with black eye stripe and mustache, red nape on male. Length of bill is equal to width of head.

Habitat: Pine scrub; hardwood swamps; cypress swamps; mesic hammocks; mixed pine and hardwood forests; urban environments; pine flatwoods; sandhills.

Jan	Feb	Mar	Apr	May	June	July	Aug	Sep	Oct	Nov	Dec

Downy Woodpecker *(Picoides pubescens)* L 6½″   **p. 85**

Similar to Hairy, but smaller. Length of bill is equal to ½ width of head.

Habitat: Pine scrub; mangrove; hardwood swamps; cypress swamps; mesic hammocks; mixed pine and hardwood forests; urban environments; pine flatwoods; sandhills.

Jan	Feb	Mar	Apr	May	June	July	Aug	Sep	Oct	Nov	Dec

    ▫ Present in Florida   ▨ Breeding in Florida

Yellow-bellied Sapsucker
male
female

Red-cockaded Woodpecker
male

Hairy Woodpecker
male

Red-headed Woodpecker
adult

Downy Woodpecker
female
male

juvenile

Eastern Kingbird *(Tyrannus tyrannus)* L 8″   p. 90

Black upper parts, white below; white-tipped black tail.
Habitat: Dry prairies; mixed pine and hardwood forests; urban environments; agricultural environments.

Jan	Feb	Mar	Apr	May	June	July	Aug	Sep	Oct	Nov	Dec

Gray Kingbird *(Tyrannus dominicensis)* L 9″   p. 90

Gray above, white below; black ear patch; large dark bill.
Habitat: Mangroves; mesic hammocks; urban environments.

Jan	Feb	Mar	Apr	May	June	July	Aug	Sep	Oct	Nov	Dec

Eastern Phoebe *(Sayornis phoebe)* L 7″   p. 88

Gray-black above, white or yellowish below; dark wash on breast; pumps tail consistently. Habitat: Dry prairies; mesic hammocks; mixed pine and hardwood forests; urban environments; sandhills; agricultural environments.

Jan	Feb	Mar	Apr	May	June	July	Aug	Sep	Oct	Nov	Dec

Scissor-tailed Flycatcher *(Tyrannus forficatus)* L13″   p. 90

Very long black and white tail feathers, pale gray overall, dark wings, pinkish-red wash on belly. Habitat: Urban environments; agricultural environments.

Jan	Feb	Mar	Apr	May	June	July	Aug	Sep	Oct	Nov	Dec

Western Kingbird *(Tyrannus verticalis)* L 9″   p. 89

Gray head and breast, yellow belly, black tail with white outer feathers.
Habitat: Dry prairies; urban environments; agricultural environments.

Jan	Feb	Mar	Apr	May	June	July	Aug	Sep	Oct	Nov	Dec

Acadian Flycatcher *(Empidonax virescens)* L 6″   p. 88

Olive-green upperparts, lighter below; buffy wing bars and eye ring.
Habitat: Hardwood swamps; cypress swamps; mesic hammocks; mixed pine and hardwood forests; sandhills.

Jan	Feb	Mar	Apr	May	June	July	Aug	Sep	Oct	Nov	Dec

Least Flycatcher *(Empidonax minimus)* L 5″   p. 88

Gray-green above, lighter below; buff wing bars and eye ring.
Habitat: Mesic hammocks; mixed pine and hardwood forests; sandhills.

Jan	Feb	Mar	Apr	May	June	July	Aug	Sep	Oct	Nov	Dec

Vermilion Flycatcher *(Pyrocephalus rubinus)* L 6″   p. 89

Male: Bright red, black back and eyestripe. Female: Gray-brown above, streaked belly. Habitat: Dry prairies; mesic hammocks; mixed pine and hardwood forests; urban environments; sandhills; agricultural environments.

Jan	Feb	Mar	Apr	May	June	July	Aug	Sep	Oct	Nov	Dec

Great Crested Flycatcher *(Myiarchus crinitus)* L 9″   p. 89

Olive-brown crest and back, gray throat and breast, yellow belly, rufous on wings and tail, white wing bars. Habitat: Pine scrub; hardwood swamps; cypress swamps; mesic hammocks; mixed pine and hardwood forests; urban environments; pine flatwoods; sandhills; agricultural environments.

Jan	Feb	Mar	Apr	May	June	July	Aug	Sep	Oct	Nov	Dec

Eastern Wood-Pewee *(Contopus virens)* L 6″   p. 87

Olive-brown or gray above, whitish wing bars and underparts, no eye ring.
Habitat: Mesic hammocks; mixed pine and hardwood forests; pine flatwoods; sandhills.

Jan	Feb	Mar	Apr	May	June	July	Aug	Sep	Oct	Nov	Dec

   Present in Florida   Breeding in Florida

Eastern Kingbird

Gray Kingbird

Eastern Phoebe

Scissor-tailed Flycatcher

Western Kingbird

Acadian Flycatcher

Least Flycatcher

Vermilion Flycatcher

Great Crested Flycatcher

Eastern Wood-Pewee

Bank Swallow *(Riparia riparia)* L 5″   **p. 91**

Dark brown above; white throat with brown band across chest; white belly.
Habitat: Open freshwater; dry prairies; wet prairies and marshes; urban environments; agricultural environments.

Jan	Feb	Mar	Apr	May	June	July	Aug	Sep	Oct	Nov	Dec

Northern Rough-winged Swallow *(Stelgidopteryx serripennis)* L 5½″   **p. 91**

Light brown above, whitish below with brownish wash on breast.
Habitat: Open freshwater; wet prairies and marshes; urban environments; agricultural environments.

Jan	Feb	Mar	Apr	May	June	July	Aug	Sep	Oct	Nov	Dec

Cliff Swallow *(Hirundo pyrrhonota)* L 5½″   **p. 92**

Pale white or buff forehead, blue cap, rufous throat, buff rump.
Habitat: Open freshwater; urban environments; agricultural environments.

Jan	Feb	Mar	Apr	May	June	July	Aug	Sep	Oct	Nov	Dec

Barn Swallow *(Hirundo rustica)* L 7″   **p. 92**

Deeply forked tail, blue-black back, buff to cream underparts, chestnut above bill and on throat.
Habitat: Open freshwater; dry prairies; wet prairies and marshes; urban environments; agricultural environments.

Jan	Feb	Mar	Apr	May	June	July	Aug	Sep	Oct	Nov	Dec

Tree Swallow *(Tachycineta bicolor)* L 6″   **p. 91**

Metallic green or blue upperparts, white below, notched tail.
Habitat: Coastal beaches; salt marshes; open freshwater; dry prairies; wet prairies and marshes; urban environments; agricultural environments.

Jan	Feb	Mar	Apr	May	June	July	Aug	Sep	Oct	Nov	Dec

Cave Swallow *(Hirundo fulva)* L 5½″   **p. 92**

Rufous forehead, dark blue cap, buff throat, rufous rump.
Habitat: Urban environments; agricultural environments.

Jan	Feb	Mar	Apr	May	June	July	Aug	Sep	Oct	Nov	Dec

Purple Martin *(Progne subis)* L 8″   **p. 90**

Male: Metallic purplish-black, black wings.
Female: Dull purplish-black upperparts, gray collar, gray underparts.
Habitat: Mangrove; dry prairies; mixed pine and hardwood forests; wet prairies and marshes; urban environments; agricultural environments.

Jan	Feb	Mar	Apr	May	June	July	Aug	Sep	Oct	Nov	Dec

☐ Present in Florida   ▨ Breeding in Florida

Bank Swallow

Northern Rough-winged Swallow

Cliff Swallow

Barn Swallow

Tree Swallow

Cave Swallow

Purple Martin

male

Karl E. Karalus

Scrub Jay *(Aphelocoma coerulescens)* L 11″   **p. 93**

Blue upperparts, gray back, dark eye-ear patch, whitish forehead, white throat, breast with blue-gray streaks, gray underparts.
Habitat: Pine scrub.

Jan	Feb	Mar	Apr	May	June	July	Aug	Sep	Oct	Nov	Dec

Blue Jay *(Cyanocitta cristata)* L 11″   **p. 92**

Blue crest, black collar, blue above, white spots on wings and tail, white underparts.
Habitat: Pine scrub; hardwood swamps; cypress swamps; mesic hammocks; mixed pine and hardwood forests; urban environments; pine flatwoods; sandhills; agricultural environments.

Jan	Feb	Mar	Apr	May	June	July	Aug	Sep	Oct	Nov	Dec

Fish Crow *(Corvus ossifragus)* L 15″   **p. 94**

All black. Call: *cah, cah,* or a 2-note *uh-oh.*
Habitat: Coastal beaches; salt marshes; mangrove; mesic hammocks; mixed pine and hardwood forests; urban environments; agricultural environments.

Jan	Feb	Mar	Apr	May	June	July	Aug	Sep	Oct	Nov	Dec

American Crow *(Corvus brachyrhynchos)* L 17″   **p. 93**

All black. Call: A full, broad *caw, caw.*
Habitat: Coastal beaches; pine scrub; hardwood swamps; dry prairies; cypress swamps; mesic hammocks; mixed pine and hardwood forests; urban environments; pine flatwoods; sandhills; agricultural environments.

Jan	Feb	Mar	Apr	May	June	July	Aug	Sep	Oct	Nov	Dec

Red-whiskered Bulbul *(Pycnonotus jocosus)* L 7″   **p. 204**

Large black crest, red ear patch, red undertail coverts.
Habitat: Urban environments.

Jan	Feb	Mar	Apr	May	June	July	Aug	Sep	Oct	Nov	Dec

Present in Florida   Breeding in Florida

Scrub Jay

Blue Jay

American Crow

Fish Crow

Red-whiskered Bulbul

Tufted Titmouse *(Parus bicolor)* L 6″ p. 94

Gray upperparts and crest, black forehead.
Habitat: Pine scrub; hardwood swamps; cypress swamps; mesic hammocks; mixed pine and hardwood forests; urban environments; pine flatwoods; sandhills.

Jan	Feb	Mar	Apr	May	June	July	Aug	Sep	Oct	Nov	Dec

Carolina Chickadee *(Parus carolinensis)* L 4½″ p. 94

Black cap and bib, white cheeks.
Habitat: Pine scrub; hardwood swamps; cypress swamps; mesic hammocks; mixed pine and hardwood forests; urban environments; pine flatwoods; sandhills.

Jan	Feb	Mar	Apr	May	June	July	Aug	Sep	Oct	Nov	Dec

Brown-headed Nuthatch *(Sitta pusilla)* L 4½″ p. 95

Brown head, gray back, whitish throat, buff-gray below.
Habitat: Pine flatwoods; sandhills.

Jan	Feb	Mar	Apr	May	June	July	Aug	Sep	Oct	Nov	Dec

Red-breasted Nuthatch *(Sitta canadensis)* L 4½″ p. 94

Black (male) or gray (female) crown, white eyebrow, black eyeline, rusty below.
Habitat: Mixed pine and hardwood forests; pine flatwoods.

Jan	Feb	Mar	Apr	May	June	July	Aug	Sep	Oct	Nov	Dec

Brown Creeper *(Certhia americana)* L 5″ p. 95

Brown above, streaked with white; thin decurved bill; white below.
Habitat: Mesic hammocks; mixed pine and hardwood forests; pine flatwoods; sandhills.

Jan	Feb	Mar	Apr	May	June	July	Aug	Sep	Oct	Nov	Dec

White-breasted Nuthatch *(Sitta carolinensis)* L 5½″ p. 95

Black crown, white face and underparts.
Habitat: Mesic hammocks; mixed pine and hardwood forests; pine flatwoods; sandhills.

Jan	Feb	Mar	Apr	May	June	July	Aug	Sep	Oct	Nov	Dec

Present in Florida Breeding in Florida

Tufted Titmouse

Carolina Chickadee

Brown-headed Nuthatch

Red-breasted Nuthatch

White-breasted Nuthatch

Brown Creeper

Brown Thrasher *(Toxostoma rufum)* L 11″   **p. 209**

Rufous-brown above, white wing bars, gray face, white below streaked with brown; long tail.
Habitat: Mesic hammocks; mixed pine and hardwood forests; urban environments; sandhills; agricultural environments.

Jan	Feb	Mar	Apr	May	June	July	Aug	Sep	Oct	Nov	Dec

Northern Mockingbird *(Mimus polyglottos)* L 10″   **p. 208**

Gray above, black wings with white wing bars and white patches, long tail with white outer feathers.
Habitat: Pine scrub; dry prairies; mesic hammocks; mixed pine and hardwood forests; urban environments; pine flatwoods; sandhills; agricultural environments.

Jan	Feb	Mar	Apr	May	June	July	Aug	Sep	Oct	Nov	Dec

Gray Catbird *(Dumetella carolinensis)* L 8″   **p. 208**

All gray, black cap, rufous undertail coverts.
Habitat: Pine scrub; hardwood swamps; cypress swamps; mesic hammocks; mixed pine and hardwood forests; urban environments; pine flatwoods.

Jan	Feb	Mar	Apr	May	June	July	Aug	Sep	Oct	Nov	Dec

House Wren *(Troglodytes aedon)* L 5″   **p. 205**

Brown upperparts with fine barring on wings and tail, grayish-white below.
Habitat: Pine scrub; mesic hammocks; mixed pine and hardwood forests; urban environments; pine flatwoods; sandhills.

Jan	Feb	Mar	Apr	May	June	July	Aug	Sep	Oct	Nov	Dec

Carolina Wren *(Thryothorus ludovicianus)* L 5½″   **p. 204**

Rufous-brown above, white eyebrow, buff below.
Habitat: Pine scrub; hardwood swamps; cypress swamps; mesic hammocks; mixed pine and hardwood forests; urban environments; pine flatwoods; sandhills; agricultural environments.

Jan	Feb	Mar	Apr	May	June	July	Aug	Sep	Oct	Nov	Dec

Bewick's Wren *(Thryomanes bewickii)* L 5″   **p. 204**

Brownish-gray above, gray below; white eyebrow stripe; white in outer tail feathers.
Habitat: Mesic hammocks; mixed pine and hardwood forests.

Jan	Feb	Mar	Apr	May	June	July	Aug	Sep	Oct	Nov	Dec

Marsh Wren *(Cistothorus palustris)* L 5″   **p. 205**

Dark brown, gray brown, or rusty brown upperparts with white streaks on back, whitish below, white eyebrow.
Habitat: Salt marshes; freshwater marshes in winter, migration.

Jan	Feb	Mar	Apr	May	June	July	Aug	Sep	Oct	Nov	Dec

Sedge Wren *(Cistothorus platensis)* L 4½″   **p. 205**

Brown-tan above, streaked head and back, buff-orange below.
Habitat: Salt marshes; dry prairies; wet prairies and marshes; agricultural environments.

Jan	Feb	Mar	Apr	May	June	July	Aug	Sep	Oct	Nov	Dec

Winter Wren *(Troglodytes troglodytes)* L 4″   **p. 205**

Dark brown above, paler below; heavy barring on flanks; buff eyebrow.
Habitat: Mesic hammocks; mixed pine and hardwood forests.

Jan	Feb	Mar	Apr	May	June	July	Aug	Sep	Oct	Nov	Dec

Present in Florida   Breeding in Florida

Northern Mockingbird

Brown Thrasher

Gray Catbird

Carolina Wren

Bewick's Wren

House Wren

Marsh Wren

Sedge Wren

Winter Wren

Hermit Thrush *(Catharus guttatus)* L 7″   **p. 207**

Olive-brown above, reddish tail, spotted breast.
Habitat: Hardwood swamps; mesic hammocks; mixed pine and hardwood forests.

Jan	Feb	Mar	Apr	May	June	July	Aug	Sep	Oct	Nov	Dec

Wood Thrush *(Hylocichla mustelina)* L 8″   **p. 207**

Rufous-brown head and nape, olive-brown back and tail, large brown spots on
white breast.
Habitat: Hardwood swamps; mesic hammocks; mixed pine and hardwood forests.

Jan	Feb	Mar	Apr	May	June	July	Aug	Sep	Oct	Nov	Dec

Gray-cheeked Thrush *(Catharus minimus)* L 7″   **p. 207**

Plain olive-brown above, gray cheeks, indistinct gray eye ring, spotted breast.
Habitat: Mesic hammocks; mixed pine and hardwood forests.

Jan	Feb	Mar	Apr	May	June	July	Aug	Sep	Oct	Nov	Dec

American Robin *(Turdus migratorius)* L 10″   **p. 208**

Gray-brown above, gray or black head, pale to bright russet breast, incomplete
white spectacles. Juveniles have speckled breasts and backs.
Habitat: Hardwood swamps; cypress swamps; mesic hammocks; mixed pine and
hardwood forests; urban environments; pine flatwoods; agricultural environments.

Jan	Feb	Mar	Apr	May	June	July	Aug	Sep	Oct	Nov	Dec

Swainson's Thrush *(Catharus ustulatus)* L 7″   **p. 207**

Plain olive-brown above, orange-buff on throat and side of head, buff eye ring,
spotted breast.
Habitat: Hardwood swamps; cypress swamps; mesic hammocks; mixed pine and
hardwood forests; pine flatwoods.

Jan	Feb	Mar	Apr	May	June	July	Aug	Sep	Oct	Nov	Dec

Veery *(Catharus fuscescens)* L 7″   **p. 207**

Reddish-brown above, gray sides, buff on breast with light spotting.
Habitat: Mesic hammocks; mixed pine and hardwood forests.

Jan	Feb	Mar	Apr	May	June	July	Aug	Sep	Oct	Nov	Dec

Eastern Bluebird *(Sialia sialis)* L 7″   **p. 206**

Blue above, reddish-brown throat and breast, white belly. Female duller and
grayer. Juveniles spotted.
Habitat: Mixed pine and hardwood forests; pine flatwoods.

Jan	Feb	Mar	Apr	May	June	July	Aug	Sep	Oct	Nov	Dec

Present in Florida   Breeding in Florida

Hermit Thrush

Wood Thrush

American Robin

Gray-cheeked Thrush

adult

juvenile

Swainson's Thrush

male

female

Veery

Eastern Bluebird

Ruby-crowned Kinglet *(Regulus calendula)* L 4″   **p. 206**

Olive-green back, two white wing bars, incomplete eye ring, yellowish-gray underparts.

Habitat: Hardwood swamps; cypress swamps; mesic hammocks; mixed pine and hardwood forests; pine flatwoods; sandhills.

Jan	Feb	Mar	Apr	May	June	July	Aug	Sep	Oct	Nov	Dec

Golden-crowned Kinglet *(Regulus satrapa)* L 4″   **p. 206**

Tiny; orange or yellow striped crown bordered by black; whitish underparts; two white wing bars.

Habitat: Hardwood swamps; cypress swamps; mesic hammocks; mixed pine and hardwood forests; pine flatwoods; sandhills.

Jan	Feb	Mar	Apr	May	June	July	Aug	Sep	Oct	Nov	Dec

Blue-gray Gnatcatcher *(Polioptila caerulea)* L 4½″   **p. 206**

Tiny; blue-gray above, white below; white eye ring; long black tail with white outer feathers.

Habitat: Hardwood swamps; cypress swamps; mesic hammocks; mixed pine and hardwood forests; urban environments; pine flatwoods; sandhills.

Jan	Feb	Mar	Apr	May	June	July	Aug	Sep	Oct	Nov	Dec

Loggerhead Shrike *(Lanius ludovicianus)* L 9″   **p. 210**

Hooked bill; gray cap and back, white below; black mask, wings, tail; white in wings and outer tail feathers.

Habitat: Dry prairies; sandhills; agricultural environments.

Jan	Feb	Mar	Apr	May	June	July	Aug	Sep	Oct	Nov	Dec

American Pipit *(Anthus rubescens)* L 6½″   **p. 209**

Brown above, white or buff below; streaked breast and flanks.

Habitat: Wet prairies and marshes; agricultural environments.

Jan	Feb	Mar	Apr	May	June	July	Aug	Sep	Oct	Nov	Dec

Cedar Waxwing *(Bombycilla cedrorum)* L 7″   **p. 210**

Brownish-tan crest and back, black mask, yellowish belly, yellow-tipped tail.

Habitat: Hardwood swamps; cypress swamps; mesic hammocks; mixed pine and hardwood forests; urban environments; pine flatwoods; sandhills.

Jan	Feb	Mar	Apr	May	June	July	Aug	Sep	Oct	Nov	Dec

  Present in Florida   Breeding in Florida

Ruby-crowned Kinglet

female

male

Golden-crowned Kinglet

male

female

Blue-gray Gnatcatcher

Loggerhead Shrike

American Pipit

Cedar Waxwing

Karl E. Karalus

Solitary Vireo *(Vireo solitarius)* L 5½″   **p. 211**

Slate-gray head, white spectacles, olive-green back, white wing bars, white underparts with yellowish flanks.
Habitat: Hardwood swamps; cypress swamps; mesic hammocks; mixed pine and hardwood forests; urban environments; pine flatwoods; sandhills.

Jan	Feb	Mar	Apr	May	June	July	Aug	Sep	Oct	Nov	Dec

Yellow-throated Vireo *(Vireo flavifrons)* L 5½″   **p. 211**

Bright yellow throat, breast, spectacles; olive-green back; white wing bars.
Habitat: Hardwood swamps; cypress swamps; mesic hammocks; mixed pine and hardwood forests; urban environments.

Jan	Feb	Mar	Apr	May	June	July	Aug	Sep	Oct	Nov	Dec

European Starling *(Sturnus vulgaris)* L 8½″   **p. 210**

Summer: Iridescent black, yellow bill, short tail.
Winter: Black plumage speckled with white; dark bill.
Habitat: Urban environments; agricultural environments.

Jan	Feb	Mar	Apr	May	June	July	Aug	Sep	Oct	Nov	Dec

Bananaquit *(Coereba flaveola)* L 4″   **p. 219**

Black upperparts; yellow rump and belly; white throat, breast, eyebrow; decurved bill.
Habitat: Urban environments.

Jan	Feb	Mar	Apr	May	June	July	Aug	Sep	Oct	Nov	Dec

Red-eyed Vireo *(Vireo olivaceus)* L 6″   **p. 211**

Blue-gray crown bordered with black, white eyebrow, red eye.
Habitat: Hardwood swamps; mesic hammocks; mixed pine and hardwood forests.

Jan	Feb	Mar	Apr	May	June	July	Aug	Sep	Oct	Nov	Dec

Black-whiskered Vireo *(Vireo altiloquus)* L 6″   **p. 212**

Gray crown, white eyebrow, black whisker stripe on side of throat.
Habitat: Mangrove; mesic hammocks.

Jan	Feb	Mar	Apr	May	June	July	Aug	Sep	Oct	Nov	Dec

White-eyed Vireo *(Vireo griseus)* L 5″   **p. 211**

Gray-green above, white wing bars, yellow spectacles, white eye (dark in immature), yellowish sides.
Habitat: Pine scrub; hardwood swamps; cypress swamps; mesic hammocks; mixed pine and hardwood forests; pine flatwoods; sandhills.

Jan	Feb	Mar	Apr	May	June	July	Aug	Sep	Oct	Nov	Dec

   ⬚ Present in Florida   ▨ Breeding in Florida

Yellow-throated Vireo

Solitary Vireo

Bananaquit

European Starling

winter

summer

Red-eyed Vireo

Black-whiskered Vireo

White-eyed Vireo

Karl E. Karalus

Black-and-white Warbler *(Mniotilta varia)* L 5¼″   **p. 216**

Black and white streaked overall, black (male) or white (female) throat.
Habitat: Pine scrub; hardwood swamps; cypress swamps; mesic hammocks; mixed pine and hardwood forests; urban environments; pine flatwoods; sandhills.

Jan	Feb	Mar	Apr	May	June	July	Aug	Sep	Oct	Nov	Dec

Prothonotary Warbler *(Protonotaria citrea)* L 5½″   **p. 217**

Bright yellow head, breast, sides; blue-gray wings and tail.
Habitat: Hardwood swamps; cypress swamps.

Jan	Feb	Mar	Apr	May	June	July	Aug	Sep	Oct	Nov	Dec

Swainson's Warbler *(Limnothlypis swainsonii)* L 5½″   **p. 217**

Brown above, reddish-brown cap, light eyebrow, yellowish-white below.
Habitat: Hardwood swamps; mesic hammocks; mixed pine and hardwood forests.

Jan	Feb	Mar	Apr	May	June	July	Aug	Sep	Oct	Nov	Dec

Tennessee Warbler *(Vermivora peregrina)* L 5″   **p. 212**

Olive-green above, blue-gray head, white eyebrow, white or yellowish below, white undertail coverts.
Habitat: Pine scrub; mesic hammocks; mixed pine and hardwood forests; pine flatwoods; sandhills.

Jan	Feb	Mar	Apr	May	June	July	Aug	Sep	Oct	Nov	Dec

Worm-eating Warbler *(Helmitheros vermivorous)* L 5″   **p. 217**

Black and buff head stripes, buff underparts, brown above.
Habitat: Mesic hammocks; mixed pine and hardwood forests.

Jan	Feb	Mar	Apr	May	June	July	Aug	Sep	Oct	Nov	Dec

Orange-crowned Warbler *(Vermivora celata)* L 5″   **p. 212**

Olive-green overall with yellowish underparts, incomplete eye ring, yellow undertail coverts.
Habitat: Mesic hammocks; mixed pine and hardwood forests; sandhills.

Jan	Feb	Mar	Apr	May	June	July	Aug	Sep	Oct	Nov	Dec

   Present in Florida   Breeding in Florida

Prothonotary Warbler

female

male

Black-and-white Warbler

Tennessee Warbler

male

immature

Swainson's Warbler

Orange-crowned Warbler

Karl E. Karalus

Worm-eating Warbler

Yellow Warbler *(Dendroica petechia)* L 5"   p. 213

Male: Bright yellow below with reddish streakings, yellow-green above. Female duller with faint or no streaks.
Habitat: Mangrove; hardwood swamps; agricultural environments.

Jan	Feb	Mar	Apr	May	June	July	Aug	Sep	Oct	Nov	Dec

Cape May Warbler *(Dendroica tigrina)* L 5"   p. 213

Male: Chestnut cheek patch, yellow collar and throat, white wing patch, yellow rump. Female lacks chestnut patch, is duller.
Habitat: Mesic hammocks; mixed pine and hardwood forests; urban environments.

Jan	Feb	Mar	Apr	May	June	July	Aug	Sep	Oct	Nov	Dec

Magnolia Warbler *(Dendroica magnolia)* L 5"   p. 213

Spring: Lemon-yellow underparts with black streaking, gray crown, black face and back, yellow rump.
Winter: Gray head and breast, olive-green above, yellow below with faint stripes.
Habitat: Hardwood swamps; mesic hammocks; mixed pine and hardwood forests.

Jan	Feb	Mar	Apr	May	June	July	Aug	Sep	Oct	Nov	Dec

Yellow-rumped Warbler *(Dendroica coronata)* L 5½"   p. 214

Winter: Brownish above, white throat, yellow rump.
Habitat: Pine scrub; hardwood swamps; cypress swamps; mesic hammocks; mixed pine and hardwood forests; urban environments; pine flatwoods; sandhills; agricultural environments.

Jan	Feb	Mar	Apr	May	June	July	Aug	Sep	Oct	Nov	Dec

Northern Parula *(Parula americana)* L 4½"   p. 212

Blue above, white wing bars, yellow throat and breast; male has a rufous-orange and blue band on breast.
Habitat: Hardwood swamps; mesic hammocks; mixed pine and hardwood forests.

Jan	Feb	Mar	Apr	May	June	July	Aug	Sep	Oct	Nov	Dec

Present in Florida   Breeding in Florida

Yellow Warbler

male

female

Cape May Warbler

male

female

Magnolia Warbler

male

female

Northern Parula

male

female

Yellow-rumped Warbler

male

female

Black-throated Green Warbler *(Dendroica virens)* L 5″   **p. 214**

Olive-green above, yellow face, black on throat and breast (male).
Habitat: Pine scrub; hardwood swamps; mesic hammocks; mixed pine and hardwood forests; urban environments; pine flatwoods.

Jan	Feb	Mar	Apr	May	June	July	Aug	Sep	Oct	Nov	Dec

Yellow-throated Warbler *(Dendroica dominica)* L 5″   **p. 215**

Black and white head, bright yellow throat.
Habitat: Mesic hammocks; mixed pine and hardwood forests; urban environments; pine flatwoods.

Jan	Feb	Mar	Apr	May	June	July	Aug	Sep	Oct	Nov	Dec

Black-throated Blue Warbler *(Dendroica caerulescens)* L 5″   **p. 214**

Male: Gray-blue above; black face, throat; white wing patch.
Female: Olive-green above; white eyebrow, wing patch.
Habitat: Pine scrub; hardwood swamps; cypress swamps; mesic hammocks; mixed pine and hardwood forests; urban environments; pine flatwoods.

Jan	Feb	Mar	Apr	May	June	July	Aug	Sep	Oct	Nov	Dec

Blackburnian Warbler *(Dendroica fusca)* L 4½″   **p. 214**

Male: Bright orange throat, eyebrow, crown patch; white wing patch; black crown and back.
Female and fall male: Yellow replaces orange; brownish-olive replaces black.
Habitat: Mesic hammocks; mixed pine and hardwood forests.

Jan	Feb	Mar	Apr	May	June	July	Aug	Sep	Oct	Nov	Dec

Chestnut-sided Warbler *(Dendroica pensylvanica)* L 4½″   **p. 213**

Spring: Yellow crown, black and white face, chestnut sides and flanks, yellow wing bars.
Fall: Yellow-green above, yellow wing bars, chestnut flanks (immatures may lack chestnut).
Habitat: Mesic hammocks; mixed pine and hardwood forests; sandhills; agricultural environments.

Jan	Feb	Mar	Apr	May	June	July	Aug	Sep	Oct	Nov	Dec

Present in Florida   Breeding in Florida

Black-throated Green Warbler

female

male

Yellow-throated Warbler

Black-throated Blue Warbler

male

female

Blackburnian Warbler

male

female

Chestnut-sided Warbler

spring

fall

Blackpoll Warbler *(Dendroica striata)* L 5″ — **p. 216**

Spring: Black cap, white cheeks, black and white streaking overall.
Female and fall male: Olive-green above, yellowish underparts with streaking, pale legs.
Habitat: Mesic hammocks; mixed pine and hardwood forests; urban environments; agricultural environments.

Jan	Feb	Mar	Apr	May	June	July	Aug	Sep	Oct	Nov	Dec

Bay-breasted Warbler *(Dendroica castanea)* L 5″ — **p. 216**

Spring: Chestnut crown, throat, flanks; buff neck patch.
Fall: Buff undertail coverts, black legs, olive-green streaked back.
Habitat: Mesic hammocks; mixed pine and hardwood forests.

Jan	Feb	Mar	Apr	May	June	July	Aug	Sep	Oct	Nov	Dec

Prairie Warbler *(Dendroica discolor)* L 4½″ — **p. 215**

Yellow-green above, yellow underparts with black streaks on sides and face. Female paler. Wags tail.
Habitat: Mangrove; pine flatwoods; agricultural environments.

Jan	Feb	Mar	Apr	May	June	July	Aug	Sep	Oct	Nov	Dec

Pine Warbler *(Dendroica pinus)* L 5″ — **p. 215**

Unstreaked olive-green above, yellow underparts, white wing bars, yellow eyebrow. Female paler.
Habitat: Pine scrub; mixed pine and hardwood forests; pine flatwoods; sandhills.

Jan	Feb	Mar	Apr	May	June	July	Aug	Sep	Oct	Nov	Dec

Palm Warbler *(Dendroica palmarum)* L 5″ — **p. 216**

Yellow undertail coverts, wags tail.
Spring: Chestnut crown, yellow throat and breast, streaked.
Fall: Brown crown, white eyebrow, whitish-buff underparts, streaked.
Habitat: Pine scrub; mangrove; hardwood swamps; dry prairies; cypress swamps; mesic hammocks; mixed pine and hardwood forests; wet prairies and marshes; urban environments; pine flatwoods; sandhills; agricultural environments.

Jan	Feb	Mar	Apr	May	June	July	Aug	Sep	Oct	Nov	Dec

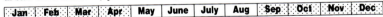

 Present in Florida   Breeding in Florida

Blackpoll Warbler

male

female

Bay-breasted Warbler

female

male

Prairie Warbler

male

Pine Warbler

male

female

Palm Warbler

breeding

winter

Karl E Karalus

Common Yellowthroat *(Geothlypis trichas)* L 5″   **p. 218**

Male: Black mask bordered with gray, olive-brown back, yellow below.
Female: Lacks mask and is duller.
Habitat: Mesic hammocks; mixed pine and hardwood forests; wet prairies and marshes; agricultural environments.

Jan	Feb	Mar	Apr	May	June	July	Aug	Sep	Oct	Nov	Dec

Yellow-breasted Chat *(Icteria virens)* L 7″   **p. 219**

Large; heavy bill; bright yellow throat, breast; white spectacles; olive above.
Habitat: Hardwood swamps; mixed pine and hardwood forests.

Jan	Feb	Mar	Apr	May	June	July	Aug	Sep	Oct	Nov	Dec

Northern Waterthrush *(Seiurus noveboracensis)* L 6″   **p. 218**

Brown above, narrow yellow or whitish eyebrow that tapers behind the eye, throat spotted.
Habitat: Hardwood swamps; cypress swamps; mesic hammocks; mixed pine and hardwood forests.

Jan	Feb	Mar	Apr	May	June	July	Aug	Sep	Oct	Nov	Dec

Ovenbird *(Seiurus aurocapillus)* L 6″   **p. 217**

Olive-green above, orange crown stripe, white eye ring, streaked breast.
Habitat: Hardwood swamps; cypress swamps; mesic hammocks; mixed pine and hardwood forests.

Jan	Feb	Mar	Apr	May	June	July	Aug	Sep	Oct	Nov	Dec

Louisiana Waterthrush *(Seiurus motacilla)* L 6″   **p. 218**

Brown above, white eyebrow that widens behind the eye. White throat unspotted.
Habitat: Hardwood swamps; cypress swamps; mesic hammocks; mixed pine and hardwood forests.

Jan	Feb	Mar	Apr	May	June	July	Aug	Sep	Oct	Nov	Dec

   Present in Florida   Breeding in Florida

female

male

immature male

Common Yellowthroat

Yellow-breasted Chat

Northern Waterthrush

Ovenbird

Louisiana Waterthrush

Karl E. Karalus

Hooded Warbler *(Wilsonia citrina)* L 5″   p. 218

Male: Black hood, yellow face and underparts, olive-green above, white spots in tail. Female lacks black hood.
Habitat: Hardwood swamps; pine flatwoods.

Jan	Feb	Mar	Apr	May	June	July	Aug	Sep	Oct	Nov	Dec

Wilson's Warbler *(Wilsonia pusilla)* L 4½″   p. 219

Male: Black cap; yellow forehead, eyebrow, and underparts; olive-green above; no white in tail. Female usually lacks black cap.
Habitat: Mesic hammocks; mixed pine and hardwood forests; agricultural environments.

Jan	Feb	Mar	Apr	May	June	July	Aug	Sep	Oct	Nov	Dec

American Redstart *(Setophaga ruticilla)* L 5″   p. 216

Male: Black head, back, breast; orange patches on wings and tail.
Female: Gray-brown with yellow on wings and tail.
Habitat: Pine scrub; mangrove; hardwood swamps; cypress swamps; mesic hammocks; mixed pine and hardwood forests; urban environments; pine flatwoods; sandhills; agricultural environments.

Jan	Feb	Mar	Apr	May	June	July	Aug	Sep	Oct	Nov	Dec

House Sparrow *(Passer domesticus)* L 6″   p. 232

Male: Black throat and breast, gray crown, white check, chestnut nape.
Female: Streaked above, gray below, buff eyebrow.
Habitat: Urban environments; agricultural environments.

Jan	Feb	Mar	Apr	May	June	July	Aug	Sep	Oct	Nov	Dec

Bobolink *(Dolichonyx oryzivorus)* L 7″   p. 227

Spring: Black head and underparts, yellow-buff nape, white scapulars and rump.
Female and fall male: Buffy with dark streaks on back, rump, sides; striped head.
Habitat: Dry prairies; wet prairies and marshes; agricultural environments.

Jan	Feb	Mar	Apr	May	June	July	Aug	Sep	Oct	Nov	Dec

    Present in Florida   Breeding in Florida

Hooded Warbler

male

female

Wilson's Warbler

male

female

House Sparrow

male

female

immature male

American Redstart

male

female

Bobolink

female

male (spring)

Karl E. Karalus

Red-winged Blackbird *(Agelaius phoeniceus)* L 8″   **p. 227**

Male: All black with red and yellow shoulder patch.
Female: Smaller, dark brown, heavily streaked.
Habitat: Salt marshes; dry prairies; wet prairies and marshes; agricultural environments.

Jan	Feb	Mar	Apr	May	June	July	Aug	Sep	Oct	Nov	Dec

Boat-tailed Grackle *(Quiscalus major)* L 15″   **p. 229**

Male: Large; glossy black; long keeled tail; eyes may be yellow or brown.
Female: Smaller, buff breast, dark brown above.
Habitat: Salt marshes; wet prairies and marshes; urban environments; agricultural environments.

Jan	Feb	Mar	Apr	May	June	July	Aug	Sep	Oct	Nov	Dec

Brown-headed Cowbird *(Molothrus ater)* L 7″   **p. 230**

Male: Brown head, black glossy body.
Female: Gray-brown overall.
Habitat: Pine scrub; dry prairies; mesic hammocks; mixed pine and hardwood forests; wet prairies and marshes; urban environments; pine flatwoods; sandhills; agricultural environments.

Jan	Feb	Mar	Apr	May	June	July	Aug	Sep	Oct	Nov	Dec

Common Grackle *(Quiscalus quiscula)* L 12″   **p. 229**

Black with iridescent purple; yellow eyes; keeled tail. Female is similar, but duller in color.
Habitat: Dry prairies; mesic hammocks; mixed pine and hardwood forests; urban environments; agricultural environments.

Jan	Feb	Mar	Apr	May	June	July	Aug	Sep	Oct	Nov	Dec

Eastern Meadowlark *(Sturnella magna)* L 9″   **p. 227**

Throat, breast, belly yellow with a black V on breast; striped head.
Habitat: Dry prairies; agricultural environments.

Jan	Feb	Mar	Apr	May	June	July	Aug	Sep	Oct	Nov	Dec

⬜ Present in Florida   ▨ Breeding in Florida

Red-winged Blackbird

male

immature male

female

Boat-tailed Grackle

female

male

male

female

Brown-headed Cowbird

Common Grackle

Eastern Meadowlark

Orchard Oriole *(Icterus spurius)* L 7″   **p. 230**

Male: Black head, throat, upperparts; chestnut rump and underparts.
Female: Olive-green above, yellow below. First-year male: Same as female, but with black throat and breast.
Habitat: Mesic hammocks; mixed pine and hardwood forests; urban environments; agricultural environments.

Jan	Feb	Mar	Apr	May	June	July	Aug	Sep	Oct	Nov	Dec

Northern Oriole *(Icterus galbula)* L 8½″   **p. 231**

Male: Black head, throat, back, wings; orange rump and underparts, white bars on wings.
Female: Olive-brown above, orange-yellow below, white wing bars.
Habitat: Mesic hammocks; mixed pine and hardwood forests; urban environments; agricultural environments.

Jan	Feb	Mar	Apr	May	June	July	Aug	Sep	Oct	Nov	Dec

Spot-breasted Oriole *(Icterus pectoralis)* L 9″   **p. 230**

Orange overall; black throat, back, wings, tail. Spots on breast; orange and white patches on wings.
Habitat: Urban environments.

Jan	Feb	Mar	Apr	May	June	July	Aug	Sep	Oct	Nov	Dec

Scarlet Tanager *(Piranga olivacea)* L 7″   **p. 220**

Male: Brilliant red with black wings and tail.
Female: Olive-green above, yellowish below; dark wings.
Habitat: Mesic hammocks; mixed pine and hardwood forests.

Jan	Feb	Mar	Apr	May	June	July	Aug	Sep	Oct	Nov	Dec

Summer Tanager *(Piranga rubra)* L 7½″   **p. 219**

Male: All red; large pale bill.
Female: Yellow-buff overall, darker above; pale bill.
Habitat: Mesic hammocks; mixed pine and hardwood forests; pine flatwoods.

Jan	Feb	Mar	Apr	May	June	July	Aug	Sep	Oct	Nov	Dec

192   Present in Florida   Breeding in Florida

Orchard Oriole

first-year male

female

male

Northern Oriole

female

male

Spot-breasted Oriole

Scarlet Tanager

male

female

Summer Tanager

male

female

Karl E. Karalus

Rose-breasted Grosbeak *(Pheucticus ludovicianus)* L 8″ p. 220

Male: Black head and upperparts, red breast, white belly and rump, white patches on wing, pale bill.
Female: Brown above, striped head, white eyebrow and underparts, streaked with brown.
Habitat: Pine scrub; mesic hammocks; mixed pine and hardwood forests; urban environments; pine flatwoods.

Jan	Feb	Mar	Apr	May	June	July	Aug	Sep	Oct	Nov	Dec

Evening Grosbeak *(Coccothraustes vespertinus)* L 8″ p. 232

Male: Dark brown and yellow; large pale bill; white in black wings, tail.
Female: Grayish-tan; white in wings and tail.
Habitat: Mixed pine and hardwood forests; urban environments; pine flatwoods.

Jan	Feb	Mar	Apr	May	June	July	Aug	Sep	Oct	Nov	Dec

Northern Cardinal *(Cardinalis cardinalis)* L 8″ p. 220

Male: All red, with crest, black face, orange bill.
Female: All brown or buff; reddish crest, wings, tail; black face; orange bill.
Immature: Like female, but bill dark.
Habitat: Pine scrub; mesic hammocks; mixed pine and hardwood forests; urban environments; pine flatwoods; sandhills; agricultural environments.

Jan	Feb	Mar	Apr	May	June	July	Aug	Sep	Oct	Nov	Dec

Indigo Bunting *(Passerina cyanea)* L 5½″ p. 221

Male: Indigo blue with blackish wings.
Female: All brown with faint breast streakings.
Habitat: Mixed pine and hardwood forests; agricultural environments.

Jan	Feb	Mar	Apr	May	June	July	Aug	Sep	Oct	Nov	Dec

Blue Grosbeak *(Guiraca caerulea)* L 6″ p. 220

Male: All blue with rusty wing bars, large stout bill.
Female: All brown with rusty wing bars.
Habitat: Mesic hammocks; mixed pine and hardwood forests; agricultural environments.

Jan	Feb	Mar	Apr	May	June	July	Aug	Sep	Oct	Nov	Dec

Present in Florida   Breeding in Florida

Rose-breasted Grosbeak

male

female

Evening Grosbeak

Northern Cardinal

male

female

Indigo Bunting

male

female

Blue Grosbeak

male

female

Purple Finch *(Carpodacus purpureus)* L 6″ p. 231

Male: Rosy red head, throat, breast, back; notched tail.
Female: Overall brown; heavily streaked white breast; brown and white striped head.
Habitat: Hardwood swamps; cypress swamps; urban environments; agricultural environments.

Jan	Feb	Mar	Apr	May	June	July	Aug	Sep	Oct	Nov	Dec

House Finch *(Carpodacus mexicanus)* L 5½″ p. 231

Male: Brown cap with red forehead, throat, and breast; brown face and back with heavily streaked underparts; square tail.
Female: Brown streaked; unpatterned head.
Habitat: Urban environments; agricultural environments.

Jan	Feb	Mar	Apr	May	June	July	Aug	Sep	Oct	Nov	Dec

Pine Siskin *(Carduelis pinus)* L 5″ p. 232

Brown upperparts and white underparts heavily streaked. Yellow at base of primaries.
Habitat: Urban environments; pine flatwoods.

Jan	Feb	Mar	Apr	May	June	July	Aug	Sep	Oct	Nov	Dec

Painted Bunting *(Passerina ciris)* L 5″ p. 221

Male: Blue head; greenish-yellow back; green wings, tail; red rump and underparts; red eye ring.
Female: Greenish above, yellowish below; yellow eye ring.
Habitat: Mesic hammocks; mixed pine and hardwood forests; urban environments; pine flatwoods.

Jan	Feb	Mar	Apr	May	June	July	Aug	Sep	Oct	Nov	Dec

American Goldfinch *(Carduelis tristis)* L 5″ p. 232

Spring male: Black cap, wings, tail; yellow body; white wing bars.
Winter male: Olive-brown above, no cap, yellowish head.
Female: Dull olive-yellow; black wings, tail; no cap.
Habitat: Mixed pine and hardwood forests; urban environments; pine flatwoods; sandhills; agricultural environments.

Jan	Feb	Mar	Apr	May	June	July	Aug	Sep	Oct	Nov	Dec

Dickcissel *(Spiza americana)* L 6″ p. 221

Male: Gray head; black V on yellow breast; rufous shoulders.
Female: Browner, less yellow, no V on breast.
Habitat: Dry prairies; urban environments; agricultural environments.

Jan	Feb	Mar	Apr	May	June	July	Aug	Sep	Oct	Nov	Dec

Present in Florida   Breeding in Florida

House Finch
male

male
female

Purple Finch

Pine Siskin

male
female

Painted Bunting

American Goldfinch
spring male

winter male

Dickcissel
male

female

Sharp-tailed Sparrow *(Ammodramus caudacutus)* L 5″   **p. 224**

Gray crown stripe and nape; buff-orange and gray face; buffy breast and sides.
Habitat: Salt marshes.

Jan	Feb	Mar	Apr	May	June	July	Aug	Sep	Oct	Nov	Dec

Grasshopper Sparrow *(Ammodramus savannarum)* L 5″   **p. 223**

Striped head, plain buff face and underparts, streaked buff-brown back.
Habitat: Dry prairies.

Jan	Feb	Mar	Apr	May	June	July	Aug	Sep	Oct	Nov	Dec

Savannah Sparrow *(Passerculus sandwichensis)* L 5½″   **p. 223**

Brown upperparts and white breast heavily streaked, pinkish legs, yellowish eyebrow.
Habitat: Dry prairies; agricultural environments.

Jan	Feb	Mar	Apr	May	June	July	Aug	Sep	Oct	Nov	Dec

Henslow's Sparrow *(Ammodramus henslowii)* L 5″   **p. 224**

Olive, almost green head; heavily streaked back; rust on wings; streaked breast and sides.
Habitat: Dry prairies; pine flatwoods.

Jan	Feb	Mar	Apr	May	June	July	Aug	Sep	Oct	Nov	Dec

Rufous-sided Towhee *(Pipilo erythropthalmus)* L 8″   **p. 222**

Male: Black head, breast, upperparts; rufous sides and flanks; white belly.
Female: Brown replaces black of male.
Habitat: Pine scrub; mesic hammocks; mixed pine and hardwood forests; pine flatwoods; sandhills.

Jan	Feb	Mar	Apr	May	June	July	Aug	Sep	Oct	Nov	Dec

    Present in Florida   Breeding in Florida

Sharp-tailed Sparrow

Grasshopper Sparrow

Savannah Sparrow

Henslow's Sparrow

male

female

Rufous-sided Towhee

Karl E. Karalus

Vesper Sparrow *(Pooecetes gramineus)* L 6″   **p. 223**

Gray-brown streaked above, streaked breast, white outer tail feathers.
Habitat: Dry prairies; pine flatwoods; agricultural environments.

Jan	Feb	Mar	Apr	May	June	July	Aug	Sep	Oct	Nov	Dec

Seaside Sparrow *(Ammodramus maritimus)* L 5½″   **p. 224**

Varies from grayish-olive to dark brown above with a light grayish breast marked with buff or plain streaking. Dark whisker stripe on white throat.
Habitat: Salt marshes.

Jan	Feb	Mar	Apr	May	June	July	Aug	Sep	Oct	Nov	Dec

Dark-eyed Junco *(Junco hyemalis)* L 6″   **p. 226**

Gray head, back, breast; white belly; pink bill; white outer tail feathers. Female is duller.
Habitat: Dry prairies; urban environments; pine flatwoods; agricultural environments.

Jan	Feb	Mar	Apr	May	June	July	Aug	Sep	Oct	Nov	Dec

Bachman's Sparrow *(Aimophila aestivalis)* L 6″   **p. 222**

Reddish-brown above, buff or grayish below, buff eyebrow, brown line behind eye.
Habitat: Pine flatwoods.

Jan	Feb	Mar	Apr	May	June	July	Aug	Sep	Oct	Nov	Dec

Chipping Sparrow *(Spizella passerina)* L 5½″   **p. 222**

Rufous cap (brown in winter), white eyebrow, black eye line and lores.
Habitat: Dry prairies; urban environments; agricultural environments.

Jan	Feb	Mar	Apr	May	June	July	Aug	Sep	Oct	Nov	Dec

   Present in Florida   Breeding in Florida

Vesper Sparrow

Seaside Sparrows

Dusky

Cape Sable

Northern

Scott's

Dark-eyed Junco

Bachman's Sparrow

Chipping Sparrow

breeding

winter

Karl E. Karalus

Field Sparrow *(Spizella pusilla)* L 5½" p. 223

Pink bill, rusty crown, white eye ring.
Habitat: Dry prairies; agricultural environments.

Jan	Feb	Mar	Apr	May	June	July	Aug	Sep	Oct	Nov	Dec

White-throated Sparrow *(Zonotrichia albicollis)* L 6½" p. 226

Black and white or black and tan striped head, white throat, yellow lores.
Habitat: Hardwood swamps; dry prairies; mesic hammocks; mixed pine and hardwood forests; urban environments; pine flatwoods; sandhills; agricultural environments.

Jan	Feb	Mar	Apr	May	June	July	Aug	Sep	Oct	Nov	Dec

White-crowned Sparrow *(Zonotrichia leucophrys)* L 6½" p. 226

Black and white head; gray face, neck, breast. Head is brown and buff striped in immatures.
Habitat: Dry prairies; mixed pine and hardwood forests; agricultural environments.

Jan	Feb	Mar	Apr	May	June	July	Aug	Sep	Oct	Nov	Dec

Swamp Sparrow *(Melospiza georgiana)* L 5½" p. 226

Chestnut crown, gray face, white throat, reddish-brown wings.
Habitat: Hardwood swamps; dry prairies; wet prairies and marshes; agricultural environments.

Jan	Feb	Mar	Apr	May	June	July	Aug	Sep	Oct	Nov	Dec

Song Sparrow *(Melospiza melodia)* L 6" p. 225

Brown and gray streaked head, heavily streaked breast with large central spot, heavy dark stripe borders white throat.
Habitat: Dry prairies; mixed pine and hardwood forests; sandhills; agricultural environments.

Jan	Feb	Mar	Apr	May	June	July	Aug	Sep	Oct	Nov	Dec

Present in Florida   Breeding in Florida

White-throated Sparrow

immature

Field Sparrow

adult
(tan-striped
phase)

adult

White-crowned Sparrow

immature

adult

Swamp Sparrow

Song Sparrow

Karl E. Karalus

Family Pycnonotidae: Bulbuls

Red-whiskered Bulbul *(Pycnonotus jocosus)* **p. 166**

This is one of Florida's more picturesque exotic birds. An inhabitant of greater Miami suburbs and parks, the Red-whiskered Bulbul is a native of Asia. Its establishment in south Florida followed intentional releases or escapes from captivity in 1960, an origin shared with most of the state's exotic avifauna. Red-whiskered Bulbuls are about the size of Eastern Phoebes. A flycatcherlike bill, long black crest, red ear patch, red undertail coverts, brown upperparts, and white underparts distinguish this species. Immature birds have brown crests and lack red ear patches. Males sing a distinctive, musical song. Nesting begins in early February after the breakup of large winter roosts. Nests are composed of woven grasses, plant fibers, and bits of refuse. Bulbuls use a variety of small trees and shrubs characteristic of Miami suburbs. The rapid increase of this new Florida resident is in part due to a wide assortment of exotic fruits such as Brazilian pepper, figs, lantana, jasmine, loquat, and blossoms such as bottlebrush, melaleuca, coconut palm, cecreopias, and umbrella trees. A variety of insects is also eaten. Fears that this introduced bird may become an agricultural pest have not materialized to date.

Family Troglodytidae: Wrens

Carolina Wren *(Thryothorus ludovicianus)* **p. 170**
Other names: Florida Wren

This is one of our most abundant and widespread woodland birds. More often heard than seen, the bell-like *teakettle, teakettle, teakettle* often is the best way of finding the Carolina Wren during any season. Largest of the Florida wrens, it is reddish-brown above, buff below, with a white throat and eye stripe. This year-round resident is a cavity-nester that makes use of small tree holes, upturned roots, open nest boxes, hanging plants, and an array of unexpected man-made objects from hanging laundry to old shoes. The nesting season extends from late February into July or August. Nests are an oven-shaped ball of fine material on a foundation of large leaves and twigs. Three to 6 white eggs with red-brown spotting are laid, and as many as three broods may may be raised by a single pair each year. Carolina Wrens are woodland birds inhabiting dense understory vegetation. They are also very tolerant of human activity, provided nest sites are not disturbed. Foods are almost entirely insects.

Bewick's Wren *(Thryomanes bewickii)* **p. 170**

This rare winter visitor is slightly smaller than the Carolina Wren, with white undersides, darker brown upperparts, white eye stripe, and long, fan-shaped tail ending in white spots. Bewick's Wrens have occurred in central and north Florida from October through March, but with increased rarity in recent years. Winter habitats are similar to those of the Carolina Wren, but it seems to prefer relatively hilly country. Insects make up the bulk of the diet.

House Wren *(Troglodytes aedon)* **p. 170**

Other names: Eastern House Wren, Jenny Wren

House Wrens are common winter visitors throughout Florida from October to April. The drab brown upperparts are marked with subtle black barring. Light gray underparts are barred from lower belly to tail. House Wrens are common in fence rows, brush piles, and in a variety of woodlands and wooded parks. A distinctive chattering call often gives away this small bird's presence. Food consists mainly of insects.

Winter Wren *(Troglodytes troglodytes)* **p. 170**

Other names: Eastern Winter Wren

This is our smallest wren, only 4 inches long, with an extremely stubby tail. Similar in markings to the House Wren, Winter Wrens exhibit more dark barring on the belly. They are seldom seen in south Florida, and are uncommon elsewhere in the state. Winter Wrens usually visit between October and March. This secretive bird inhabits a variety of woodlands and feeds on insects.

Sedge Wren *(Cistothorus platensis)* **p. 170**

Other names: Short-billed Marsh Wren

Sedge Wrens are common winter residents in Florida and may be seen in a variety of grassy wetlands both inland and coastal from October through April. Occasionally, drier pastures and fields will contain a few birds. Sedge Wrens exhibit finer white streaking on the back than Marsh Wrens, and a less distinct eye line. Underparts are mostly buff. When disturbed, Sedge Wrens will flutter a short distance before disappearing into thick grassy cover. Foods are mostly insects.

Marsh Wren *(Cistothorus palustris)* **p. 170**

Other names: Long-billed Marsh Wren, Tomtit

In Florida, Marsh Wrens inhabit salt marshes on both the Gulf and Atlantic coasts. The dominance of mangrove in south Florida restricts these small wrens to the northern two-thirds of the state. The Marsh Wren is mostly brown above with white eye line, black upper back streaked with white, and mostly white undersides. The breeding wren of our northeastern coast is a dull gray-brown color, that of the Gulfcoast subspecies is dark brown. In winter the lighter brown or reddish brown-plumaged birds are from northern populations and occur in freshwater marshes also. The song consists of a series of bubbly gurgles ending in a trill. Our permanent residents build a large, globe-shaped nest made of marsh grasses and attached to stems of *Spartina* or *Juncus*. Pairs of Marsh Wrens often nest in a clumped arrangement, leaving apparently suitable habitat vacant. Several "dummy" or courtship nests are made by the male but lack the lining of finer grasses and feathers. Eggs are brown with dark spots and number 3 to 5. Foods are almost entirely insects and spiders with an occasional snail or other small invertebrate.

Family Muscicapidae: Muscicapids

Subfamily Sylviinae: Old World Warblers, Kinglets, Gnatcatchers

Golden-crowned Kinglet *(Regulus satrapa)*   p. 174

Kinglets are about the size of gnatcatchers with much shorter tails and bills. The Golden-crowned Kinglet is strictly a winter visitor seen most commonly in the panhandle from October through March. Greenish upperparts are highlighted with black wings, white wing bars, and striped crown terminating with a brightly colored patch: orange in the male, yellow in the female. Underparts are a dull white. The call is an extremely high-pitched *tsee* which may be difficult to detect. The Golden-crowned Kinglet seems always to be in motion. It feeds primarily upon small forest-dwelling insects.

Ruby-crowned Kinglet *(Regulus calendula)*   p. 174

This small active bird is a common winter visitor throughout Florida woodlands. Similar in size to the Golden-crowned Kinglet, the Ruby-crowned Kinglet is greenish above, pale below, with white wing bars, and no distinct facial marks. The ruby crown of the male is rarely seen in the field. A two-note, wrenlike call and a habit of flicking its wings will help detect it. Ruby-crowned Kinglets appear in a variety of forest types in early October and may remain through April. Food consists mainly of small insects.

Blue-gray Gnatcatcher *(Polioptila caerulea)*   p. 174

Blue-gray Gnatcatchers are often described as miniature mockingbirds. The male is bluish-gray above with dark wings; long, black tail with white outer tail feathers; black forehead; white eye ring and white undersides. Females and immatures lack black on the head and do not show a bluish cast above. The call is an insectlike *zee-ee*. This diminutive forest-dweller is at home in a number of forest types, from live oak hammocks to pine flatwoods and willow swamps. Nests are compact cups of woven grasses, leaves, spider webs, and lichen straddling a horizontal twig. The 4 to 5 eggs, bluish with fine brown dots, are laid in April or May. Gnatcatchers are extremely active birds and can be observed cocking and fanning their long tails while calling or pursuing small foliage-dwelling insects. South Florida is an important wintering range for many northern gnatcatchers.

Subfamily Turdinae: Thrushes

Eastern Bluebird *(Sialia sialis)*   p. 172

Other names: Florida Bluebird

In Florida, bluebirds are characteristic of dry pinelands where nest cavities are available. With extensive timber harvesting throughout the state's extensive pinewoods, natural cavities have become less available. However, nest boxes, erected in suitable habitats, are used readily by these attractive Florida residents. Bright blue upperparts contrast with the robin-red throat and chest and white belly. Females are duller overall with a grayish head. During the breeding season from March through June the distinctive *churlee* or *cheerily* song can be heard. Three to 5 pale blue eggs are laid on a mat of pine needles or grass. Two clutches may be raised each year by the same pair.

Bluebirds are fond of sitting on tall exposed perches and are frequently seen gathered above roadsides along telephone wires. During winter, Florida's resident population is augmented by an influx of northern migrants. Food consists of grasshoppers, caterpillars, and other insects during spring and summer, while small fruits dominate the winter diet.

Veery *(Catharus fuscescens)*   p. 172
Other names: Wilson's Thrush

The Veery is a light or tawny-brown thrush with fine, indistinct breast spots and a white belly. These migrants are seen chiefly in spring during April and May and less frequently in September and October. Veeries inhabit mixed deciduous hardwoods and are usually seen on or near the ground. Food habits are similar to other thrushes.

Gray-cheeked Thrush *(Catharus minimus)*   p. 172
The Gray-cheeked Thrush is similar to Swainson's Thrush but has grayish cheek patches and lacks any buff coloration. The white undersides are heavily spotted on the breast. Immature Graycheeks may possess considerable buff coloring and can be mistaken for Swainson's Thrushes in the fall. Gray-cheeked Thrushes can be seen throughout the state in a variety of wooded areas and are regular visitors during migration at Ft. DeSoto Park in Pinellas County and the Dry Tortugas. Spring birds may be seen in April and May while fall birds pass through the state in September and October. Foods include small fruits and insects.

Swainson's Thrush *(Catharus ustulatus)*   p. 172
Other names: Olive-backed Thrush

This spring and fall migrant is a rather plain thrush. Olive-brown above and white below, the Swainson's Thrush has a streaked breast and distinct buff eye rings and cheeks. Its habits are somewhat secretive but can be looked for in moist woodlands and swamp edges from mid-April through early May, then again from September into October. A variety of fruits and insects constitute this bird's diet.

Hermit Thrush *(Catharus guttatus)*   p. 172
Other names: Eastern Hermit Thrush, Swamp Sparrow

This common winter visitor is brown above with a moderately spotted breast and a rusty tail that is often bobbed up and down. The Hermit Thrush arrives in late October and may remain in Florida until early May. It can be looked for in moist woodlands and thickets. Foods include insects such as beetles, ants, and grasshoppers as well as fruits of dogwood, holly, and poison ivy.

Wood Thrush *(Hylocichla mustelina)*   p. 172
Other names: Brown Thrush, Swamp Sparrow, Branch Bird

The Wood Thrush is similar in appearance to the Brown Thrasher but has a shorter tail and bill. In addition the head is redder than the back and the breast spots are dark and conspicuous. The song is a varied, melodious flutelike series of rounded phrases. Resident birds nest from April to June in deciduous woodlands across north Florida, but they are nowhere abundant in Florida. Nests, constructed of twigs, leaves, paper shreds, and plastic are lined with mud, pine needles, and grass, and usually placed in a shrub. Clutches average 4 greenish-blue eggs. Spring migrants may be seen from March through April, while fall birds usually pass through during October. Foods are similar to those eaten by other thrushes.

American Robin *(Turdus migratorius)*   **p. 172**

Other names: Robin Redbreast

The American Robin is one of Florida's most abundant winter visitors and is becoming an increasingly common nester around some north Florida cities such as Jacksonville, Tallahassee, and Pensacola. A "colony" of robins has been nesting in Tampa for several years. Dark gray upperparts, red breast, and yellow bill distinguish this large, familiar songbird. Immatures are spotted below and lighter above. The song is a melodius series of notes: *cheerily-cheery-cheerio.* Nests are placed on horizontal tree limbs and are constructed of a mixture of mud, grass, and twigs. Eggs, numbering 3 or 4 are greenish-blue and may be laid from March through June. Huge flocks are seen frequently throughout Florida during winter as Robins search for abundant food supplies. Winter foods include fruits of swamp tupelo, Brazilian pepper, dahoon holly, gallberry, cabbage palm, sugarberry, and poison ivy. Insects and invertebrates (chiefly earthworms) are eaten more frequently in spring and summer. Winter residents may be seen from November through April.

Family Mimidae: Mockingbirds, Thrashers, and Allies

Gray Catbird *(Dumetella carolinensis)*   **p. 170**

Other names: Black Mockingbird

This inconspicuous bird is most abundant during winter but also nests sporadically in north Florida. Because of their secretive habits, Catbirds are more often heard than seen, uttering their distinctive catlike *meow.* Catbirds possess their own musical, jumbled song and are not imitators like the closely related Mockingbird. Plumage is mostly dark gray with black tail, black cap, and red undertail coverts. The preferred habitats are dense tangles of greenbriar, fetterbush, or other thick growth often associated with large swamps. The nests are loosely constructed cups located near the ground in dense shrubs. Blue eggs number 3 or 4 and are usually laid in April or May. Food is mainly vegetable and includes fruits of dogwood, greenbriar, wild grape, and mulberry.

Northern Mockingbird *(Mimus polyglottos)*   **p. 170**

Other names: Mockingbird, Eastern Mockingbird

The widely distributed and well known Mockingbird is Florida's official state bird. A resident of habitat edges, city parks, suburbs, orange groves, and other agricultural areas, Mockingbirds have benefitted from man's increasing presence in the state. Often described as "ordinary-looking," Mockingbirds are gray above with darker wings and tail, white wing bars and outer tail feathers, and whitish underneath. Perhaps its best known trait is the ability to imitate nearly any sound familiar to it. The calls, usually repeated in threes, most often imitate other birds but may also include domestic animals and a variety of man-made sounds. In spring, the male may sing long into the evening, especially on moonlit nights. Nests, constructed of small twigs, are lined with rootlets or other fine material and usually located within a dense, concealing shrub. Eggs number 3 to 5 and are greenish-blue with brown spots and splotches. The breeding season extends from March to August with some pairs raising two or more clutches. Foods include some insects and other invertebrates and fruits such as greenbriar, dahoon holly, gallberry, Brazilian pepper, elderberry, cabbage palm, etc.

Brown Thrasher *(Toxostoma rufum)*   p. 170

Other names: Brown Thrush, Sandy Mocker, Thrash, Fence Corner Bird

Although resembling some of our wintering thrushes, the Brown Thrasher is another relative of the Mockingbird. Rusty brown upperparts, tawny wing bars highlighted with black, heavy brown streaking on whitish belly, and long bill and tail distinguish both sexes of this common Florida resident. Brown Thrashers are nearly as skilled at imitating as Mockingbirds, but do not imitate as frequently. Phrases are usually repeated only twice and in a much more musical voice. Nesting occurs in April or May when 3 to 5 bluish-white eggs marked with fine brown dots are laid. The nest, constructed with twigs, leaves, and rootlets is usually placed in dense shrubbery or thickets. Brown Thrashers are quite tolerant of humans and may be found in suburban backyards, city parks, citrus groves and other agricultural lands. In less disturbed settings it is a bird of the edge, inhabiting vegetation on the borders of woodlands and clearings. Foods consist of locally abundant insects and wild fruits.

Family Motacillidae: Wagtails and Pipits

American Pipit *(Anthus rubescens)*   p. 174

Other names: Water Pipit, Titlark, Prairie Sparrow

Pipits are easily-overlooked, ground-dwelling birds that superficially resemble sparrows. Buff undersides with brown streaking on breast contrasts with greenish-brown upperparts. A thin bill and longish tail bordered in white distinguish the American Pipit from sparrows. Migrants arrive during October and usually depart by March. Pipits inhabit open landscapes such as plowed fields, lake edges, mud flats, and golf courses in north and central Florida, where they can be seen walking, not hopping, in search of food. The call, a repeated *pip-pit*, is uttered while taking flight or flying. Pipits often feed on agricultural pests such as weevils, beetles, and grasshoppers, as well as weed seeds, grains, and mollusks. Occasionally, Sprague's Pipit (*Anthus spragueii*) appears in Florida, and one has wintered off and on along the causeway to St. George Island in recent years. It is generally lighter in color than the American Pipit, with a scaly patterned back, a pale buff face with distinct dark eye, and whitish underparts with a buff wash and some streaking.

Family Bombycillidae: Waxwings

Cedar Waxwing *(Bombycilla cedrorum)* **p. 174**

Other names: Cedar Bird, Seal, Hammerlock, Cherry Robin, Canadian Robin

The Cedar Waxwing is a characteristic winter bird seen in large flocks from suburban backyards to deep, remote swamps throughout the state. A variety of distinctive markings and its call, a high-pitched buzzy squeal, make this bird nearly unmistakable. The light brown body is highlighted with a crest, black mask, yellow belly, and yellow-tipped tail. Wing feathers of some adults bear a red spot that looks like nail polish. Immature birds resemble adults but are streaked above and below. In Florida, Cedar Waxwings are most common in winter and spring but may arrive as early as mid-October and linger until May. Fruits are the mainstay of its diet and include sugarberries, mulberries, holly, cedars, cherries, and greenbriar.

Family Laniidae: Shrikes

Loggerhead Shrike *(Lanius ludovicianus)* **p. 174**

Other names: Butcher Bird, French Mockingbird, Catbird

This predatory Florida songbird inhabits agricultural lands and other open areas. While resembling the Northern Mockingbird at a distance, the Loggerhead Shrike is a stockier bird with a bold black mask, black tail, and white wing patches. The heavy bill is short and hooked. The infrequent call consists of short mechanical notes. Its song is more varied and musical. Nests are often in open-growing shrubs or small trees and are constructed of twigs, feathers, rootlets, and other plant fibers. The Loggerhead Shrike is an early nester, laying an average of 5 light gray, brown-spotted eggs from early March through June. During winter, northern migrants inflate the Florida population. Shrikes often are seen perched on telephone wires and fences while hunting for small animals. Rodents, lizards, small birds, grasshoppers, caterpillars, and other insects make up its completely animal diet. Shrikes are incapable of grasping prey with their small feet but frequently impale food items on long thorns or barbed wire. Because of their heavy dependence upon insects, Loggerhead Shrikes recently have experienced a decline in numbers due to pesticides.

Family Sturnidae: Starlings

European Starling *(Sturnus vulgaris)* **p. 176**

Other names: Blackbird.

Starlings are glossy, black birds with needlelike yellow bills, short tails, and reddish legs. Winter birds are generously speckled with white, and the bill is dark. Immature birds are grayish-brown overall. Starlings were introduced into New York City in 1890 and have since spread throughout the continental United States. In Florida they are residents of cities, suburbs, and agricultural lands where they nest in woodpecker holes or man-made cavities. Twigs, paper, plastic, feathers and other materials line the nest where 4 to 6 bluish-green eggs are laid. The nesting season extends from March to July. This aggressive exotic is capable of displacing native cavity nesters from natural and man-made structures. During winter, Starlings may congregate in the thousands, often with other blackbirds. These large, noisy flocks may occur in backyard shade trees, on powerlines, or farm structures. Starlings often imitate other birds but their voice also includes a variety of whistles, squeaks, and clicks. Foods eaten include grasshoppers, earthworms, grains, cherries, and other fruits.

Family Vireonidae: Vireos

White-eyed Vireo *(Vireo griseus)*   p. 176

This small vireo is a common resident of Florida's woodlands. Gum swamps, oak hammocks, and pine flatwoods seem equally suitable to the White-eyed Vireo. Greenish upperparts, yellow spectacles, white wing bars, and white irises characterize adults; juveniles have dark eyes. It is a perpetual singer, the song a syncopated series of 5 to 7 notes ending in a staccato *chick*. The nest is composed of grass, bark, Spanish moss, and leaves and is hung from a V-shaped twig. Three to 5 brown-spotted, white eggs are laid in May or June. Migrants arrive in Florida in mid-September on their way to South America, although many winter in Florida. Spring migrants pass through in March and April. Foods are mostly insects but also include fruits of greenbriar, dogwood, and other woodland plants.

Solitary Vireo *(Vireo solitarius)*   p. 176

Other names: Blue-headed Vireo

The Solitary Vireo is a fairly common migrant and winter bird in Florida. Blue-gray head with white spectacles, greenish upperparts, white wing bars, yellowish flanks, and white underparts distinguish this woodland bird. Solitary vireos are found in a variety of situations from pine flatwoods and hardwood hammocks to suburban backyards. Foods are mostly tree-dwelling insects with a few fruits such as dogwood and wax myrtle. Solitary Vireos can be found in Florida from mid-October through April.

Yellow-throated Vireo *(Vireo flavifrons)*   p. 176

The Yellow-throated Vireo is a common summer resident through most of Florida north of Orlando. It prefers deciduous or mixed deciduous-pine woodlands for nesting. Yellow spectacles, breast, and throat are contrasted by a white belly, gray rump, and greenish upperparts. The song is a repeated series of 2- and 3-note phrases resembling the Red-eyed Vireo's, but slower and more deliberate. The nest is a hanging, woven cup placed high in a tall pine or hardwood. The eggs, numbering 3 to 5 and pinkish with brown spots concentrated on one end, are usually laid in April. Yellow-throated Vireos are most common in Florida between March and October. A few birds overwinter in south Florida. Insects dominate the diet.

Red-eyed Vireo *(Vireo olivaceus)*   p. 176

Other names: Hanging Bird

In eastern North America the Red-eyed Vireo is one of the most abundant woodland birds. Its distinctive song, *how-are-you? I'm fine*, may be repeated incessantly, and is a characteristic sound of spring and summer. Upperparts are grayish with a black-bordered, white eye stripe. Underparts are white with pale yellow flanks. The red eyes are visible only at close range. In Florida, Red-eyed Vireos are common in mixed hardwood forests throughout central and north Florida. They breed less frequently in south Florida. Nests are woven cups suspended from a forked branch of a shrub or tree. Eggs numbering from 3 to 5 are laid during May, and are white with brown spots on the large end. Spring migrants arrive in mid or late March while the last fall migrants pass through during October. The wintering ground of this common species is in South America. Insects form the bulk of this vireo's diet although fruits such as dogwood and Virginia creeper are also taken.

Black-whiskered Vireo *(Vireo altiloquus)* p. 176

This Florida specialty's distribution is restricted to the state's southern coasts and keys. It is similar to the Red-eyed Vireo but has a heavier bill and distinctive black "whiskers." The song also resembles the Red-eyed Vireo but is hoarser and is sung in couplets, i.e., 2 phrases and a pause. The Black-whiskered Vireo is a bird of Florida's mangrove forests and tropical hardwoods. Like other vireos its nest is a shallow woven cup. Eggs usually number 3 and are white with brown spots. Nesting occurs in May or June. Most birds depart for South America by mid-September and begin their return to Florida in late March. Although breeding occurs only south of Cedar Key, migrant Black-whiskered Vireos are frequently seen on the upper Gulf coast. Insects and spiders form the bulk of its diet.

Family Emberizidae: Emberizids

Subfamily Parulinae: Wood Warblers

Tennessee Warbler *(Vermivora peregrina)* p. 178

The Tennessee is a nondescript drab-green warbler with white eye line and yellow-green undersides. It is an abundant fall migrant during October and again passes through Florida in April. Tennessee Warblers use a variety of woodland and brushy habitats while hunting for insects.

Orange-crowned Warbler *(Vermivora celata)* p. 178

Orange-crowned Warblers are greenish-gray above and below with yellow beneath the tail. The breast is faintly streaked and the bill is narrow and slightly down-curved. The orange crown is not visible in the field. The Orange-crowned Warbler is a common winter visitor and can be seen in hardwoods, especially live oaks, as well as in shrubs and tall weeds. It occurs in Florida from late September to mid-April.

Northern Parula *(Parula americana)* p. 180

Other names: Southern Parula Warbler

The Northern Parula is widespread in Florida and breeds south to northern Monroe County. Although it is our smallest warbler its bright coloration and loud incessant song, described as an ascending trill increasing in volume towards an explosive *zip*, make this bird conspicuous. Upperparts are bluish with light green back, two white wing bars, and a white eye ring divided by a black eye stripe. The white belly is contrasted by a yellow breast. Reddish and blue bands highlight the adult male's breast. The nest is usually constructed within a hanging clump of Spanish moss. Eggs numbering 4 to 6 are white with brown spots on the large end, and are laid between early April and June. Fall migrants depart Florida as early as mid-August and begin their return in mid-February. Some Parulas also winter in Florida. Food consists primarily of caterpillars, spiders and small flying insects.

Yellow Warbler *(Dendroica petechia)*   **p. 180**

Other names: Cuban Golden Warbler, Wild Canary, Summer Yellow-bird
Throughout most of Florida the Yellow Warbler is encountered as a fall and spring migrant. However, the West Indies race is a permanent resident in the Keys. The golden yellow plumage is highlighted by chestnut streaking on the breast and darker wings. Females are lemon-yellow and unstreaked below. Yellow patches on outer tail feathers help differentiate immatures from immature Hooded Warblers (white patches) and Wilson's Warblers (no patches). The song consists of 3 to 4 *sweet* notes followed by several more in rapid succession. Nests are placed in a forked branch of a dense shrub or tree. They are constructed of grasslike materials and finished with a soft lining. The 2 to 4 blotched, white eggs are laid in April or May. Migrants are most common during the fall and can be seen from July through October. Spring migrants are seen from early March to early May. It is usually seen in willows but also in old fields and other moderately open vegetation. Yellow Warblers feed mostly on insects.

Chestnut-sided Warbler *(Dendroica pensylvanica)*   **p. 182**

The drab fall colors of the Chestnut-sided Warbler are a sharp contrast to its colorful breeding plumage. Greenish head and back, two white wing bars, and light underparts characterize fall birds. The spring bird has a yellow crown, black eye line and whiskers, white underparts, and chestnut flanks. Females are less boldly marked but have the same pattern. Chestnut-sided Warblers frequent old pastures and brushy woodlands in Florida from April to May and in September and October. It feeds mainly on insects.

Magnolia Warbler *(Dendroica magnolia)*   **p. 180**

In fall, the bright yellow and black breeding plumage of the male Magnolia Warbler is replaced by much grayer coloring. In Florida males exhibit yellow undersides with black flecks on the flanks, gray head with faint white eye line, greenish back, yellow rump, white tail patches, and two white wing bars. Females are grayer overall and lack the white tail patches. Fall migrants arrive in Florida during late September on their way to Central America. A few birds winter in extreme south Florida. Spring birds are seen occasionally in April and May. They seem partial to hardwood habitats where they hunt insects.

Cape May Warbler *(Dendroica tigrina)*   **p. 180**

The burnt-orange or chestnut ear of the male Cape May Warbler is its most distinctive feature. Underparts are bright yellow with heavy black streaking. Upperparts are olive-green streaked with black. The rump is yellow and the wings have large white wing bars. The female is duller colored, but also has a yellow rump, heavily streaked breast and white wing bars. In both sexes the bill is slightly down-curved. Cape Mays are abundant spring migrants passing through Florida during April and May. Fall migration occurs from late August through October. A few birds spend the winter in extreme south Florida. It feeds primarily on insects and is most frequent in deciduous woodlands.

Black-throated Blue Warbler *(Dendroica caerulescens)*   p. 182

Audubon considered the female Black-throated Blue Warbler a species distinct from the male. Olive-drab upperparts, white eye line, white wing patch and buff underparts identify the female. Males are dark blue above with black cheeks, throat and flanks, and are white below with white wing patches. The wing patches are the most consistent field mark for both sexes, although some immature females may lack these. During migration it can be seen in a variety of forest types from late August to late October and from mid-March through May. A few overwinter in south Florida. Foods are predominantly insect.

Yellow-rumped Warbler *(Dendroica coronata)*   p. 180

Other names: Myrtle Warbler, Audubon's Warbler

The Yellow-rumped is the most abundant wintering warbler in Florida. This is in part due to its habit of feeding upon fruit of the widely distributed wax myrtle during the colder parts of winter. It is a rather drab warbler with brownish upperparts, white eye line, and streaked undersides. The best field mark is the bright yellow rump patch characteristic of both sexes. In early spring a few males may exhibit various stages of breeding plumage development, but most birds depart Florida before completing their molt. Yellowrumps appear in Florida during October and may remain until April. It is not unusual to encounter large flocks of this species particularly during the colder months. Under these circumstances its call, a distinctive *chip*, is easily identified. Aside from wax myrtle fruit, insects also are eaten.

Black-throated Green Warbler *(Dendroica virens)*   p. 182

This is the only eastern warbler with a black throat and yellow cheek patches. White underparts have black-streaked flanks, upperparts are olive-green, and wings have two white wing bars. Females are similar but less boldly marked. Although the Black-throated Green Warbler nests as close as north Georgia, it is seen only briefly in most of Florida as a migrant. A few birds regularly winter in extreme south Florida and the Keys. Spring birds may be encountered from late March to early May. In fall they migrate between early September and late October. The Black-throated Green Warbler uses a variety of woodlands and feeds on small insects and a few small fruits.

Blackburnian Warbler *(Dendroica fusca)*   p. 182

A large white wing patch and orange throat are the best field marks for the adult Blackburnian Warbler. Upperparts are black, with light undersides and streaked flanks. Immatures and adult females exhibit similar color patterns but are duller overall with two white wing bars. This is not a common bird in Florida, but can be expected in migration in September and

October and in April and May. Blackburnians are seen chiefly in deciduous hardwoods while foraging for insects.

Yellow-throated Warbler *(Dendroica dominica)* p. 182
Other names: Sycamore Warbler

Gray upperparts are highlighted by two white wing bars, white eye line, white ear patch, and black cheeks. Underparts are white with black-streaked flanks and yellow throat and chest. The bill is long compared to others of the genus. The song is a series of *sweet* notes with the last three repeated more rapidly than the first three. The Yellow-throated Warbler is a common year-round resident in north Florida and is a winter resident in the rest of the state. It is most abundant in mixed pine-hardwoods habitats where it can be seen foraging along trunks and branches probing for insects. Nests are most frequently built in clumps of hanging Spanish Moss. The 3 to 5 white eggs are marked on the large end with brown and lavender flecking, and are laid in April or early May. The "Sutton's" Warbler is a hybrid between the Yellow-throated Warbler and Northern Parula. This rare form exhibits a greenish back and little streaking on flanks.

Pine Warbler *(Dendroica pinus)* p. 184
Other names: Pine-creeping Warbler

The male Pine Warbler is greenish above with dark wings, 2 white wing bars, yellow breast and streaked flanks. Females have grayish undersides while immature birds are browner above than adults. The song is a single-pitched trill—like a musical sewing machine—that carries a considerable distance. Pine Warblers may be seen hawking for flying insects or creeping, nuthatch-fashion, along trunks and tree limbs. During the breeding season, from March through April, Pine Warblers are usually associated with pine trees. Nests are concealed cups attached to narrow branches and constructed of pine needles and grass with a lining of finer materials. The 3 to 4 eggs are white with brownish spotting on the large end. Pine Warblers are year-round residents in Florida. In addition to insects, a variety of small seeds also are eaten.

Prairie Warbler *(Dendroica discolor)* p. 184
Other names: Northern Prairie Warbler, Florida Prairie Warbler

The Prairie Warbler is greenish above with buff wing bars, chestnut streaking on back, a black eye line, yellow undersides, and black streaking on the flanks. Males are somewhat more brightly colored than females and also have a black crescent beneath each eye. Immatures are much duller. The song is an ascending series of flutelike *zee* notes. Its habit of tail bobbing is a good aid to identification. Despite its name, open grasslands are not used. During the breeding season in Florida the resident Prairie Warbler is essentially a bird of coastal mangrove swamps. However, a few birds breed at inland locations in north Florida among shrubs and young, densely grown pine stands. Nests are composed of local plant fibers and placed up to 10 feet in a mangrove or other shrub. The 3 to 5 white eggs are speckled brown and laid from March through May. Northern birds migrate through Florida from late July through early November and from early March to early May. Prairie Warblers feed mainly on insects.

Palm Warbler *(Dendroica palmarum)*   p. 184

Other names: Yellow Palm Warbler, Western Palm Warbler

As a winter warbler in Florida the Palm is second in abundance only to the Yellow-rumped. Spring birds are yellow below with brownish streaking, olive above, with a pale eye line and rufous cap. Fall and winter birds are paler overall with yellow undertail coverts. Palm Warblers continually bob their tails. Fall migrants arrive in late September and may reside in Florida through April. They may be seen in a variety of habitats from woodland edges to agricultural lands and marshes. Foods are mostly insects such as small beetles, caterpillars, and grasshoppers. During colder weather small fruits and seeds are eaten.

Bay-breasted Warbler *(Dendroica castanea)*   p. 184

Spring males exhibit chestnut crown, throat, and flanks, black face, cream ear patch and undersides, two white wing bars and grayish upperparts. Females lack the black face and are less boldly colored. While breeding individuals are unmistakable, fall birds are olive-gray overall with black wings and two white wing bars. Adult males usually retain some bay coloration on the sides. Bay-breasted Warblers closely resemble the fall Blackpoll Warbler but lack distinct streaking underneath and have black rather than brown legs. Fall birds pass through Florida primarily in October. Spring migrants have been recorded from mid-March to early May. The Bay-breasted Warbler is not common in Florida but can be looked for in deciduous hardwoods. Foods are mostly insects.

Blackpoll Warbler *(Dendroica striata)*   p. 184

White cheeks, two white wing bars, black cap and throat, and streaked undersides distinguish the spring adult male Blackpoll. The female has a greenish-brown head and is less boldly marked. The fall bird has a streaked, greenish-yellow head, back, and throat. During fall it is an uncommon migrant from late September to late October. Spring migrants are abundant and have been recorded from mid-April to late May. As West Indian migrants, they are not often seen in northwestern Florida during either season. The Blackpoll Warbler inhabits a variety of woodland types and may also be seen in gardens, orchards, and wooded suburbs. Like most warblers its food is mostly insects.

Black-and-white Warbler *(Mniotilta varia)*   p. 178

Heavy black streaking with white belly and white stripe on the crown distinguish this common winter visitor. The Black-and-white is one of our "creeping" warblers and may be seen hanging upside down, nuthatchlike on tree limbs. The call is a high, thin, two-noted whistle. Fall migrants arrive in late July, while the last spring migrants depart in May. In Florida, they can be found throughout winter in a variety of habitats but show a preference for hardwoods. Black-and-white Warblers feed exclusively on insects.

American Redstart *(Setophaga ruticilla)*   p. 188

Other names: Flamebird

This colorful warbler is a common spring and fall migrant. It has nested in northwest Florida and is an uncommon winter resident in south Florida. The adult male is white below and black above with orange patches on the sides, wings, and tail. The female is grayish above with yellow instead of orange patches. The second-year male resembles the female with dark flecking on the throat and light orange side patches. Redstarts make a habit of fanning their tails and exposing these brightly colored feathers. It is frequently seen in hardwood forests and woodland edges. Fall migrants arrive between late July and early November. Spring birds pass through between late March and early June. Redstarts actively hawk for flying insects.

Prothonotary Warbler *(Protonotaria citrea)*   **p. 178**

Other names: Golden Swamp Warbler, Swamp Yellowbird

The Prothonotary is a stocky, bright yellow warbler with bluish wings and tail. There are no wing bars but the tail has distinctive white patches. The song is a series of ringing notes: *sweet, sweet, sweet, sweet, sweet.* This is our only warbler that nests in cavities. Preferred habitats are forested wetlands such as gum swamps, cypress swamps, and hardwood bottomlands in Florida south to northern Monroe County. Occasionally, nest boxes are used. The nest consists of moss, grasses, and small leaves. Eggs, numbering 3 to 6, are cream-colored and boldly speckled. Laying may occur between mid-April and early June. Migrants leave Florida between July and September and return in March. Insects form the bulk of its diet.

Worm-eating Warbler *(Helmitheros vermivorus)*   **p. 178**

Olive-brown back, buff head with two black stripes and buff-orange underparts make this a distinctive warbler. The song is a brief, unmusical buzz. In Florida, the Worm-eating Warbler is most often encountered as a migrant from late March to early May and from late August to early October. A few birds overwinter in south Florida. As a breeder it is found only in the western panhandle in late April and May. The nest is built of leaves and placed in dense vegetation on the ground. Eggs are white with brown flecking on the large end. Worm-eating Warblers are mostly found in deciduous hardwood habitats. Foods are primarily insects and spiders.

Swainson's Warbler *(Limnothlypis swainsonii)*   **p. 178**

This olive-brown warbler is white below with a dark eye line, pale stripe above the eye, and dark crown. The song is a loud, slurred series of 5 notes ending with 2 ascending notes. The Swainson's Warbler is an uncommon breeder throughout north Florida. It favors densely vegetated rivers and swamps where it fastens a nest to a shrub, cane, or vine. Three to 4 white eggs are laid in April or May. Fall migration takes place from August through October. Spring birds arrive during late March. Swainson's Warblers frequently forage on the ground. They eat a variety of small insects.

Ovenbird *(Seiurus aurocapillus)*   **p. 186**

Other names: Golden-crowned Thrush

This ground-dwelling warbler gives the impression of a small thrush. Olive upperparts are highlighted by a black-bordered orange cap. White underparts are marked boldly with black spots. Immatures lack the orange crown. Although less common in north Florida, the Ovenbird is a widespread winter resident. Fall migrants arrive in mid-August; the last birds in spring are seen in late April or early May. Ovenbirds exhibit a preference for deciduous woodlands where they feed on spiders, caterpillars, flies, and other insects. Fruits and seeds are occasionally eaten.

Northern Waterthrush *(Seiurus noveboracensis)*   p. 186

This is another ground-dwelling migrant and winter resident warbler. Olive-brown upperparts are contrasted by white or cream underparts that are heavily streaked and lack contrasting flank color. The narrow eyebrow is white or buff. The Northern Waterthrush is a common fall and spring migrant, travelling south from late August through September and north from April through May. A few birds winter in scattered south Florida locations. This is a bird of deciduous or broadleaf woodlands and is usually not far from water. Northern Waterthrushes usually walk, instead of hop, and bob their tails rapidly. The song begins with loud distinctive notes and trails off at the end but is rarely heard in Florida. Insects make up the bulk of its diet.

Louisiana Waterthrush *(Seiurus motacilla)*   p. 186

Other names: Large-billed Waterthrush, Water Wagtail

The Louisiana Waterthrush closely resembles its relative the Northern Waterthrush. The unspotted white throat, white eyebrow that becomes broader behind the eye, tannish flanks, and a larger bill separate the Louisiana from the Northern. The sexes appear similar. While foraging, the Louisiana bobs its head and tail continuously. The song consists of 5 to 6 slurred notes followed by 3 or 4 sharper notes. It is an inhabitant of wooded streams and seems to be expanding its breeding range into north-west Florida. Nests are placed in protected spots along stream banks and are constructed of leaves and grass. The 4 to 6 white eggs are laid from early May to June. Migration occurs earlier than that of most other warblers. Spring birds pass through Florida in March and early April, while fall migrants are seen from mid-July through September. A few scattered individuals have been reported during winter. Food consists of snails, insects, and other invertebrates that are associated with streams.

Common Yellowthroat *(Geothlypis trichas)*   p. 186

Other names: Maryland Yellowthroat

This abundant, resident warbler is one of Florida's most widespread birds. Both sexes are olive-green above and yellow below. Males have white-bordered black masks and are brighter yellow beneath. The song is a loud *wichity-wichity*, and the call a *churr-churr*. Nests may be located in marshes, swamps, or dry woodlands but usually are placed near the ground and constructed of dry grass and stems. The 3 to 5 white eggs are speckled around the large end and are laid from early April to early June. Many northern birds either winter in Florida or pass through in spring and fall. Common Yellowthroats feed on a variety of aquatic and terrestrial insects.

Hooded Warbler *(Wilsonia citrina)*   p. 188

The Hooded Warbler is olive-green above, with yellow cheeks, large black eyes, and yellow underparts. Adult males exhibit a distinctive black hood that extends from the top of the head to the throat. The song is a ringing *weet-a, weet-a, wee-tee-o.* In Florida the Hooded Warbler inhabits swamps and moist pine flatwoods in the panhandle and northern peninsula south to Ocala. Nests are made of woven plant fibers and placed in dense shrubs. Eggs numbering 3 or 4 are white and splotched in shades of gray and brown. Laying takes place from May to July. During fall migration they are seen in Florida from July through October and in spring from mid-March through April. Foods consist of insects and other invertebrates.

Wilson's Warbler *(Wilsonia pusilla)* p. 188
The Wilson's is an uncommon unpredictable migrant in Florida. The male is bright yellow below, greenish above, and has a black cap. The female is similar but lacks black plumage and is duller overall. During migration Wilson's Warblers utilize forest edge and shrub vegetation while foraging for insects.

Yellow-breasted Chat *(Icteria virens)* p. 186
This largest of North American warblers is a summer resident in north Florida. Not only is its size unusual for a warbler but its behavior is also unique. The yellow breast grades to a white underbelly; upperparts are olive green. The black between the eye and bill is bordered in white. Some of the Chat's unusual behavior includes nighttime singing, song mimicry, and aerial feats of contortion. Hal Harrison described one variation of the song as "the alarm call of a Wren, a foghorn, and a chuckling, high-pitched laugh." The nest is placed no more than 6 feet off the ground in dense vegetation and is a bulky, well concealed structure. The large eggs number 3 to 5, are white with splotches of brown and lavender, and are laid between May and July. Foods include caterpillars, beetles, wasps, and a variety of fruits and berries.

Subfamily Coerebinae: Bananaquits

Bananaquit *(Coereba flaveola)* p. 176
Bahama Honeycreeper, Sugarbird
An abundant inhabitant of the Bahama Islands only 50 miles east of south Florida, it is strange that so few Bananaquits ever reach Florida, and the few that do remain only a few days before disappearing. The Bananaquit is a warbler-sized bird with a decurved bill. The adult has a black back with a yellow rump, black tail, white eyebrow and yellow underparts. White highlights appear on the wings and tail. Bananaquits feed primarily on nectar and nectar-eating insects.

Subfamily Thraupinae: Tanagers

Summer Tanager *(Piranga rubra)* p. 192
Other names: Summer Redbird
Although not so brightly colored as the Scarlet Tanager, this summer resident is one of Florida's most distinctive birds. The Summer Tanager exhibits red plumage, with darker red wings, and heavy bill. Females are orange-yellow below and greenish brown above. The song is robinlike and the call is a staccato *chick-a-tick-a-tuck.* Nests are usually built in large trees in hardwood hammocks or oak-pine woodlands. The 3 or 4 eggs are bluish-green

with brown spots and laid in April or May. Nests are constructed with Spanish moss, grass, and other fine materials. Summer Tanagers return to Florida in early March and may remain until early November. A few birds may overwinter. Foods include caterpillars, beetles, wasps, and many small, fleshy fruits.

Scarlet Tanager *(Piranga olivacea)* p. 192

The male Scarlet Tanager is unmistakable with its brightly colored red plumage and contrasting black wings and tail. Females are greenish yellow below and olive green above. Winter males resemble females with black wings and tail. During fall some males may exhibit red splotches while molting into winter plumage. Scarlet Tanagers are encountered only during migration in Florida. Fall birds can be seen from early September through October. Spring migration lasts from late March through early May. While this bird may be seen throughout the state it seems most common in the panhandle. Scarlet Tanagers prefer deciduous woodlands and feed upon a variety of insects and spiders.

Subfamily Cardinalinae: Cardinals and Grosbeaks

Northern Cardinal *(Cardinalis cardinalis)* p. 194

Other names: Cardinal, Redbird

One of our most common suburban inhabitants and backyard feeder visitors, the Cardinal is also one of our most easily recognized birds. The bright red plumage of the male is highlighted by a black mask. Females are brown overall with red highlights. Both sexes are heavy-billed and crested. The song, a rich, whistled *cheer, cheer, cheer* is performed by both the male and female. Northern Cardinals are nonmigratory inhabitants of woodland edges, gardens, and suburbs. Nests are loosely constructed of small twigs, leaves, and grasses, and are usually placed in a wild or landscaped shrub. Eggs, numbering 2 to 4, are greenish-blue with brown and reddish markings and can be found from March through August. Cardinals are primarily seed and fruit eaters, but also will eat insects when abundant and when feeding their young. In particular, fruits of dogwood, beautyberry, sugarberry, cherry, poison ivy, and holly are eaten. Sunflowers are favorite items at feeding stations.

Rose-breasted Grosbeak *(Pheucticus ludovicianus)* p. 194

This large finch is seen occasionally in Florida during migration. The male is black above with white rump and wing patches. Underparts are white with a red breast. The female is brown with white wing bars, white eye line, and streaked, buff-colored underparts. Rose-breasted Grosbeaks are seen in open woodlands, swamps, and second-growth timber, especially in the panhandle. Spring migrants can be seen from late March through early May, and in fall from early September through October. Some birds overwinter. Foods include a variety of fruits, seeds, and insects.

Blue Grosbeak *(Guiraca caerulea)* p. 194

The Blue Grosbeak is a summer resident in north Florida inhabiting brushy vegetation bordering streams, marshes, fields, woodlands, and roadsides. Males are purplish-blue with a black face mask and chestnut wing bars. Females are light brown with dark wings, buff wing bars, and dark tail. Blue Grosbeaks are somewhat larger and heavier-billed than the similar Indigo Bunting. The song is a series of long melodious warbles. Nests are found in shrubs or small trees and are constructed with grass, leaves, and other pliable material. Three to 4 light blue eggs are laid from late April through July. Breeding records occur southward into Polk and Highlands Counties. Migrants return to Florida in early or mid-April and the last fall migrants depart in September. Insects, spiders, snails, weed seeds, and grains are eaten.

Indigo Bunting *(Passerina cyanea)* p. 194

Other names: Indigo Bird, Swamp Bluebird

No other Florida bird is entirely blue or as iridescent as the male Indigo Bunting. The female is mostly brown with faint streaks on breast and back and has faint blue plumage on tail and wings. Winter adult males resemble females but have more blue. The song is a musical series of paired phrases. Indigo Buntings are summer residents in north Florida, nesting in open woodlands, field edges, and old fields. The cupped nest is woven with fine grasses and leaves. The 2 to 4 pale blue eggs are laid from May to August. Spring migrants return to Florida in mid-April while fall birds are seen from August through October. A few overwinter in central and south Florida. Indigo Buntings primarily are seed eaters but also will consume a variety of berries and insects.

Painted Bunting *(Passerina ciris)* p. 196

Other names: Nonpareil

The Painted Bunting is one of Florida's most colorful birds. The male has a blue head, red undersides and rump, greenish yellow back, and dark wings and tail. Females are dull yellow below and green above. First-year males look similar to females. The song is a loud, high-pitched and varied warble. Painted Buntings prefer dense, brushy vegetation along roads, woodland edges, and backyard gardens. It breeds from northern Brevard County northward along the St. Johns River and the Atlantic coastal counties. Nests are similar to those of Indigo Buntings, usually placed at the end of a branch in Spanish moss. Eggs number 3 or 4, are white with brown speckling, and are laid from May through June. Foods are primarily seeds but may include small fruits and insects. In some locations Painted Buntings are frequent visitors at feeding stations. Although numerous birds overwinter in central and south Florida, most Painted Buntings leave the state by late October. Spring migrants begin their return in mid-April.

Dickcissel *(Spiza americana)* p. 196

This sparrow-sized finch is a regular migrant in Florida, and numerous individuals overwinter, when they may be found with House Sparrows. Upperparts are brown above and light below with yellow eye line and yellow breast. The male shows a gray to black throat patch. Immatures are duller overall and are streaked below. The song is *dick, dick, dickcissel.* Dickcissels are inhabitants of grasslands, prairies, old fields, and suburbs during their visits to Florida. Migrants are seen primarily during April along the west coast. Foods are mostly seeds and grains.

Subfamily Emberizinae: Emberizines

Rufous-sided Towhee *(Pipilo erythrophthalmus)*   p. 198

Other names: Red-eyed Towhee, White-eyed Towhee, Alabama Towhee, Joree, Ground Robin, Chewink, Bullfinch

The Rufous-sided Towhee is a widespread resident in a variety of woodlands and wooded suburbs in Florida. The male is black above, white below, with orange-red flanks, and white wing and tail spots. Females have brown plumage in place of the males' black. Juveniles are brownish-gray with streaking above and below. Towhees in Florida exhibit white eyes in most of peninsular Florida and red eyes in the western panhandle. Wintering Towhees from northern areas have red eyes. Intergradations between shades of red and white also occur. The song is a ventriloqual *drink-your teeee*, and the call an ascending *tuwee*. Towhees nest in dense shrubbery or palmettos in pine flatwoods, deciduous hardwoods, sand pine scrub, and other forested uplands. The cupped nest is made of leaves, twigs, bark, and other plant fibers. Each of as many as 3 clutches usually contain 3 eggs that are pink-white with brown markings. The breeding season extends from April through August. This extremely active and inquisitive bird often gives the impression of a larger animal as it noisily scratches through dry leaves and palmetto fronds in search of a meal. It moves both feet together when it scratches. Foods include ground dwelling beetles, grubs, ants, earthworms, and a variety of seeds and berries.

Bachman's Sparrow *(Aimophila aestivalis)*   p. 200

Other names: Pine-woods Sparrow

As its other name indicates, the Bachman's Sparrow is a resident of dry pine-dominated woodlands. Brown upperparts are highlighted with gray; underparts are unstreaked with white belly and gray breast. The crown is dark brown with gray streaks, and gray cheeks are bordered with brown. The musical song is a long, high whistle followed by an extended trill, its ending reminiscent of the trill of the Rufous-sided Towhee. Nests are grassy domes placed on or near the ground in a palmetto clump or dense shrub. Eggs, numbering 3 or 4, are white and laid from early April through July. The Bachman's Sparrow is a permanent resident throughout Florida north of Lake Okeechobee in scattered locations usually dominated by longleaf pine and saw palmetto. A few birds winter in extreme south Florida. Foods include seeds and a variety of insects and other invertebrates.

Chipping Sparrow *(Spizella passerina)*   p. 200

This abundant winter resident is also an infrequent nester in panhandle Florida. Upperparts are brown and underparts are gray. The head is gray with black eye line, white eyebrow, and rufous cap. Winter birds have less distinct head plumage. Immatures are streaked below. The song is a single-pitched trill, like a sewing machine. Nests are placed low in small trees or shrubs. Eggs are greenish-blue with brown-red markings, and laid from early April through June. Chipping Sparrows are much more likely to be seen as wintering residents from mid-October through mid-May. Small flocks are common in weedy fields, woodland edges, and suburban lawns and gardens. Foods include caterpillars, beetles, ants, grains, and weed seeds.

Field Sparrow *(Spizella pusilla)* p. 202

Other names: Grass Sparrow

The Field Sparrow is primarily a winter visitor but also nests in the panhandle and north Florida. Upperparts are brown and gray with white wing bars. Underparts are buff-gray, and the head is gray with light brown face highlights and reddish-brown crown. The immature bird is browner overall with a streaked breast. The song is a series of slow whistles increasing to a trill. Nests are made of grasses or other fibers and placed in a tall shrub, bush, or on the ground. Three or 4 eggs, laid from early April through June, are bluish-green with brown spots. Most birds in Florida are northern visitors that occur from early November through early April. Field Sparrows use pastures, old fields, woodland edges, and other open areas where they feed upon weed seeds and insects. In winter they often may be seen in the company of Chipping Sparrows.

Vesper Sparrow *(Pooecetes gramineus)* p. 200

This large sparrow is streaked brown and buff above, and white below with streaking on breast and sides. White outer tail feathers are conspicuous when in flight and distinguish it from the similar Savannah Sparrow. Vesper Sparrows remain close to the ground in dry grasslands, woodland edges, and other open areas. Winter visitors are found in Florida from early October through early April. Foods in winter are primarily seeds and waste grains.

Savannah Sparrow *(Passerculus sandwichensis)* p. 198

This winter resident is a common inhabitant of grasslands, sand dunes, old fields, and other dry, open areas. The breast is heavily streaked and the back varies from light to medium brown with dark streaking. A light yellowish eyebrow is visible at close range. When disturbed, Savannah Sparrows often fly a short distance then run. The call note is a staccato *chip*. Migrants arrive in Florida in late September and may remain through early May. The Savannah Sparrow is primarily a weed seed eater.

Grasshopper Sparrow *(Ammodramus savannarum)* p. 198

This highly variable, widespread sparrow is represented in Florida by an isolated endangered subspecies. The Florida resident is darker than other forms with a white crown stripe, orange lores, buff breast, white belly and thinly streaked flanks. The juvenile is less colorful with streaking on the breast. The song consists of 2 chips followed by a grasshopperlike buzz. Grasshopper sparrows are not easily viewed and if flushed, fly a short distance, then run. The breeding season extends from April through June when 3 or 4 white, brown-speckled eggs are laid. Nests are constructed of fine grass and placed on or near the ground. Preferred habitat is treeless and poorly drained. Typical plants include saw palmetto, cordgrass, and scattered shrubs. Grasshopper Sparrows apparently were abundant in south-central Florida, but now have a patchy distribution. The conversion of their nesting habitat to cattle rangeland has caused this species to decline. Northern birds overwinter in Florida and may be seen throughout the state from mid-October through early May. Foods shift from insects during summer to seeds during winter.

Henslow's Sparrow *(Ammodramus henslowii)* p. 198

The Henslow's Sparrow is an extremely secretive bird, rarely assuming an exposed perch. The greenish, flat-topped head has a yellowish central stripe with black borders. The brown upperparts are streaked with white and black. Underparts are white with buff breast streaked with brown. Henslow's Sparrows prefer open grasslands with scattered shrubs or small trees. The wet savannahs of Apalachicola National Forest are a typical wintering ground. They can be expected in north and central Florida from early November through mid-April. Foods include, seeds, insects, and other small invertebrates.

LeConte's Sparrow *(Ammodramus leconteii)* L 5″

Jan	Feb	Mar	Apr	May	June	July	Aug	Sep	Oct	Nov	Dec

This small sparrow has a white crown stripe bordered by black, with a pale orange eyebrow, gray ear patch, buff breast and sides with dark streaks. A scaly-appearing back with faintly streaked nape separate it from the similar Sharp-tailed Sparrow. This rarely seen wintering species prefers to run rather than fly in its preferred habitat of moist, grassy fields. LeConte's Sparrows may be found in north and central Florida between November and early May. Weed seeds and insects are eaten.

Sharp-tailed Sparrow *(Ammodramus caudacutus)* p. 198

Other names: Nelson's Sparrow

This is a relatively common, but secretive sparrow that winters in salt marshes along both coasts of Florida. Upperparts are reddish brown with white streaking, the belly is white, and sides and breast are buff with faint brown streaking. The tail is short and pointed. An orange triangle surrounds a gray cheek patch in birds from the northeast. In all forms, a gray crown is bordered by broad, dark brown stripes. Sharp-tailed Sparrows can be seen from mid-October through May in Florida. Foods consist of marsh grass seeds, spiders, grasshoppers, and other insects.

Seaside Sparrow *(Ammodramus maritimus)* p. 200

Other names: Dusky Seaside Sparrow, Cape Sable Seaside Sparrow, Scott's Seaside Sparrow, Northern Seaside Sparrow, Wakulla Seaside Sparrow, Louisiana Seaside Sparrow, McGillavray's Seaside Sparrow

The Seaside Sparrow is an inhabitant of coastal saltwater marshes from Massachusetts to Texas. Variability in plumages has led to the description of nine subspecies, seven of which occur in Florida (see other names above). Seaside Sparrows on the Atlantic coast are grayish-olive above, with a light grayish breast marked with faint streaking. On Gulf coast marshes adults are darker with brown backs and more buff-colored breasts. The Cape Sable Seaside Sparrow appears more greenish gray than the other subspecies. The most distinctive race of Seasides in Florida—the black and white streaked

Dusky Seaside Sparrow from Merritt Island and the St. Johns valley in Brevard County—became extinct in 1987. All races have a dark whisker stripe on a white throat and yellow lores. The tail is short and pointed and the bill is relatively long and conical. Because Seasides molt only once annually in late summer or early fall, feathers are heavily worn by May and June, at which time the adult appears dull brown with dark gray breast. The song is a buzzy *spitsch-sheer* which resembles the song of a distant Red-winged Blackbird. Nests are constructed of marsh grass and often have a roof or canopy woven over the top. Three or 4 white, brown-spotted eggs are laid from March through August. Florida nesters are year-round residents while northern migrants overwinter from November through March. Foods primarily are snails, spiders, grasshoppers, small crabs, beetles, and seeds.

Fox Sparrow *(Passerella iliaca)* L 7"

Jan	Feb	Mar	Apr	May	June	July	Aug	Sep	Oct	Nov	Dec

This is a species of the far north that occasionally winters in north Florida. It derives its name from its reddish plumage. The Fox Sparrow has a gray head streaked with brown, reddish rump and tail, heavily streaked underparts, and a large breast spot. It inhabits dense undergrowth of mixed hardwood-pine forests, usually between November and February. Seeds and insects are eaten.

Song Sparrow *(Melospiza melodia)* p. 202

This familiar northern songster is a common winter resident in Florida. Brown upperparts are contrasted by white undersides. The heavily streaked flanks and breast usually surround a large, central spot. The white throat is bordered by dark stripes and the head is streaked brown with a lighter central stripe. The tail is long and rounded and pumped in flight. In Florida only its call note, a staccato *chip* can be heard. Song Sparrows are regular winter visitors except in the southern third of the state. They may be seen in grasslands, woodland edges, and old fields from early October through April. Foods include insects and a variety of weed seeds.

Lincoln's Sparrow *(Melospiza lincolnii)* L 5½"

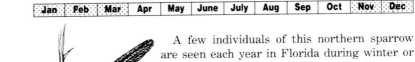

Jan	Feb	Mar	Apr	May	June	July	Aug	Sep	Oct	Nov	Dec

A few individuals of this northern sparrow are seen each year in Florida during winter or while migrating. The adult has a buff breast band with fine brown streaks, white belly, gray-brown upperparts, gray central crown stripe bordered in reddish brown, and a wide gray eyebrow. It usually is seen along brushy ditches, canal banks, and thickets. The diet consists of seeds and insects.

Swamp Sparrow (*Melospiza georgiana*)   **p. 202**

The Swamp Sparrow is a common winter resident in Florida using brushy fields, lake borders, swamp edges, and other wet areas. Brown upperparts are highlighted with reddish wing patches, white throat, gray cheeks, and gray crown. Underparts are grayish with brown streaking on breast and flanks. The call is a metallic *chip*. Swamp Sparrows can be seen in Florida from early October–April. Weed seeds and insects make up most of its diet.

White-throated Sparrow (*Zonotrichia albicollis*)   **p. 202**

Unstreaked, grayish underparts, bright white throat patch and head stripes distinguish this winter visitor. The immature has a buff throat patch and head stripe. The call is a thin *zeep*. Occasionally its song, *old-sam-peabody, peabody, peabody*, is heard on warm winter days. White-throated Sparrows are common in north and central Florida from late October through April. They can be found in a variety of habitats from hardwood forest and swamp edges to old fields and suburban backyards. Foods include seeds, small fruits, and insects.

White-crowned Sparrow (*Zonotrichia leucophrys*)   **p. 202**

Black and white striped crown, gray, unstreaked underparts and grayish-brown upperparts distinguish this unpredictable winter visitor. Immatures are browner and duller overall, without the white striped crown. White-crowned Sparrows use woodland edges, brushy fields, and other open areas. Although uncommon, this large sparrow may be looked for from early October through early May. Foods are mostly seeds but include a variety of insects when available.

Dark-eyed Junco (*Junco hyemalis*)   **p. 200**

Other names: Slate-colored Junco, Blue Snowbird, White-tailed Sparrow

The Dark-eyed Junco winters in unpredictable numbers in Florida. Its unsparrowlike plumage is slate-gray with white belly and white outer tail feathers. The bill is flesh-colored. Wintering flocks may be seen, primarily in north Florida, from late October through April. Juncos occasionally may use feeding stations but are more often seen in open woodlands, grain fields, dry grasslands, and brushy vegetation. Dark-eyed Juncos forage on the ground in search of exposed seeds and insects.

Lapland Longspur (*Calcarius lapponicus*) L 6"

Jan	Feb	Mar	Apr	May	June	July	Aug	Sep	Oct	Nov	Dec

A rare winter visitor to Florida, this long-spur has a broad buff eye brow, a buff ear patch with black border, reddish-brown nape and neck, white belly, and streaked flanks. The male has black barring on the chest while the female exhibits a buff chest. Lapland Longspurs have been seen in Florida on sand dunes, at airports, in pastures, and along grassy road shoulders.

Snow Bunting *(Plectrophenax nivalis)* L 6½"

Jan	Feb	Mar	Apr	May	June	July	Aug	Sep	Oct	Nov	Dec

During some winters, this Arctic species spends a few days or weeks in northeast Florida in the grassy dune area of Ward's Bank between the St. Johns River and Fort George River Inlets. Its winter plumage is mostly white with a buff or rusty cap, black and white wings, and a black and white streaked tail. Its occurence in Florida is unpredictable.

Subfamily Icterinae: Blackbirds and Orioles

Bobolink *(Dolichonyx oryzivorus)*   p. 188
Other names: Ricebird

During spring the male Bobolink is the only North American songbird that is black below and light above. Fall males and juveniles resemble females and are buff-colored with dark eye line and head streaks, darker wings and tail, and streaking on flanks. During migration, Bobolinks travel high overhead in large flocks emitting a characteristic *clink* call. They are found in Florida from mid-April through late May and again from late August through October. Preferred habitats include agricultural lands, pastures, and green grasslands. During fall principal foods include grains and seeds. Insects also are taken when available.

Red-winged Blackbird *(Agelaius phoeniceus)*   p. 190
Other names: Florida Red-wing, Redwing

This is one of North America's most widespread and abundant birds. In Florida it is found throughout the state from salt and freshwater marshes to agricultural lands. Males are a glossy black with bright red wing patches or epaulets bordered in golden yellow. Females and immatures are sparrowlike, brown above, and streaked below. Females are somewhat smaller than males. The male's song is a melodious *konk-ler-eee*, which may vary in different parts of the state. Nests are woven-grass structures attached to shrubs or tall annuals. Eggs, numbering 3 or 4, are bluish with black and purple markings and laid from April to June. During fall and winter, migrant and resident Redwings congregate in huge numbers with other blackbirds (starlings, cowbirds, grackles). Flocks with thousands of individuals can be seen feeding in agricultural fields and grasslands or descending upon productive marshes. Food consists of seeds such as rice, corn, oats, and wild grasses as well as grasshoppers, dragonflies, and other insects.

Eastern Meadowlark *(Sturnella magna)*   p. 190
Other names: Field Lark, Southern Meadowlark

Bright yellow underparts accented by a broad, black bib are the most obvious field marks of the resident Eastern Meadowlark. The head is marked in alternating brown and buff streaks, the back appears mottled brown, and the flanks are streaked. When flying, the Meadowlark displays conspicuous white borders on the tail. The song consists of 2 descending, ventriloqual phrases. Meadowlarks are grassland birds and construct a woven grass nest on the ground. Eggs are white with brownish spots and number from 3 to 5. Egg laying occurs as early as February and as late as June. Insects such as crickets, grasshoppers, beetles, and caterpillars form the bulk of its diet. Small seeds and grains also are eaten.

Yellow-headed Blackbird *(Xanthocephalus xanthocephalus)* L 9″

Jan	Feb	Mar	Apr	May	June	July	Aug	Sep	Oct	Nov	Dec

This western species usually appears somewhere in Florida each winter, often a single immature, rarely an adult male, in a flock of Red-winged Blackbirds at a cattle feed lot, a horse barn, or pasture. Adult males are black with a bright yellow head, neck, and upper breast, and have white wing patches that show in flight. Females are smaller with yellow throat and no white in the wings. Immature males are brownish with a pale yellow head. Foods consist of grains, seeds, and insects.

Rusty Blackbird *(Euphagus carolinus)* L 9″

Jan	Feb	Mar	Apr	May	June	July	Aug	Sep	Oct	Nov	Dec

The Rusty Blackbird occasionally is seen in flocks of mixed blackbird species during winter in central and north Florida. The feathers of wintering birds are edged with rust color. Females exhibit buff undersides. By spring the rusty tips wear away leaving a glossy green plumage in the male and a grayish plumage in the female. A bright yellow eye is present in all plumages. These fruit and insect eaters can be seen in a varity of open and woodland settings from October through April.

Brewer's Blackbird *(Euphagus cyanocephalus)* L 9″

Jan	Feb	Mar	Apr	May	June	July	Aug	Sep	Oct	Nov	Dec

Brewer's Blackbirds can occasionally be seen in large flocks or with Red-winged Blackbirds in pastures, cropland, golf courses, or parks from November through April. Males have glossy, purple-green plumage and yellow eyes, while females are gray-brown with dark eyes. A variety of seeds and insects are eaten.

Boat-tailed Grackle *(Quiscalus major)*   p. 190
Other names: Jackdaw

This large grackle appears still larger with its long, deep-keeled tail. Males are black with a purplish iridescence. Females are smaller and brown with dark wings and a shorter, dark tail. The population in peninsular Florida south of Gainesville has brown eyes unlike the yellow-eyed birds of the northeast coast. The male's song consists of a complicated array of noisy twitters, clucks, and rattles. Boat-tailed Grackles are common year-round residents except in the extreme northern panhandle and the Keys. They nest in loose colonies in freshwater and saltwater marshes as well as along lake and stream borders and in towns. Grasses are used to construct a bulky nest placed in trees and other vegetation. Eggs are white with purplish mottling and number 3 to 4. The nesting season extends from February through July; however, Boattails occasionally will nest again in October through December. Foods include beetles, crayfish, crabs, corn, and other grains and insects.

Common Grackle *(Quiscalus quiscula)*   p. 190
Other names: Jackdaw, Florida Grackle, Crow Blackbird

This blackbird is smaller and shorter-tailed than the similar Boat-tailed Grackle. The male is black with a purplish head and bronze iridescence elsewhere. Females appear duller, and immatures are brownish. The eyes have light-colored irises. This permanent resident is distributed throughout Florida. Nesting occurs in a variety of habitats from open woodlands to citrus groves, prairies, and buildings. The bulky, mud-lined nests are placed in tree cavities, forked branches, shrubs, or man-made structures. Eggs number 3 to 6, are greenish white with splotches of black, gray, and brown, and are laid from mid-March through May. During winter common Grackles may form large flocks with other blackbirds. The diet is highly variable and includes many insects, mollusks, crustaceans, berries, and wild and cultivated grains.

Shiny Cowbird *(Molothrus bonariensis)* L 7"
Other names: Glossy Cowbird

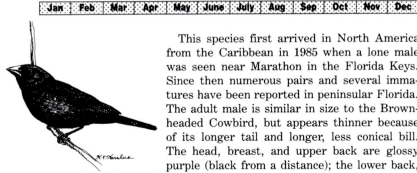

Jan	Feb	Mar	Apr	May	June	July	Aug	Sep	Oct	Nov	Dec

This species first arrived in North America from the Caribbean in 1985 when a lone male was seen near Marathon in the Florida Keys. Since then numerous pairs and several immatures have been reported in peninsular Florida. The adult male is similar in size to the Brown-headed Cowbird, but appears thinner because of its longer tail and longer, less conical bill. The head, breast, and upper back are glossy purple (black from a distance); the lower back, wings, and tail a duller black. The female and immatures are almost indistinguishable from female and immature Brown-headed Cowbirds, except for the longer, less conical bill. Some female Shiny Cowbirds exhibit a faint but distinct eye stripe.

Bronzed Cowbird *(Molothrus aeneus)* L 8½"
Other names: Red-eyed Cowbird

Jan	Feb	Mar	Apr	May	June	July	Aug	Sep	Oct	Nov	Dec

The frequency of recurrence of this species in Florida has been increasing and in winter the Bronzed Cowbird may show up anywhere in the state. The male is black with a bronze gloss on the head and back, blue-black wings and tail, and a bright red eye. The female is a dull black, and immatures are brown with less distinctive red eyes. Bronzed Cowbirds are inhabitants of open country in their native southwestern U.S. range. Foods consist of seeds and insects.

Brown-headed Cowbird *(Molothrus ater)*   p. 190

The Brown-headed Cowbird is a small blackbird with brown head and greenish-black body. Females are gray overall with faint streaks below. The male's song is a series of thin, wavering squeaks. Brown-headed Cowbirds are most often seen in Florida as a fall and winter visitor; however, breeding birds have been found south to St. Lucie County on the east coast and Lee County on the west coast. The Cowbird has earned a notorious reputation because of its parasitic nesting habits. Not building its own nest, the female lays 4 to 5 white, brown-spotted eggs each in a different bird's nest. The victimized species include a variety of warblers, vireos, tanagers, buntings, orioles, and sparrows. Because the egg and young cowbird is larger than its nest mates, it is often the only nest survivor. The diet is mostly grains and seeds but also includes grasshoppers and other insects. Brown-headed Cowbirds often congregate with other fall-flocking blackbirds.

Orchard Oriole *(Icterus spurius)*   p. 192

The Orchard Oriole is a characteristic summer resident in open deciduous woodlands and suburbs in north Florida. The adult male's black head, breast, tail, back, and wings contrast with rusty red undersides, flanks, and rump. Females are greenish-yellow with grayish wings and buff wing bars. First-year males resemble females but sport a black bib. The song is a musical warble ending with a down-slurred note. The Orchard Oriole has been extending its breeding range southward in Florida and now breeds in Orlando. Nests are usually high off the ground and may be concealed in a clump of Spanish Moss. They are constructed of fine grasses that contain 3 to 5 light blue eggs streaked with brown and purple. Laying may occur from early April through June. Migrants pass through Florida from mid-March through early May and in fall from late August through October. The diet is composed mostly of insects.

Spot-breasted Oriole *(Icterus pectoralis)*   p. 192

South Florida's only regularly breeding oriole is the exotic Spot-breasted. Introduced in the 1950s, this Central American native makes its home in heavily landscaped yards in Dade, Broward, and Palm Beach counties. The song is a series of loud, bubbling, and musical whistles. The male is orange with black tail and back, and wings with white patches. The black bib separates into scattered spots above the breast. Females are similar but somewhat duller. Spot-breasted Orioles build pendulous nests in their native tropical haunts, but in Florida, nests are cup-shaped structures placed in a tree or shrub. Eggs, numbering 3 to 5 are pale blue with brown spots and can be found from May through September. This colorful exotic is an inhabitant of Florida's urbanized southeast coast and does not seem to have displaced any native species. Individuals have been seen as far north as Brevard County. Foods include a variety of tropical fruits and insects.

Northern Oriole *(Icterus galbula)* p. 192
Other names: Baltimore Oriole, Bullock's Oriole
The distinctively marked male Northern Oriole has a black hood, tail, and wings with contrasting orange undersides, rump, and outer tail feathers. The female is dull orange to yellow with dark tail, back, head, and wings. Both sexes show some white in the wings. Spring migrants can be seen in Florida from early April through mid-May. Fall birds are not commonly seen here and wintering birds occur at scattered locations throughout the state. Each winter several orioles from the western population (Bullock's) also winter in Florida. One nesting record exists for a pair in Key West in the 1970s. Foods consist of insects, seeds, and small fruits. It occasionally will appear at feeding stations if orange sections are offered.

Family Fringillidae: Finches

Purple Finch *(Carpodacus purpureus)* p. 196
The Purple Finch has become an increasingly common winter visitor to north Florida, and in some cold winters can be seen in south Florida. Males are rose red, especially on the head, rump, and breast. The back is streaked with brown and the tail is distinctly notched. The female is brown above with heavy streaking on a white breast, and has a distinctive white eyebrow and brown ear patch. The diet primarily consists of seeds found in a variety of woodland habitats. These finches can be frequent visitors at feeding stations.

House Finch *(Carpodacus mexicanus)* p. 196
This western species was introduced on Long Island, New York, in the early 1940s when 100 birds were released by a department store. It now breeds west into the Great Lake states and south to Georgia. Wintering flocks recently have been found in Florida where it also may become an established breeder. House finches are similar to Purple Finches; however, the male has a brown cap with a red forehead, throat, and breast along with brown-streaked underparts. The female is brown streaked and lacks the ear patch and white eyebrow characteristic of the female Purple Finch. In both sexes the tip of the tail is square, not notched, as in the Purple Finch. The song is a very musical series of 3-note phrases that occasionally can be heard in winter. In some parts of the east the House Finch has become the most frequent visitor at feeders. As its name implies, it adapts well to urban and

suburban settings, wherever trees and shrubs abound. Nests, constructed of grass and small twigs, are built in conifers. In the absence of evergreens House Finches will nest on ledges of porches, sheds, barns, and other structures. Food consists primarily of seeds.

Pine Siskin *(Carduelis pinus)*   **p. 196**

The Pine Siskin's sharp, pointed bill is uncharacteristic for a finch. The boldly streaked plumage is grayish-brown above and white or buff below. The dark wings and tail are highlighted with bright yellow bands. Pine Siskins are unpredictable winter visitors in Florida. Severe northern weather seems to account for occasionally high numbers in the state. Most birds remain in north Florida during their stay, although a few have been recorded in south Florida as well. It feeds chiefly on pine and sweetgum seeds, and in south Florida, Australian pine seeds.

American Goldfinch *(Carduelis tristis)*   **p. 196**

Other names: Wild Canary, Thistle Bird, Eastern Goldfinch

This colorful bird appears in its drab winter plumage during its stay in Florida. The male has yellow cheeks and throat, brown back, black wings and tail, and white wing bars. Females are duller overall. Its call, *chick-chick-a-ree*, is often given in flight. When the bird is perched, its call is a question: *chick-a-ree?* Flocks of goldfinches can be seen from early November through April in most parts of Florida. It is a bird of open woodlands, brushy areas, and old fields, and may be an abundant visitor at feeding stations. Foods include seeds of sunflowers, pines, buttonbush, thistle, and other weeds. A few insects also are taken.

Evening Grosbeak *(Coccothraustes vespertinus)*   **p. 194**

This large, chunky finch is an unpredictable visitor but can be expected during some cold winters and has occurred south to Gainesville. The male is yellow with black wings and tail, brown head with yellow eyebrow, and white inner wing patch. The female is buff-colored with an additional white wing patch. Evening Grosbeaks will visit backyard feeding stations as well as pine and hardwood forests. Seeds and fruits form the bulk of its diet.

Family Passeridae: Old World Sparrows

House Sparrow *(Passer domesticus)*   **p. 188**

Other names: English Sparrow, Weaver Finch

The House Sparrow was released at hundreds of locations in eastern North America during the late 1800s. This European native now is widespread in the Western Hemisphere, especially in urban settings. A study of residential birds in St. Petersburg in the 1960s revealed that House Sparrows comprised 45% of the avian population. The male has a black bib, gray cap, white cheeks, dirty white belly, brown and black streaked back and wings with a single white wing bar. Females and immatures are dingy brown with a faint eye stripe. In Florida nests may be found at any time, although most breeding occurs from March to September. Nests are bulky masses of dry grass, pine straw, feathers, plastic, paper, and string, and are built in bird houses, crevices in buildings, signs, light fixtures, rain gutters, and in leafy tree branches. The 3 to 5 whitish eggs are heavily speckled with brown and black. Several broods may be raised each year. Young remain in the nest until almost fully grown, enhancing their survivorship. It feeds primarily on seeds and grains but also is fond of bread crumbs and other food discarded by people. During nesting young birds are fed insects.

BIRDING AND BIRD STUDY

Birding

In historic times the term birding meant bird hunting or shooting, but today, it means the act of watching birds. Some people prefer the term bird watching to birding and bird watcher to birder, and occasionally, if you introduce yourself to a nonbirding person as a birder, you have to explain the term. Were you to say "I am a bird watcher," no further explanation would be necessary. Take your choice, both terms are acceptable.

Birding has become a major outdoor activity, and its growth has stimulated much economic activity in sales of binoculars, spotting scopes, bird guides, bird seed, feeders, and associated items, as well as in the nature-tour business. One can engage in this "sport" at any desired level, ranging from simply observing birds frequenting a backyard feeder to spending most of your waking hours visiting birding spots and chasing rarities throughout your state or region, or taking expert-guided tours to various parts of the world.

Basic Equipment

Basic equipment for birding is a good pair of binoculars and a field guide covering the birds of the region. As your interest and involvement develop, you will want to acquire a good spotting scope for observing some birds—ducks, shorebirds, raptors, for example—from a distance.

Many brands and models of binoculars are available, ranging from useless dime-store glasses costing under $50, to good binoculars at moderate prices costing $75-$300, to top-of-the-line glasses especially designed for birding costing from $400 to $1000 or more. Before purchasing a pair of binoculars you should know a few basic facts about them. Power of magnification, the first number listed in a description, indicated by 7x, or 8x, or 10x, for example, means that the object being viewed is enlarged by a factor of 7, 8, or 10, respectively. Magnification above 10 requires such large glasses and such steady hands that a tripod may be required, thus making them useless for most bird watching.

The second number, 35 up to 50 (7x35, 7x50, for example) refers to the diameter (in millimeters) of the opening, and thus to the light-gathering ability of the lenses. The higher the number, the more light is admitted, and, thus, the better one can see. Thus 7x35 (say "7 by 35") binoculars magnify seven times and the diameter of the opening is 35mm. However, wider openings mean larger and heavier binoculars. Thus, in addition to the price, you need to consider the size and weight with which you are most comfortable. Because of the greater light-gathering ability, 7x50 binoculars are probably the best type; however, the size and weight are undesirable for most folks. A good pair of 7x35 binoculars will suffice for most people, for either casual or more intensive birding. Price should range from $75 to $200 or thereabouts. Occasionally, dealers may have used, higher-priced binoculars available at considerably reduced prices.

The best source of information for suggestions and advice about binoculars is from experienced birders. Your local Audubon chapter probably has several active birders among its membership who would be willing to assist. Several periodicals catering to birders occasionally publish articles comparing the advantages and disadvantages of the most popular brands and models. A list of these publications appears at the end of this section.

Where to Observe Birds

Birds occur in almost every habitat on earth, in cities as well as in fields and forests, so a good beginning point to observe birds is in your own backyard and neighborhood. Every Florida town is home to an array of species—Northern Mockingbird, Northern Cardinal, Blue Jay, Mourning Dove, Red-bellied Woodpecker, Common Grackle, and the ever-present Domestic Pigeon, European Starling, and House Sparrow, just to mention a few of the more common species. A bird feeder and a bird bath will attract many species and allow close-up viewing. (See Chapter 5 on attracting birds to your yard.)

Ponds and lakes, especially if the shoreline vegetation has not been totally obliterated by aggressive landowners or park departments, provide habitat for gallinules, ducks, waders, and other species. In most communities, city or county parks and old cemeteries provide good bird watching habitat. Regionally, state and national parks and national wildlife refuges are easily accessible. Inlets and bays attract large numbers and varieties of birds.

One of the best ways to learn bird identification is to accompany experienced birders in the field. The Florida Audubon Society has chapters located throughout the state. Each chapter schedules monthly, sometimes more frequent, field trips to nearby birding areas, holds monthly meetings, and usually publishes a monthly newsletter. Newcomers are always welcomed. The address of the chapter nearest to your town may be obtained from your local Chamber of Commerce, or by contacting the Florida Audubon Society in Maitland, or the National Audubon Society's Southeastern Regional office in Tallahassee.

Many county and state parks conduct periodic guided tours to observe their birds and other wildlife. Information about these can be obtained from county park departments, and a list of state parks, preserves, reserves, and recreational areas can be obtained from the Florida Department of Natural Resources in Tallahassee. Chapters of the Sierra Club and the Nature Conservancy also sponsor field trips to various parts of the state (see Chapter 7 for addresses of these organizations).

For more information on birding sites in Florida refer to Chapter 4.

Birding References

The growing sport of bird watching in North America has resulted in a number of excellent books and periodicals devoted to the subject. We highly recommend each of the titles listed below.

Books

A.B.A. Checklist: Birds of Continental United States and Canada. American Birding Association, P.O. Box 6599, Colorado Springs, CO 80934.

The Birder's Handbook: A Field Guide to the Natural History of North American Birds by Paul R. Ehrlich, David S. Dobkin, and Darryl Wheye. Simon & Schuster, Inc., New York. 1988.

Birds of South Florida: An Interpretive Guide by Connie Toops and Willard E. Dilley. River Road Press, Conway, AR. 1986.

Checklist of Florida's Birds by Henry M. Stevenson. Nongame Wildlife Program, Florida Game & Fresh Water Fish Commission. (Available free from FG&FWFC, 620 S. Meridian St., Tallahassee, FL 32399-1600.)

Check-list of North American Birds, 6th Ed. American Ornithologists' Union. Allen Press, Lawrence, KS. 1983.

The Complete Birder: A Guide to Better Birding by Jack Conner. Houghton Mifflin Co., Boston. 1988.

The Country Journal Book of Birding and Bird Attraction by Alan Pistorius. W. W. Norton Co., Inc., New York. 1981.

A Field Guide to the Nests, Eggs, and Nestlings of North American Birds by Colin Harrison. Collins, NY. 1978.

First Guide to Birds by Roger Tory Peterson. Houghton Mifflin Co., Boston. 1986.

Florida Bird Life by Alexander Sprunt, Jr. Coward-McCann, Inc. New York. 1954 (Out of print, but occasionally available from some dealers.)

The Habitat Guide to Birding by Thomas P. McElroy, Jr. Alfred A. Knopf, New York. 1974.

How to Know the Birds by Roger Tory Peterson. Signet Key Books, The New American Library of World Literature, New York. 1949.

The Illustrated Bird Watcher's Dictionary by Donald S. Heintzelman. Winchester Press, Tulsa, OK. 1980.

An Introduction to Bird Life for Bird Watchers by Aretas A. Saunders. Dover Publs., Inc., New York. 1964.

SCANS Key to Birdwatching by Virginia C. Holmgren. Timber Press, Portland, OR. 1983.

Vertebrates of Florida: Identification and Distribution by Henry M. Stevenson. University Presses of Florida, Gainesville. 1976.

Watching Birds: An Introduction to Ornithology by Roger F. Pasquier. Houghton Mifflin Co., Boston, 1977.

General Periodicals for Birders

American Birds. National Audubon Society, 950 Third Ave., New York, NY 10022.

Birding. American Birding Association, P.O. Box 6599, Colorado Springs, CO 80934.

Bird Watcher's Digest. Box 110, Marietta, OH 45750.

Birder's World. P.O. Box 1347, Elmhurst, IL 60126-8347.
Wildbird. P.O. Box 483, Mt. Morris, IL 61054-8044.
The Living Bird. Cornell Laboratory of Ornithology, 159 Sapsucker Woods Road, Ithaca, NY 14850.
Nature Society News. Griggsville, IL 62340.

Ornithology—The Study of Birds

Because birds are so widespread and so visible—unlike most other vertebrates—people have observed and studied them for centuries. The earliest students of birds probably were hunters whose main interest in learning their habits was to obtain them or their eggs for food, and their feathers for ornamentation and clothing. Much of the early information on the natural history of birds was recorded by egg collectors, or oologists, people who collected eggs as a hobby (now illegal) in the 1800s and early years of this century.

Biologists study birds as subjects of research in anatomy, physiology, endocrinology, evolution, behavior, and ecology. The American Ornithologists' Union, organized in 1883, is the professional organization for ornithologists in North America, and publishes *The Auk*, a quarterly journal. Young people considering a possible career in the field of ornithology may write to the A.O.U., U.S. Museum of Natural History, Smithsonian Institution, Washington, DC 20560, for a brochure on this subject.

Several institutions of higher education in Florida offer educational programs in ornithology leading toward undergraduate and advanced degrees in biology, wildlife ecology, and zoology. These include the University of Florida in Gainesville, Florida State University in Tallahassee, Florida Atlantic University in Boca Raton, University of Central Florida in Orlando, University of South Florida in Tampa, the University of Miami in Coral Gables, and the Florida Institute of Technology in Melbourne. Most of these universities also maintain research collections of bird skins, skeletons, and eggs.

Three institutions, one public and two private, that maintain study collections and foster research are the Florida Museum of Natural History (FMNH) in Gainesville, Archbold Biological Station near Lake Placid, and Tall Timbers Research Station near Tallahassee. The FMNH also houses one of the top collections in North America of bird sounds, both songs and calls.

The abundance and visibility of birds has enabled a large number of amateurs to make important contributions to the science of ornithology. National organizations that foster amateur participation in the field are the Wilson Ornithological Society, which publishes the quarterly *Wilson Bulletin;* the Cooper Ornithological Society, which publishes the quarterly *Condor;* and the Association of Field Ornithologists, which publishes the *Journal of Field Ornithology*. The majority of the membership of the three major bird banding organizations in North America (Eastern, Inland, and Western Bird Banding Associations) is comprised of amateurs. These associations jointly publish the *North American Bird Bander*.

High interest in bird watching and bird study has led to the organization of state ornithological societies. In 1972, Florida Audubon Society sponsored the founding of the Florida Ornithological Society (F.O.S.) to promote the study and enjoyment of birds by professional and amateur ornithologists and birders in Florida. The F.O.S. publishes a quarterly journal, the *Florida*

Field Naturalist, a quarterly newsletter, and a special publication series. It holds semiannual meetings in the spring and fall at various localities in the state, and, through its Allan D. and Helen G. Cruickshank Research Fund annually supports one or more basic bird research projects. The F.O.S. sponsors a Rare Bird Alert, a telephone circuit to inform participants about the appearance of rare species in Florida. The organizations's permanent address is Florida Ornithological Society, Florida Museum of Natural History, University of Florida, Gainesville, FL 32611.

Bird Banding

Sometimes, in the study of birds, it is desirable or necessary to be able to identify each individual in the population. This can be done by placing a numbered band on one leg, so that it can be observed and recorded the next time it is captured, or, with the use of additional colored bands one may be able to identify marked individuals without needing to physically recapture them. This study technique is called bird banding (bird ringing in Europe) and in North America the banding program is administered by the U.S. Fish & Wildlife Service (USF&WS). The Service issues permits and bands to qualified persons and research facilities and maintains the records of *wild* birds banded annually. We have emphasized the word "wild" because the USF&WS does not maintain records of banded pet-store birds or pigeons. The USF&WS also, however, does not maintain records of state game department bandings of nonmigratory game birds even though they are indeed wild birds. In Florida such nonmigratory game birds are the Bobwhite Quail and the Wild Turkey.

Each USF&WS band bears a number and the message (either on the same side, or, for small bands, in the inside surface) "Avise Wash DC," so that in the event a banded bird is recovered by recapture, death, or injury, the finder can send it or a report about it to the bird banding office. The word "advise" is purposely spelled "Avise" to insure that Spanish-speaking people will understand the message. Information that should accompany the band or report is the date found, location (including state, county, and nearest city), circumstances, if known, and your name and address if you desire a report on where and when the bird was banded. Finders may send the band and report to the Bird Banding Laboratory, USF&WS, Laurel, MD 20708, directly, or give the band and information to any ornithologist, bird bander, or local office of the USF&WS or Florida Game & Fresh Water Fish Commission and ask them to send it on to Washington. Do not remove a band from a live bird if it can be rehabilitated and released back to the wild.

Over the years the banding program has contributed much knowledge about the migratory habits of birds, including distances traveled, directions and routes, wintering and breeding sites (and fidelity to these) and age and longevity. The first inkling about where Chimney Swifts wintered in South America came from the observation of Indians in the high Andes wearing necklaces made of bird bands.

It may be a bit more difficult to track down banded pigeons. Two organizations of pigeon fanciers administer this program—the American Racing Pigeon Union (AU) and the International Federation of Homing Pigeon Fanciers (IF). Annually, the secretary of each local club in these two organizations is issued a series of numbered bands to be placed on a leg of each nestling being raised for racing by individual club members. Often, a pigeon is seen with additional markers—usually a colored rubber band placed on the bird just prior to being released for a race. Ideally, when the bird is released it flies straight home, enters its coop, and is a "winner." Sometimes obstacles may be encountered: a storm or adverse winds may exhaust the flyer, or a predator may cripple it. If a tired bird appears in your yard, feed it some bird seed and water for a day or two and it will probably recover and fly home. If injured it should be taken to a rehabilitation center and treated or put out of its misery. A report of your finding can be made to the national secretary of the organization that issued the band. For bands with the letters AU followed by a combination of letters and numbers write The American Racing Pigeon Union, Inc., P.O. Box 2713, South Hamilton, MA 01982. For bands with the letters IF followed by a combination of letters and numbers write International Federation of American Homing Pigeon Fanciers, Inc., 107 Jefferson St., Belmont Hills, PA 19004.

Books on the Biology of Birds

The Audubon Society Encyclopedia of North American Birds by John K. Terres. Alfred A. Knopf, New York. 1980.

Bird Migration by Chris Mead. Facts on File Publs., New York. 1983.

Birds: Their Life, Their Ways, Their World by Christopher Perrins and C.J.O. Harrison. Reader's Digest Assoc., Inc. Pleasantville, NY. 1979.

The Dictionary of American Bird Names (Rev. Ed.) by Ernest A. Choate, revised by R. A. Paynter, Jr. The Harvard Common Press, Boston. 1985.

A Dictionary of Birds edited by Bruce Campbell and Elizabeth Lack. Buteo Books, Vermillion, SD. 1985.

Fundamentals of Ornithology, 2nd Ed., by Josselyn Van Tyne and Andrew J. Berger. John Wiley & Sons, New York. 1975.

A Guide to Bird Behavior, Vol. I, by Donald W. Stokes. Little, Brown & Co., Boston. 1979.

A Guide to Bird Behavior, Vol. II, by Donald W. Stokes and Lillian Q. Stokes. Little, Brown & Co., Boston. 1983.

A Guide to Bird Behavior, Vol III, by Donald W. Stokes and Lillian Q. Stokes. Little, Brown & Co., Boston. 1989.

How Birds Work: A Guide to Bird Biology by Ron Freethy. Blandford Press, Sterling Publ. Co., New York. 1982.

An Introduction to Ornithology, 3rd Ed., by George J. Wallace and H. D. Mahan. MacMillan Co., New York. 1975.

The Life of Birds, 4th Ed., by Joel Carl Welty and Luis F. Baptista. W. B. Saunders, New York. 1988.

Ornithology: An Ecological Approach, by John Faaborg. Prentice Hall, Englewood Cliffs, NJ. 1988.

Ornithology in Laboratory and Field, 5th Ed., by Olin Sewall Pettingill, Jr. Academic Press, Orlando, FL. 1985.

Treasury of North American Birdlore edited by Paul S. Eriksson and Alan Pistorius. Paul S. Eriksson Publ., Middlebury, VT. 1987.

The Wonder of Birds edited by Robert M. Poole. National Geographic Society, Washington, D.C. 1983.

Words for Birds: A Lexicon of North American Birds with Biographical Notes by Edward S. Gruson. Quadrangle Books, New York. 1972.

Bird Finding In Florida

An excellent guide to birding sites in Florida was published by Jim Lane in 1981. This was revised and updated by Harold Holt in 1984 and most recently in 1989. We recommend it to every serious birder in Florida: "A Birder's Guide to Florida" by James A. Lane and Harold R. Holt, L & P Press, POB 21604, Denver, CO 80221. Copies are available from the Florida Audubon giftshop, 1101 Audubon Way, Maitland, FL 32751, and from L & P Press in Denver.

The use of a screech-owl call is often most helpful in calling birds to the observer. For some reason, many species respond to the call of the screech-owl when given during daylight hours. It is one way to learn what species are in the neighborhood. Another technique, especially effective during the breeding season when males are defending territories, is to play a tape of the song of the species you desire to see. Territorial males will usually respond immediately to the "intruder." Great care must be taken not to play the song so frequently that it disturbs breeding activities. In some areas, such as Everglades National Park, the use of a tape recorder to attract birds is prohibited.

During spring migration in April and May (the peak period in Florida is mid-April to mid-May) several places in Florida are worth visiting to see the transients passing through the state on their way to their northern breeding grounds. One of the best is Fort DeSoto Park, a Pinellas County park on the southern tip of the Pinellas peninsula. Also called Mullet Key, this site is famous for the variety and number of birds that occur there in migration.

Other spring "traps" for migrating birds are St. George Island State Park in the Panhandle; Ft. Pickens State Park on Santa Rosa Island on the upper Gulf coast; Cedar Key on the Gulf coast about halfway up the peninsula; and the Dry Tortugas, 67 miles west of Key West.

One of the better fall migration sites worth visiting early in October for transient vireos, warblers, tanagers, and grosbeaks, is Saddlecreek Park, a former phosphate mine, now a Polk County park near Lakeland. Another site is Cape Florida Bill Baggs State Recreation Area on Virginia Key, near Miami, where numerous raptors, including accipiters, hawks, and falcons may be seen migrating south toward the Keys in late September and early October.

In winter, excellent birding is found at Merritt Island National Wildlife Refuge in Brevard County; Loxahatchee National Wildlife Refuge in Palm Beach County; Everglades National Park in Dade and Monroe counties;

National Audubon's Corkscrew Swamp Sanctuary, near Immokalee, Collier County; Ding Darling National Wildlife Refuge on Sanibel Island in Lee County; St. Marks National Wildlife Refuge and Wakulla Springs State Park, both in Wakulla County.

Florida Specialties

Visiting birders from other states usually want to see those species that are either restricted to Florida or are easier to find here. For example, in North America, the Snail Kite, Short-tailed Hawk, Smooth-billed Ani, Mangrove Cuckoo, Black-whiskered Vireo, and White-crowned Pigeon occur regularly only in Florida. Florida is the only state in eastern North America where the Crested Caracara, Burrowing Owl, and Scrub Jay may be seen.

A list of the Florida "specialties" in our opinion should include the following:

White-tailed Tropicbird	Sooty Tern
Magnificent Frigatebird	Brown Noddy
Great White Heron	Black Noddy
Reddish Egret	White-crowned Pigeon
Roseate Spoonbill	Eurasian Collared-Dove
Wood Stork	Mangrove Cuckoo
Greater Flamingo	Smooth-billed Ani
Mottled Duck	Burrowing Owl
Masked Duck	Antillean Nighthawk
American Swallow-tailed Kite	Red-cockaded Woodpecker
Snail Kite	Gray Kingbird
Short-tailed Hawk	Cave Swallow
Crested Caracara	Florida Scrub Jay
Limpkin	Red-whiskered Bulbul
Spot-breasted Oriole	Black-whiskered Vireo
	Cape Sable Seaside Sparrow

To this list some birders would probably add a number of other exotic species (we list only two of these) now breeding in Florida.

Following are a few of the most sought-after species and suggested places to look for them.

Snail Kite

When water levels are up in south Florida and apple snails are plentiful, Snail Kites tend to concentrate and breed in the water conservation areas and near Lake Okeechobee. At this time a good place to see Snail Kites is near the Shark Valley entrance to Everglades National Park and the Miccosukee Indian Restaurant on the Tamiami Trail (U.S. 41) on the southern edge of Conservation Area 3A.

In recent years, Snail Kites have been reoccupying more of their former range in central Florida and may now be seen on Lake Kissimmee where State Road 60 crosses the southern outlet of the lake. Kites are now being seen in Lakes Tohopekaliga and East Tohopekaliga in Osceola County, and in the Fellsmere marshes on the northwest quadrant of the intersection of State Road 60 and County Road 512 in Indian River County. During times of severe drought, Snail Kites may concentrate in certain surviving wetlands sites. One such place in the mid-80s was the Palm Beach County Water Catchment Area along the Florida Turnpike, where over 300 kites—nearly half of the Florida population—fed and roosted for several weeks.

Limpkin

This species is widespread throughout central Florida and may be seen along many lakes and streams, but one of the surest places is from a Jungle Boat cruise at Wakulla Springs State Park, south of Tallahassee on State Road 267, just east of its intersection with State Road 61. Another sure site is the Wekiva River Marina, north of Orlando.

Florida Keys Specialties

Birding in Florida is not complete without one or more trips to Florida Bay, the Florida Keys, and the Dry Tortugas to see the various species that for the most part are seen only there. An excellent Keys birding guide has been produced by National Audubon's Research Department and the Florida Keys Audubon Society (available for $1.50 from National Audubon Society Research Dept., 115 Indian Mound Trail, Tavernier, FL 33070.) The Research Department is located just off U.S. 1, at Mile Marker 89.

The Great White Heron, a color morph of the Great Blue found only in the Caribbean area, may be seen feeding along the shoreline and in Florida Bay throughout the Keys. Part of its population has become adept at panhandling fish from fishermen in the Keys.

Reddish Egrets, both dark phase and white phase, are fairly common along the edges of Florida Bay and in shallow ponds on the Keys.

Roseate Spoonbills are more commonly seen in upper Florida Bay near Flamingo in Everglades National Park, but from November to March they nest on Cowpens Key, just west of Tavernier.

Four Caribbean species are found wherever mangroves and tropical hammocks occur. The White-crowned Pigeon is a year-round resident, while the other three species—the Mangrove Cuckoo, Antillean Nighthawk, and Black-whiskered Vireo—occur only during the breeding season, April through August. White-crowns inhabit all of the keys from Key Largo to Key West, and are locally abundant in places. The Antillean Nighthawk is best seen in early evening at Marathon Airport and the Key West Airport. Common Nighthawks also occur throughout the Keys, and the only way to separate the two species as they fly overhead is by their different calls. The Common Nighthawk's call is a long, drawn-out *peeent*, while that of the Antillean is a three- or four-note *kity-kay-dick*, distinctively different from that of the Common.

Throughout the Keys, Black-whiskered Vireos sing their two-phrase song *cheer-lip, cheer-lip* followed by a pause before another repetition. They are dooryard birds in residential areas, as well as being common in the undeveloped tropical hammock.

The Mangrove Cuckoo is considerably less common and takes more time and effort to locate. It too can occur in residential areas but is best searched for in the still undeveloped tropical hardwoods and mangrove habitats of the lower Keys, especially Big Pine Key, No-Name Key, Sugarloaf Key, and Saddlebunch Key. In late April and May it often responds to a taped playback of its call.

A fifth subtropical species, abundant in the Keys during the spring and summer, is the Gray Kingbird. It also occurs along the Atlantic coast north to St. Augustine (occasionally to Fernandina Beach), and on the Gulf coast north to the panhandle. Watch for these on utility lines.

A trip to the Dry Tortugas to see its specialties—Sooty Tern, Brown Noddy, Masked Booby, Brown Booby, and White-tailed Tropicbird—is best undertaken in late April or early May since that is the time of peak migration for numerous transients. The Tortugas are accessible only by boat or seaplane. Several organizations including the Florida Audubon Society, the Florida Ornithological Society, the Sierra Club, and a number of commercial nature tour groups organize trips of several days' duration to the Tortugas in late April or early May each year to observe these species and the numerous landbird migrants that stop to rest and feed enroute from the tropics. Boat tour prices range from $125-$400/person, depending on length of stay and whether or not board and lodging are included in the price.

Individuals can charter seaplane flights from Key West Seaplane Service (Phone: 305-294-6978) for about $100/person for a flight out, a two-hour visit on Garden Key and return flight to Key West. If you desire to remain longer, or to camp overnight (you must bring your own food and water), you can arrange to do so at double the flight cost.

In all the years we have been visiting the Dry Tortugas we have never met anyone who has not been ecstatic about his or her visit to these unique keys.

Florida Scrub Jay

This threatened species is restricted to sand scrub habitat in central Florida. The largest populations occur on Merritt Island and Cape Canaveral, Ocala National Forest, and the remnant patches of scrub habitat on the Florida Ridge in Polk and Highlands counties. On Merritt Island one may see Scrub Jays along the road to Cape Canaveral National Seashore. In Highlands County a healthy population lives on the grounds of Archbold Biological Station, south of Lake Placid. Scattered populations occur from Volusia County south to Palm Beach County on the east coast, and from Lake County south to Lee County on the west coast. Check with your local Audubon chapter to learn of specific locations in your immediate area.

Red-cockaded Woodpecker

This endangered species occurs in mature pine flatwoods, especially longleaf and slash pine, throughout the state, but is becoming increasingly scarce. Most of the remaining active colony sites are not readily accessible to birders. The largest populations occur in our three national forests: the Apalachicola (which has the healthiest population), the Ocala, and the Osceola (both of whose populations are dwindling). One particularly visible pair has set up housekeeping in a grove of pines on Sheppard Road, about 0.3 mile off Old State Road 8 near Venus. You should check with your local Audubon chapter to learn of any observable colonies in your vicinity.

Short-tailed Hawk

This tropical species breeds throughout peninsular Florida but is so uncommon that it is rarely seen on a regular basis during the nesting season unless someone has pinpointed a breeding pair. In winter up to six or more birds inhabit the Flamingo area of Everglades National Park. From November to late February one or more birds might be seen soaring high overhead along the road to Flamingo. Both color phases, dark and light, occur together. In April and May of 1989 two pairs were found nesting just east of Avon Park in Highlands County.

Smooth-billed Ani

This Caribbean species first appeared in Florida near Lake Okeechobee in the early 1950s, and since then has spread throughout the southern half of the peninsula as far north as Merritt Island on the east coast and the Tampa Bay area on the west coast. It remains relatively uncommon and patchy in distribution except in some local areas. It inhabits brushy thickets in residential areas and agricultural fields. Anis are frequently seen at Loxahatchee National Wildlife Refuge, the western edges of Miami and Homestead, on the Anhinga Trail and at Flamingo in Everglades National Park, and at Ding Darling National Wildlife Refuge on Sanibel Island.

Exotic Species

Like many humans who come to Florida to visit, then end up staying permanently, numerous species of birds from South America, Africa, Asia, and Australia are taking up residence in south Florida. Many of these are the colorful psittacines (parrots). For a partial list, see the chapter devoted to exotics in Florida. The urban/suburban belt from Homestead north to the Palm Beaches has become home to dozens of species of escaped and released birds. A mild climate, numerous plantings of exotic flowering and fruiting trees and shrubs, and feeding stations supplied by humans all combine to make living in Florida a successful experience for these birds.

Several members of the Tropical Audubon Society in Miami have become experts in locating and identifying most of these species. Information for finding these may be obtained from Tropical Audubon Society, 5530 Sunset Drive, South Miami, FL 33143 (Phone: 305-666-5111). A professional guide service is occasionally available. For information contact Mort Cooper, 7625 SW 79th Ct., Miami, FL 33173 (Phone: 305-271-2413).

ATTRACTING AND FEEDING BIRDS

Like all creatures, birds have three basic needs—food, water, and shelter. Shelter includes nest sites and cover for protection from predators. If your yard provides one or more of these needs, you should have some birds frequenting it. The more variety of foods and plants in your yard, the greater variety of birds you should be able to attract.

Before we suggest ways to attract birds to your property, we should discuss two basic questions that often arise concerning the feeding of wild birds. These are: (1) Is it necessary to provide food for wild birds? and (2) If I should start feeding, will it be fatal to birds if I stop feeding them? In Florida, the answer to both questions is *no*. In the absence of snow and ice, birds find sufficient natural foods to sustain them through the winter. Occasionally, when an Arctic air mass penetrates Florida and we have several days of frigid temperatures, some of the insect-eating species, such as vireos, warblers, kinglets, and wrens, may suffer losses, and for some of these a bird feeder provisioned with the proper foods could be life-saving.

In some urban areas, such as St. Petersburg, for example, where several tons of bird seed are sold each week, supplemental feeding has undoubtedly enabled larger populations of birds to exist. The three species that appear to have benefitted the most from bird feeders are the House Sparrow, European Starling, and Mourning Dove. Three other species living in St. Petersburg that are dependent on human food subsidies are the pigeon (Rock Dove), Ringed Turtle-Dove, and the Budgerigar.

We are not aware of any evidence that shows avian mortality has resulted when a person who has been feeding birds suddenly stops feeding them. It is conceivable that this could occur in the north where recent mild winters and a large number of feeding stations may have encouraged some individuals of species that usually migrate south to remain through the winter. Those individuals, however, probably have several feeding stations to choose from in the neighborhood.

In summary, no one need fear that if they don't provide unlimited food supplies, or if they stop feeding, that our wild birds will suffer. For our native species, sufficient natural foods occur in Florida so that cessation of artificial feeding will have no adverse effect on local populations.

In Florida, the primary reason for providing food for birds is to attract them to our yards where we can more readily see and enjoy them. The best way to do this is to help them meet their three basic needs—food, water, and shelter. By providing a variety of foods you should attract a variety of birds. By planting a variety of trees and shrubs you provide both food and shelter for birds.

Numerous species of birds have adapted well to living with man in cities, residential suburbs, and agricultural areas, and a bird feeder will attract most of them. They include Northern Mockingbird, Blue Jay, Mourning Dove, Northern Cardinal, Common and Boat-tailed grackles, Tufted Titmouse, House Sparrow, Red-winged Blackbird, and European Starling. Depending on the variety of foods provided, geographic location, and surrounding habitat, several additional species may also frequent feeders: Northern Bobwhite, Red-bellied Woodpecker, Downy Woodpecker, Northern Flicker, Carolina Chickadee, Carolina Wren, Brown Thrasher, Gray Catbird, Common Ground-Dove, Brown-headed Cowbird, Rufous-sided Towhee, Indigo and Painted buntings, Purple and House finches, American Goldfinch, and Pine Siskin, and chiefly in north Florida, several species of sparrows.

Feeders

Some species, for example, Northern Bobwhite, Rufous-sided Towhee, and sparrows, prefer to feed on the ground, although some of them will fly up to platform feeders or a tree stump close to the ground. Other species prefer hanging feeders, or feeders fastened to trees. So, a variety of feeder types will attract more species. In addition, it will allow more birds to feed at the same time. Often, when you maintain only one feeder, one or two individuals may exclude other visitors to the feeder.

The simplest feeder is a tray or platform either hanging from a branch or clothesline or installed atop a 2×4 or 4×4 post. It should be roofed to protect the seed from rain and should have a raised edge to keep the wind from blowing the seed away. The tray could be a piece of marine plywood or any piece of scrap wood. Another idea is to make a rectangular frame and to nail window screening to this for the bottom. This allows rain to drain through and obviates the need for a roof. A piece of quarter-inch hardware cloth can be fastened beneath the screening to give it support. If the city cuts down an old oak in your neighborhood, you might request a one- or two-foot section of the trunk (if it is solid wood and not rotten) and use this as a feeding platform.

A large variety of commercial feeders can be purchased. Some of these are expensive, but like most expensive things, they last far longer than do the cheap feeders. If you have squirrels in the neighborhood, do not buy cheap plastic feeders, because the squirrels will make short work of them.

Feeders can be made of household items, such as half-gallon or gallon-size milk cartons and jugs, bleach jugs, large plastic soda bottles, etc. Natural materials in the yard can be used—a small log with holes drilled in it or a pinecone stuffed with suet and peanut butter. These can be hung with clothes hanger wire. Again, if you have squirrels, do not use string or plastic cord.

Food

Wild Bird Seed

Mixes of wild bird seed can be purchased at most supermarkets, pet stores, feed stores, and discount department stores, and nowadays most of these are satisfactory for use in Florida. It is usually a mixture of white proso millet, milo, wheat, and sunflower seeds. Higher priced mixes are available from garden supply and feed stores. These usually contain more sunflower seeds and less milo and wheat. Many birds like finely cracked corn and this is not found in most mixes. We recommend purchasing a bag of baby chick starter scratch from a feed store and mixing this with the wild bird seed. You may also want to add more sunflower seed to the mix. Two kinds of sunflower seeds are available, the small black oil seed, preferred by most birds, or the larger black and white striped seed. Often, both kinds come in the same package. These can be added to the wild bird seed mix or fed separately in special feeders.

Niger, sometimes called thistle, is a preferred food of American Goldfinches and Pine Siskins. It is also a very expensive seed and in much of Florida a waste of time and money because these two species rarely attend feeders, especially south of the northern tier of counties.

If you feed birds on the ground, be sure to periodically rake and clean up old seed and fecal material. It would not hurt to change feeding locations periodically to prevent the development or spread of fungal diseases.

If you store your bird seed out of doors or in an open shed, be sure it is in a secure container so that squirrels and rats cannot chew their way into it. Moisture can cause the seed to go moldy and flour beetles can quickly turn it into powder, so do not store large amounts over a long period of time.

Suet

Many species of birds will eat suet—the dry hard fat from beef cattle, especially from around the heart and kidneys. This is usually available from your butcher, either free or very inexpensively. You have to ask for it specifically as it is not out on the shelves.

Fat turns rancid, especially in Florida's warm climate, so only small amounts at a time should be provided in mesh bags (onion or citrus bags) or in hardware cloth baskets placed on a tray feeder or fastened to the trunk of a tree. If the suet is cut into small pieces many birds that do not usually come to your feeder will come especially during cold spells. Brown Thrashers, Carolina Wrens, House Wrens, Yellow-rumped Warblers, Ruby-crowned Kinglets—all usually insect-eating birds—have been seen eating suet.

A number of ingredients can be added to melted fat to produce a "cake" readily eaten by many birds. Wild bird seed mix, corn meal, white or whole wheat flour, oatmeal, crushed dried dog food, chopped nuts, raisins, peanut butter—almost anything edible—can be added. The resulting cake can be poured into molds, shaped into balls, stuffed into pinecones or into holes drilled in logs. It can be refrigerated or frozen. Following are two basic recipes:

(1) 1 cup chopped suet
   1 cup peanut butter
   2 cups corn flour
   ½ cup wheat flour

Melt the suet in a pan and stir in peanut butter. Set aside to cool. Mix dry ingredients well and add to the cooling suet mixture. Shape into balls.

(2) 1 cup oatmeal
    ½ lb. suet (any fat will do)
    ½ cup peanut butter
    Corn meal, raisins, chopped nuts, dry cereal, etc.

> Cook oatmeal. While hot, add fat and peanut butter. Then add other ingredients. Form into balls. Place in mesh bags.

You should try various combinations of ingredients until you find one that your birds prefer. Empty pint-size ice cream cartons are ideal for storing suet mix.

Peanut Butter

This can be fed straight or mixed with suet, corn meal, bird seed, etc., and stuffed into holes in a log or in a pinecone. Several years ago some birds were found dead at a feeder with peanut butter in the esophagus, and since then some folks have felt that straight peanut butter is dangerous for small birds. No additional evidence has been found to confirm this. It should cause no problem when mixed with other foods.

Nuts

Peanuts and pecan pieces or crumbs are readily eaten by a number of species, especially jays, woodpeckers, and titmice.

Fruit

Dried fruits, such as raisins and currants, are loved by mockingbirds and waxwings. Most birds like fresh fruits quartered or sliced—apples, pears, grapes, bananas, and citrus. Wintering Northern Orioles will frequent feeders to feed on orange halves. A good way to offer these is to hammer one or two long nails through a board, turn the board over and impale orange halves on the points.

Doughnuts and Bread

Day-old doughnuts can be purchased from doughnut shops and placed on a dowel nailed to a board on the feeder, or suspended from an overhead wire. Small pieces and crumbs of most kinds of breads are readily eaten by several species of birds. White bread is not as nutritive as the dark breads, but may be used sparingly.

Sugar Water for Hummingbirds

Hummingbirds are attracted to specially designed feeders built to hold a sugar solution—a mixture of one part granulated sugar to three parts water. The water should be boiled first and the mixture stored in the refrigerator. Feeders should be thoroughly cleaned at least weekly, but do not use a detergent. Do not allow the sugar solution to remain in the feeder so long that mold starts growing in it. Honey should not be used because it sometimes fosters a fungus growth that can be fatal to hummingbirds.

Although most of our Ruby-throated Hummingbirds migrate to Central and South America for the winter, some do overwinter in Florida, and several western Rufous Hummingbirds winter in Florida. Hence it is worthwhile to maintain a feeder all winter long in some areas. Wintering hummingbirds have occurred in Pensacola, Destin, Tallahassee, Gainesville, Orlando, and southward.

Occasionally, other species, such as Northern Orioles, some warblers, and tanagers, will attend a hummingbird feeder. Ants can become a problem at times, but a little grease or Vaseline jelly on the wire suspending the feeder should solve that problem.

For more information on feeding birds, see the recommended reading list at the end of this chapter. An excellent, inexpensive guide on feeding wild birds, entitled "Banquets for Birds" is available from the Information Services Dept., National Audubon Society, 950 Third Ave., New York, NY 10022.

Bird Feeder Problems

Bully-birds or Hog-birds

When one or two birds seem to be hogging all the food, install several feeders to spread out the feast. Use a variety of feeder types—tray, hanging tubular, domed, etc. A cage of $1'' \times 2''$ weldwire fencing built around a feeder will allow the smaller birds to enter but excludes the larger species. By squeezing every other pair of wires you can adjust the size of the openings.

Your yard is probably within the territory of a Northern Mockingbird, and he (or she—in the winter females also defend a territory) may try to exclude any other species from the yard. By providing several feeders in different parts of the yard, your mocker's attention is so divided that it cannot exclude every visitor.

Occasionally, Blue Jays or Red-winged Blackbirds will thresh seed out of the reservoir of a feeder while searching for sunflower seeds. If you have too few ground-feeding birds to pick the spilled seeds and the seed is going to waste, you need to stop this behavior. This is easily accomplished by boring holes spaced one-inch apart in a $\frac{3}{8}''$ by $\frac{3}{4}''$ piece of wood to insert three-inch lengths of wire cut from a clothes hanger. This strip is then attached to the front of the food tray. The wires prevent the birds from swinging their heads sideways and sweeping seed out of the reservoir, yet they can still feed. (This is the suggestion of Roy M. Hoover, Apalachee Audubon Society.)

If you feel that one particular species is overwhelming your feeders, observe what those birds are eating, then stop providing those items for a week or so. Some people feed only sunflower seed and this attracts only those species that can shell and eat those seeds.

Hawks

If you have a feeder that caters to small birds, sooner or later one of the bird-eating hawks, usually a Sharp-shinned Hawk or Cooper's Hawk (small, trim, long-legged, long-tailed bluish or brownish raptors) will find your yard. You have created a concentration of their favorite prey items and they are taking advantage of it. This is, of course, natural behavior for their species and they have a right to live also. But, of course, you do not want to be the cause of birds being killed in your back yard. What do you do? The best thing is to cease providing food for a few days. As soon as the small birds stop coming to the feeder, the hawk will move on to a better feeding area (woods). Next, check to insure that you have sufficient cover in your yard to allow small birds to escape from a predator. The feeder should be no farther than 10 to 15 feet from shrubbery or a brushpile.

Cats

Cats will be cats, regardless of how well fed, and they will capture birds. You can train a dog not to do something that is in his nature to do, but rarely is this possible with a cat. So, you need to assist the birds to escape a cat's attempt to capture them. You can do this by making sure the cat is not able to sneak up undetected on birds feeding or bathing on the ground. Do not place a feeder or birdbath immediately next to dense shrubbery or ground cover. You can also bell your cat. Use two bells; some cats can learn to adjust their movements to silence a single bell.

Don't let your cat roam at night. If, no matter what you do, your cat captures too many birds, then stop making it easier for him, and simply stop feeding and attracting birds to your yard.

If you are having problems with a neighbor's cat, speak to the neighbor about the problem and see what can be worked out. Cats hate water. A garden hose might discourage the cat from entering your yard. If the cat is an untagged stray or feral cat, then try trapping it to turn over to the local animal control department or the Humane Society.

Squirrels

The Gray Squirrel is one of our common native mammals that has learned to adapt well to humans. They have as much right to live in our yards as do the birds we want to attract. However, they can monopolize a feeder and eat a lot of food. They have all day to learn how to outsmart your every move to foil them. Sometimes all you can do is keep trying. There are some excellent commercial feeders on the market designed to exclude squirrels and larger birds by closing shut whenever an animal above a certain weight settles on them. They are expensive, but effective in their job.

An inverted cone of metal placed under a feeder supported by a post will prevent a squirrel from climbing the post, and a cone over a hanging feeder will prevent access from above. But squirrels can easily jump to a feeder if it is placed only a few feet from a tree or shrub. When hanging a feeder use strong wire because a squirrel can easily chew through string or plastic.

Sometimes people trap and cart squirrels several miles away. This might solve your problem temporarily, but may be adding to the squirrel population in someone else's yard. And it is only a temporary solution because there are sufficient squirrels in the area to fill in any empty territories that occur. The senior author once decided that he had to remove the five or six squirrels in his Orlando yard, so he set a trap and over the next 15 days proceeded to capture a squirrel a day, and *still* had several squirrels coming to the feeder!

You can either spend your time trying to outwit them or resign yourself to feeding them, too. They are interesting animals in their own right, and what would our cities be like without squirrels?

Water

All birds require water for drinking and bathing. Thus, a source of water will attract several species that aren't particularly interested in the expensive food you might lay out for them. Bird baths can range from a simple inverted trashcan lid set on the ground to a commercially constructed concrete pedestal bath or a custom-built rock-walled pool or grotto with waterfalls and recycling water.

Some birds, especially warblers, are attracted to water dripping into a shallow basin, and many birds love to bathe in a fine misty spray directed at a leafy branch. The water drip is easily made by poking a small pinhole in a gallon plastic jug and suspending it over the bird bath.

It is important to clean the bird bath weekly, and every once in a while clean it with a weak solution of bleach. As with feeders, the location of the bird bath should not be too close to dense vegetation, yet not be farther than 10-15 feet from safe cover.

Cover and Food Plantings

If you want to attract a variety of birds to your yard, you may first need to change some of your present agricultural practices. Do you use a lot of pesticides? If so, either cease doing this or do all you can to chase birds *out* of your yard. Some judicious use of pesticides, especially the safer varieties, is sometimes acceptable, but for the most part, if you want to attract wildlife you need to become unhooked on pesticides.

Do you maintain an extremely manicured yard and remove all leaves, clippings, twigs, etc, from around every tree and shrub? If so, you need to stop doing this. It is fine to be neat and trim up to a point, but leaf litter should be left under shrubs. It is good for the shrubs as well as for ground-dwelling birds. Dead trees and snags should be left in place unless they pose a danger to structures, vehicles, or people.

If you have an extensive yard consider allowing some of it to revert to the wild. You can do this and still have a beautiful yard, including a lawn near the house. Expert advice about the use of native plants in home landscaping is available. Some nurseries now specialize in this and members of local chapters of the Florida Native Plant Society are willing to assist homeowners in the use of native species.

Fruit-producing trees, shrubs, and vines attract many birds, and numerous species of these are available for landscape plantings in each of the various climatic regions of Florida. The state's Nongame Wildlife Program has published a free guide entitled "Planting a Refuge for Wildlife: How to create a backyard habitat for Florida's birds and beasts." It is available from regional offices, or by writing the Florida Game and Fresh Water Fish Commission, 620 South Meridian St., Tallahassee, FL 32399-1600.

Do you live on the edge of a pond or lake? If so, do not remove all of the shoreline vegetation. The emergent vegetation along the lake edge provides important habitat for Least Bitterns, Green-backed Herons, Common Moorhens, Red-winged Blackbirds, and Boat-tailed Grackles. Insects produced from the lake and surrounding lands are important foods for numerous birds, including Purple Martins in summer and Tree Swallows in winter.

A lake shore is an ideal place to install a Purple Martin apartment house on a pole in the water, on a dock, or on the nearby land. Wood Duck boxes can be installed on a post in the lake or in trees on the uplands.

The League of Women Voters of Orange County has published a booklet for waterfront property owners in the central Florida area. It is appropriate for most Florida lakes and is entitled "Preserve Florida Waters." For a copy of this guide call (407) 894-6586 or 671-6902.

Housing for Birds

Each species of bird has a particular preference for a nest site. Some species prefer the branches of trees (for example, Blue Jay, Eastern Kingbird, Blue-gray Gnatcatcher). Others prefer cavities in trees (woodpeckers, titmice, chickadees, screech-owls) or shrubs (mockingbirds, thrashers, cardinals). Some prefer crevices and crannies (Carolina Wren, House Sparrow) or ground cover (Eastern Meadowlark, Northern Bobwhite). Several of the species that nest in tree cavities will also nest in man-made bird houses. Installation of bird houses on your property won't guarantee their occupancy, but chances are good that sooner or later some species will nest in one.

Houses may be made out of scrap lumber, but it should be a good wood that will last several years in the out-of-doors. If you paint the houses, paint only the external surfaces and use a brown or green color. Tops should be hinged and fastened with a hook and eye so that the boxes can be checked and cleaned periodically. Detailed designs for house construction may be found in some of the references listed at the end of this chapter.

Following are some suggested dimensions of houses for several Florida species:

Species	Width of Floor (in.)	Depth of Cavity (in.)	Entrance Diameter (in.)	Entrance above Floor (in.)	Height above Ground (or Water) (ft.)
Barred Owl	12 × 12	19-24	6	10-16	12-30*
Common Barn-Owl	12 × 18	17-19	6 × 9	0-7	12-30*
Carolina Chickadee Tufted Titmouse	4 × 4	8-10	1¼	6-8	5-15
Eastern Bluebird	5 × 5	8-12	1½	6-10	5-6
Great Crested Flycatcher	6 × 6	8-10	2	6-8	8-20
Red-bellied Woodpecker Red-headed Woodpecker	6 × 6	12-15	2	9-12	8-10*
Northern Flicker	7 × 7	16	2½	14	6-12*
American Kestrel Eastern Screech-Owl	7 × 7	16	3	14	10 + *
Prothonotary Warbler	4 × 4	6	1½	4	4-12 (Land) 3 (Water)
Purple Martin**	6 × 6	6	2½	1-2	15-20
Wood Duck	10 × 10	24	3 × 4	18	10-25* (Land) 5-25* (Water)

*Place sawdust in box.
**Build as multiple apartment house, or gourds may be substituted.

Carolina Wrens will nest in all sorts of containers—hanging plants and baskets, shelving, ledges, kegs, large coffee and juice cans, etc.—but rarely in a bird house. We have used No. 10 juice cans successfully in a maple swamp where natural crevices were scarce. A rectangular box, 8 to 10 inches long and 5×5 inches wide with one end left open may attract this species.

Numerous references dealing with the attracting and feeding of birds have been written, and several of these are listed below. The first two listed are, in our opinion, the best of the lot, and should be read by everyone with a serious interest in this subject.

Recommended Reading

Attracting Birds and Other Wildlife to Your Yard by William J. Weber, DVM. Holt, Rinehart and Winston, New York. 1982.

The Audubon Society Guide to Attracting Birds by Stephen Kress. Charles Scribner's Sons, New York. 1985.

Banquets for Birds. National Audubon Society, 950 Third Ave., New York, NY 10022.

A Complete Guide to Bird Feeding by John V. Dennis. Alfred A. Knopf, New York. 1983.

Feeding the Birds by Jan Mahnken. Garden Way Publishing, Pownal, Vermont 05261. 1983.

Homes for Birds. Conservation Bull. 14 (Revised). U.S. Dept. of Interior. (Available from U.S. Govt. Printing Office, Washington, DC. 1979.)

How to Attract Birds by Michael McKinley. Ortho Books, San Francisco. 1983.

The New Handbook of Attracting Birds by Thomas P. McElroy, Jr. W. W. Norton Co., New York. 1985.

Planting a Refuge for Wildlife: How to create a backyard habitat for Florida's birds and beasts by Susan Cerulean, Celeste Botha, and Donna Legare. Florida Game and Fresh Water Fish Commission, Nongame Wildlife Program. 1987. (Available from 620 S. Meridian St., Tallahassee, FL 32399-1600.)

The Wildlife Gardener by John V. Dennis. Alfred A. Knopf, New York. 1985.

SICK, INJURED, AND ORPHANED BIRDS

As more and more people populate Florida, interactions between people and birds increase. For example, more automobiles result in more bird hits, and more buildings with mirrored windows result in higher frequency of bird strikes. At the same time, a greater awareness by people of the plight of wildlife causes them to see and rescue more injured or helpless birds. As a result, a greater effort in both time and money is being spent on the care, treatment, and rehabilitation of birds in Florida.

Most of these injured and orphaned birds, of course, belong to the most widespread and abundant species in the state—Northern Mockingbird, Blue Jay, Mourning Dove, Cardinal, crows, just to mention a few—and we would be hard pressed to prove that efforts in rehabilitation had the slightest beneficial impact on those populations. On the other hand, we can say that the expertise, experience, and interest now exists to assist the injured or orphaned individuals of rare, threatened, and endangered species that occasionally come to wildlife rehabilitators.

We can also point out that most of these rehabilitators are involved with environmental education efforts in their communities, spreading greater awareness of human impact on wildlife. Wildlife rehabilitators are performing a worthwhile and valuable service to the community as well as to their wildlife patients. Few of them receive any tax dollars, and most of them end up spending their own funds to support their efforts. They need your financial support and welcome your volunteer services.

Your local Animal Control Department, Humane Society, or Audubon chapter can direct you to your nearest wildlife rehabilitator. Because both state and federal regulations govern the possession of migratory birds, game birds, and many other forms of wildlife, rehabilitators must have permits authorizing them to possess and care for the creatures in their charge. In Florida the Game & Fresh Water Fish Commission issues these permits and can provide a list of names of rehabilitators in your area. Gradually, most of the rehabilitators are becoming members of the Florida Wildlife Rehabilitation Association, which may be contacted at the Museum of Science, 3280 S. Miami Ave., Miami, FL 33129-9989.

Most of Florida's wildlife rehabilitators did not learn their profession in school, but through on-the-job training, which probably began with the first injured or orphaned bird brought to them by a neighborhood kid. Many of them are still learning, but after many failures and successes most know the basics of bird care. A reference that we highly recommend is *Wild Orphan Babies: Caring for Them, Setting Them Free* by William J. Weber, a Leesburg, Florida, veterinarian. (See the recommended reading list at the end of this chapter.)

Sick and Injured Birds

It usually takes a person with professional training and experience, such as a veterinarian, to diagnose and treat sick and injured birds. A broken wing or leg must be properly set or the limb will not heal correctly. Most rehabilitators rely on a local veterinarian interested in wildlife medicine for assistance. Many of these vets provide thousands of dollars' worth of free service annually for wildlife. Severely injured or diseased birds may require euthanasia to put them out of their misery. Hence, any birds that appear ill or injured should be delivered to your local wildlife rehabilitator for care.

Fish-hooked Birds

Several species of fish-eating waterbirds, especially Brown Pelicans, Double-crested Cormorants, and Royal Terns, frequently will take bait fish on a fisherman's line. When this occurs, do not cut the line allowing the bird to fly off trailing a streamer of monofilament line. That is a death sentence for the bird because the line usually becomes entangled in trees where pelicans and cormorants roost and nest, or, for the tern, it becomes wrapped around its body. Instead, reel in the bird, and with another person to assist you with the larger birds, grab the bird by the bill, fold the wings against the body, and carefully remove the hook without injuring the bird. You may have to cut off the barbed end first. If the hook has been swallowed, leave it in the bird, but cut the monofilament line as short as possible. Then release the bird.

Monofilament line, even without a hook, snags and kills many creatures along our waterways. Florida fishermen lose and discard miles of monofilament annually. Everyone should get into a habit of picking up this dangerous litter and disposing of it properly.

Oiled Birds

Florida's long coastline, ports of commerce, and tanker shipping lanes on both the Gulf and Atlantic coasts make it extremely vulnerable to an oil spill. As this book was being readied for publication, the *Exxon Valdez* spill occurred in Prince William Sound in Alaska, affecting, among other things, a massive number of seabirds and marine mammals. This has pointed up the need for contingency planning for a similar tragedy someday in Florida's coastal waters. The question is not *if*; it is *when*.

The American Petroleum Institute (API) has published a manual for cleaning and rehabilitating oiled waterfowl, entitled "Saving Oiled Seabirds." Single copies are available free from API, 2101 L St. NW, Washington, DC 20037. In the event this publication has not been updated since its 1978 publication, readers should note that Dawn Dishwashing Detergent can now be substituted for the recommended (but more expensive and less readily available) Lux Liquid Amber detergent.

When an oil spill occurs, speed in responding is of the essence. If you should spot an extensive sheen of oil or tar on a body of water, do not assume

that someone else has reported it. The following numbers should be called:
National Oil or Chemical Spill Hotline: 1-800-424-8802
U.S. Coast Guard: (305) 536-5611
Florida Department of Environmental Regulation, Office of Emergency
   Response: (904) 488-0190

Finding and Reporting Sick or Dead Birds

Occasionally some calamity occurs that results in the illness or death of birds. This could be caused by a naturally occurring disease—avian botulism, pox, aspergillosus, for example—or by a lethal pesticide with which the birds have come in contact—for example, diazinon sprayed on lawns to control mole crickets. If birds should land on a lawn shortly after it has been sprayed with this chemical—and in the dry season birds are sometimes attracted to a wet lawn—it is fatal to them. Because of this the Environmental Protection Agency has banned the use of diazinon on golf courses and sod farms. However, the EPA still allows its use on home lawns, and occasionally grackles, mockingbirds, and robins have been killed in Florida.

During spring and fall migration birds occasionally strike TV towers and tall buildings, especially during severe weather fronts. Other birds strike picture windows and windows coated with highly reflective materials, and others are hit by cars.

If you find an occasional sick or dead bird there is no cause for alarm, but if you find a number of sick or dead birds in one place then the Florida Game and Fresh Water Fish Commission should be notified so that an investigation can be made. (See chapter 7 for addresses and phone numbers of Commission regional offices.)

Fresh dead birds are valuable, not only because they can be studied for possible cause of death, but as material for other biological studies and for museum and educational specimens. Ornithologists located at most of the state's major universities always welcome fresh dead birds in good condition, as long as information showing date and locality and possible cause of death, if known, accompanies the specimen.

Orphaned Birds

Each year during the baby bird season—chiefly the spring and summer—newly fledged birds, some too young to fly well, appear in our neighborhoods, and many people think they are abandoned and in need of human assistance. The best policy is to leave them alone. Their parents are nearby and are still caring for them. If the baby is in some immediate danger of predation or being run over by traffic, then it should be picked up and placed in a nearby shrub or small tree.

Touching it will not cause the parents to abandon it. If the baby appears too young and wobbly, then place it in a small container, such as a berry box, and fasten it to a branch of the tree or shrub. Most of the time this should be sufficient and the parents will continue caring for the fledgling. If you have doubts about the well-being of the bird, observe it from a distance over the next hour or two to see if a parent has returned to it before you decide to rescue it permanently. Only after you have determined that the baby bird is truly abandoned should you remove it from the wild.

Baby birds require frequent feeding of specialized diets and several weeks of care until they are independent. Only as a last resort should anyone take on the task of rearing one. Do everything you can to get the baby to a rehabilitator. (Once you have gone through the experience of rearing a baby bird you will better appreciate this bit of advice!) If you must rear the bird, the first thing you need to do is determine which species it is so you will know what to feed it. Most likely it will be one of the more common species nesting in your neighborhood—Northern Mockingbird, Blue Jay, Northern Cardinal, Common Grackle, or Mourning Dove.

The above species, and most of the other bird species you may care for, are called *altricial* birds. They hatch helpless, usually naked and blind, and are dependent upon the parents for warmth and food for two or three weeks until they become fully grown and independent. Birds whose babies are fully developed when they hatch—with downy feathers, open eyes, and strong legs—are called *precocial* birds. Within a few hours after hatching they can run about or swim and feed themselves, although they still require adult protection and guidance and warmth for a few days until their contour (body) feathers form. Chickenlike birds—Northern Bobwhite and all ducks and shorebirds—are precocial.

Care of Altricial Orphans

Shelter

The baby bird should be placed in a small container, lined with a soft cloth or paper towel and several sheets of tissue. A quart-size berry box or any similar container will do. As the tissue becomes soiled remove it. Warmth can be provided by a 40- or 60-watt light bulb with the distance of the bulb being adjusted until temperature is above 95°F if the baby is naked, and 70-75° if feathered. Once the nestling is fully feathered and the ambiant nighttime temperature remains in the 70°s, then no additional heat is required. Instead of a light bulb, a heating pad could be used. In both cases, be sure not to overheat the bird.

The nest container should be placed inside a larger carton to protect the bird from accidental tipovers or a household pet or, in the case of an older fledgling, from premature escape. When the fledgling begins moving around, the nest container can be placed in a 1″ × ½″ hardware cloth cage, or if you have a secure screened porch, it can be given a corner of the porch with a perch (a tree branch) over newspaper.

Food

A number of baby bird diets have been developed by various rehabilitators, but the following, devised by Dr. Weber, is a good basic diet for most altricial birds that is relatively easy to prepare and feed. Soak pieces of dry Purina Cat Chow in one egg yolk mixed into 6 ounces of homogenized milk. The pieces of cat chow should soak in a small amount of formula only until they have absorbed sufficient moisture to soften them, but not be mushy. The softened pieces may be picked up with a pair of blunt forceps or a tooth pick and placed into the back of the throat of the begging bird. Feed the bird as much as it will take at a feeding. Younger birds need to be fed every 20-30 minutes;

older birds once filled, can go an hour between feedings. Generally, the babies will let you know when they are hungry.

Other Foods and Supplements
Offer pieces of grape, apple, banana, mulberries, blackberries, blueberries (whatever is in season), insects captured in the yard (but only in pesticide-free yards), mealworms (golden grubs, available from fish bait or pet stores), crickets, and shelled sunflower seeds, peanuts, pecans. Once or twice a week add a drop of liquid vitamins—the kind sold in pet shops for cagebirds—on a food pellet. Also about once a week crush a tablet of Vitamin B-1 and sprinkle this on a few pellets before feeding.

Water
Most baby bird diets contain sufficient water and they do not need to be given water directly. However, occasionally after you have fed the nestling, you may dip your finger in water and touch it to the tip of the beak so that it dribbles water into the mouth. This is the only way to provide water; do not use a dropper as you could accidentally place water into the air passage.

Mourning Doves
Doves feed their young a "milk" formed in the crop. An excellent substitute for this is Hi Protein baby cereal mixed with water to a soupy consistency, just thin enough to be taken up by a medicine dropper. Insert the dropper down the back of the mouth and fill the crop. Do this several times. Feed every two hours or so, depending on the hunger of the dove. As the dove becomes feathered, begin feeding it by hand a mixture of bird seed and baby chick starter scratch, but first remove the unshelled sunflower seeds and shell these before feeding them to the dove. Also provide a few grains of canary or parakeet grit with the bird seed mixture. Gradually reduce the cereal diet and increase the seed diet, but continue providing some cereal until the dove is feeding itself and drinking from a water dish. Be sure to wipe off with a damp cloth any cereal spilled on the head and neck after each feeding.

Hawks and Owls (Raptors)
Orphaned raptors should be taken to a rehabilitator trained in the care of this highly specialized group of birds. Far too many orphaned raptors have been brought to Florida Audubon's Madalyn Baldwin Center for Birds of Prey suffering from vitamin/mineral deficiencies as a result of inadequate nutrition. A diet that can be fed to raptors prior to transfer to a raptor center is the same one designed for altricial birds. Thin strips of beef heart sprinkled with a calcium-vitamin-mineral powder (Vionate, available from drug stores and some pet stores) can supplement this diet.

Care of Precocial Orphans
Because they tend to be flighty and high strung, it is sometimes difficult to successfully rear wild quail and ducks, but with care and patience, it can be done.

Northern Bobwhite

The cage should be a wooden or heavy cardboard box about 12-15 inches wide and 24-30 inches long. Insert a wire or string across the top of the box about 8 or 10 inches from one end. Over this drape a piece of cloth to form an inner chamber. The cloth should leave about a two-inch gap above the floor to allow chicks to run in and out of the chamber. Fasten a small mirror on the wall of this chamber. The mirror functions as a sibling—another chick is always there when needed. This is especially important if you have only one chick. The heat source can be a heating pad under the box or a 40-watt light bulb. Temperature should be about 90-95°F in the chamber.

Line the floor with several layers of newspaper and several layers of paper towels above this. The towels will be removed daily, the newspapers once a week, depending on need. Do not allow papers to become too wet or messy. Ideally, have two identical containers so that you can alternate their use. This way you need handle the chicks only once a week when you transfer them from one box to the other.

Feed turkey starter food. In an emergency, baby chick starter will suffice, but it is lower in protein content. After a few days begin adding a few grains of baby chick starter scratch. Also begin adding small bits of grass and clover blades, lettuce, and any insects that you can capture including small mealworms and crickets. Always keep some canary or parrot grit on the floor of the cage or in the food dish. The water dish should be the kind used for baby chicks, although a very shallow jar lid will suffice if only a few chicks are present.

As the quail become larger and fully feathered, you will need to build an outdoor predator-proof pen that allows them contact with the ground.

Wood Duck

Food and care of ducklings is similar to that for quail, except you need to provide a larger source of water and you will have to clean the cage almost daily. After the ducklings are several days old, add a shallow pan of water no more than an inch deep and allow the ducklings to play in it for 10-15 minutes, perhaps once or twice daily, but do not let them become soaked and chilled. After two or three weeks you will need to provide a large outdoor pen with a permanent pool of water (a pan buried in the dirt, or one above ground with a ramp. Be sure the ducklings can easily get out of the pool. To predator-proof a cage, the outer covering should be made of two or three thicknesses of chicken wire or hardware cloth. Once the ducklings are about three-fourths grown and are fully feathered, including wing primaries, they may be released in suitable habitat—usually a pond where you have seen other Wood Ducks.

Recommended Reading

"The care and feeding of orphan song and garden birds." A free brochure available from Suncoast Seabird Sanctuary, Inc., 18328 Gulf Blvd., Indian Shores, FL 33535.

"The Care of Orphaned Birds" by Herbert W. Kale, II. *Florida Naturalist* 52(2): 6-12 (1979).

Care of Uncommon Pets by William J. Weber, DVM. Holt, Rinehart and Winston, New York. 1979.

The Complete Care of Orphaned or Abandoned Baby Animals by C.E. Spaulding, DVM, and Jackie Spaulding. Rodale Press, Emmaus, PA. 1979.

"Saving Oiled Seabirds." International Bird Rescue Research Center. American Petroleum Institute, Washington, DC 1978. (Single copies free from API, 2101 L St. NW, Washington, DC 20037).

Wild Orphan Babies: Caring for Them, Setting Them Free by William J. Weber, DVM. 2nd Ed. Holt, Rinehart and Winston, New York. 1978.

Wild Orphan Friends by William J. Weber, DVM. Holt, Rinehart and Winston, New York, 1976.

BIRD CONSERVATION

If we enjoy seeing birds, if we appreciate their role and value as living creatures, then it follows that we should become involved with their welfare and conservation. Ever-expanding human development is destroying the habitats of numerous wildlife species in Florida, especially those that depend on natural forests, scrublands, prairies, and wetlands. Each new homesite, subdivision, or shopping plaza displaces the animals that lived there. In the past we could rationalize this by thinking, "Oh, there are plenty of undeveloped areas nearby that they can move to." This is no longer true in our highly urbanized and suburbanized areas. Most of the vacant undeveloped properties scattered here and there are being developed, and few "vacant" habitats remain nearby; if there are any, they are probably already occupied by wildlife.

When a community buys parklands for the recreational needs of its citizens—ball parks, tennis courts, picnic facilities—it too often ignores the needs of wildlife and of those citizens who enjoy passive recreation such as bird watching, nature photography, or just hiking through the woods. Wildlife, which probably has just as much "right" to live on the land as do the humans who "own" it, do not have any say about their fate. They neither vote nor pay taxes, but they do pay a high price for human development, with their lives, and, sometimes, with the extinction of their species. The need for pristine natural space and wildlife habitat within our communities and on our own lands is as important to humans as it is to wildlife.

What can you as an individual do about all this? The very least is to join one or more of the environmental organizations in your area that are actively promoting the preservation and conservation of wildlife habitat. It takes no more effort than simply to write a check and mail in your annual membership.

If you are willing and able to do more, you can become an active participant in the work of the organization. You can also take a few moments to write or phone to let your elected officials know of your interest and concern about what they are doing or not doing on behalf of wildlife. Show your support for programs and initiatives that encourage wise management of growth and development on the regional, state, and national level. You cannot assume that the agencies responsible for the management of a public resource will always do what is "right" in the discharge of their stewardship. Continual vigilance by the public is necessary to ensure the protection of our wildlife resources. It is an undertaking that is well worth the effort. The beauty and wonder of nature are rewards in themselves, and they are a precious legacy for future generations. You, individually, may feel helpless to change the course of things, but through membership in environmental organizations your name and your annual dues multiply your power manyfold.

Conservation Organizations in Florida

In addition to the following statewide organizations (many with both local and national affiliates), several regional and local organizations also exist. To learn of one in your community, check your phone directory or local chamber of commerce.

Florida Audubon Society, 1101 Audubon Way, Maitland, FL 32751 (Phone: 407-647-2615). Founded in 1900 when the slaughter of birds for the plume trade was at its peak, Florida Audubon is the largest conservation group in the state with 46 chapters and 35,000 members. A list of the chapters may be obtained on request.

National Audubon Society, Southeastern Regional Office, 928 N. Monroe St., Tallahassee, FL 32303 (Phone: 904-222-2473). National Audubon and Florida Audubon are separate, independent corporations, but share a common membership in Florida and the two groups work together on many conservation issues.

The **Nature Conservancy,** Florida Chapter, 1353 Palmetto Ave., Winter Park, FL 32789 (Phone: 407-628-5887). The primary effort of this organization is the preservation of high quality natural plant and animal habitat throughout the state through purchase or gift. Most of the acquired lands are turned over to a state or federal land agency for protection and management, while some are retained as Conservancy sanctuaries.

The **Sierra Club,** Southeastern Regional Office, 1201 North Federal Highway, Room 250H, North Palm Beach, FL 33408 (Phone: 407-775-3846). This organization focuses on a wide range of environmental concerns including air and water quality, wildlife, and scenic habitat protection.

Florida Defenders of the Environment, 1523 Northwest 4th St., Gainesville, FL 32601 (Phone: 904-372-6965). This organization specializes in scientific and economic studies of environmental issues dealing with river and lake protection, water quality, and public lands.

Florida Wildlife Federation, P.O. Box 6870, Tallahassee, FL 32314 (Phone: 904-656-7113). An affiliate of the National Wildlife Federation with 10,000 members in Florida, including hunters, fishermen, and other outdoor recreationalists, all with an interest in conservation and wise use of wildlife and the environment.

Florida Conservation Foundation, 1190 Orange Ave., Winter Park, FL 32789 (Phone: 407-644-5377). This organization operates the Environmental Information Center, publishes ENFO News on various environmental issues, and organizes conferences and workshops.

1000 Friends of Florida, P.O. Box 5948, Tallahassee, FL 32314 (Phone: 904-222-6277). A watchdog organization, founded to see that the growth planning process fulfils the long-term needs of Florida.

Florida Native Plant Society, P.O. Box 680008, Orlando, FL 32868 (Phone: 407-299-1472.) Members of this group are interested in the preservation and enjoyment of native plants and the utilization of many of these in landscape plantings.

Many of Florida's birds spend a large part of their lives in the neotropical regions of Central and South America. Thus, we cannot ignore the impacts of the habitat degradation now taking place in these countries. Again, the individual can enlarge his or her ability to help solve environmental problems through membership in organizations working in the region, or in a particular country. The International Council for Bird Preservation, through its Cambridge, U.K., headquarters and the U.S. and Pan American Sections of ICBP, fosters numerous programs in bird conservation in Central and South America. Individuals can assist in this effort through membership in the **ICBP World Bird Club,** 801 Pennsylvania Ave., S.E., Suite 301, Washington, DC 20003.

State Government Agencies

Several state and federal agencies deal with land and water resources and impact directly or indirectly on birds. The most important of these are listed here.

Department of Environmental Regulation, 2600 Blairstone Rd., Tallahassee, FL 32399 (Phone: 904-488-4805). Water quality of lakes and rivers, ground water, sewage, municipal and hazardous wastes, dredge and fill, mining, etc.

Department of Natural Resources, Marjory Stoneman Douglas Bldg., Tallahassee, FL 32399 (Phone: 904-488-1554). Marine resources, beaches and shores, mine reclamation, state lands, recreation and parks.

Florida Game & Fresh Water Fish Commission, 620 S. Meridian St., Tallahassee, FL 32399 (Phone: 904-488-1960). All game and nongame wildlife and fresh water fish come under the jurisdiction of the Game Commission, a constitutional body unlike other state agencies in that it does not come under the governor and cabinet, but is governed by a commission of five members appointed by the governor. The Commission maintains five regional offices as follow:

Northwest Region
6938 Highway 2321
Panama City, FL 32409
(904) 265-3676
Wildlife Alert 1-800-342-1676

Central Region
1239 S.W. 10th St.
Ocala, FL 32670
(904) 629-8162
Wildlife Alert: 1-800-342-9620

Northeast Region
Rt. 7, Box 440
Lake City, FL 32055
(904) 752-0353
Wildlife Alert: 1-800-342-8105

Southern Region
3900 Drane Field Rd.
Lakeland, FL 33811
(813) 644-9269
Wildlife Alert: 1-800-282-8002

Everglades Region
551 N. Military Trail
West Palm Beach, FL 33406
(407) 683-0748
Wildlife Alert: 1-800-432-2046

Water Management Districts

Northwest Florida Water Management District, Rt. 1, Box 3100, Havana, FL 32333 (Phone: 904-487-1770).

Suwanee River Water Management District, Rt. 3, Box 64, Live Oak, FL 32060 (Phone: 904-362-1001).

St. Johns Water Management District, P.O. Box 1429, Palatka, FL 32078 (Phone: 904-328-8321).

South Florida Water Management District, 3301 Gun Club Rd., P.O. Box V, West Palm Beach, FL 33402 (Phone: 407-686-8800).

Southwest Florida Water Management District, 2379 Broad St., Brooksville, FL 34609 (Phone: 904-796-7211).

Federal Agencies

U.S. Fish & Wildlife Service, Region IV., 75 Spring St. S.W., Atlanta, GA 30303 (Phone: 404-331-5872). Endangered Species Field Office, Jacksonville, FL (Phone: 904-791-2580).

Environmental Protection Agency, Region 4, 345 Courtland St., N.E., Atlanta, GA 30308 (Phone: 404-881-4727).

U.S. Army Corps of Engineers

Jacksonville District, P.O. Box 4970, Jacksonville, FL 32201 (Phone: 904-791-3697).

Mobile District, P.O. Box 2288, Mobile, AL 36628 (Phone: 205-690-2658).

Birds and the Law

Both state and federal laws regulate the taking of birds in Florida. The only species not protected are the European Starling and the House Sparrow, both exotic species introduced into North America in the nineteenth century. Many cities have ordinances prohibiting the firing of weapons within city limits. The state also has a law dealing specifically with children and guns (including air rifles or BB guns) which reads as follows:

(1) The use for any purpose whatsoever of BB guns, air or gas operated guns, or a firearm . . . by any child under the age of sixteen years is prohibited unless such use is under the supervision and in the presence of an adult.

(2) Any adult responsible for the welfare of any child under the age of sixteen years who knowingly permits such child to use or have in his possession any BB gun, air or gas operated gun, or any firearm in violation of the provisions of subsection (1) of this section is guilty of a misdemeanor of the second degree, punishable as provided (by law). Section 790.22, Florida Statutes.

If you know of a child shooting at birds, make an effort to talk with the child and/or the parents about the situation and the law. If the child persists and the parents won't cooperate, then speak to your local wildlife enforcement officer or the police or sheriff. Don't expect them to become excited and rush out to arrest the violator. Most of them feel that they have more important criminals to deal with than a kid with a BB gun. But if the child is killing or injuring numerous birds, then be persistent. Ask the officials at least to speak with the child's parents. Fortunately, with greater environmental awareness and conservation concerns being taught in elementary schools, fewer children are inclined to kill birds.

In 1979, the Florida Game and Fresh Water Fish Commission established a panel of representatives of Florida sportsmen and conservation organizations to oversee a program that offers cash awards to citizens whose reports of wildlife violations result in arrests (whether or not a conviction follows). The program, called Wildlife Alert, spreads its message via press releases and bumper stickers that read "Reward—Report Wildlife Law Violators, They Are Stealing From You!" and lists the Commission's toll-free numbers (listed under each regional office above). The program has been highly successful, and over 60% of callers decline to accept a reward.

Town Bird Sanctuaries

We frequently receive inquiries about designating a community or a particular area as a bird or wildlife sanctuary. Technically, with the state and federal laws that already protect birds, and with the prohibitions against firing of weapons within most city limits, each municipality is automatically a bird sanctuary. Today, officially designating a particular area a bird sanctuary is done primarily for publicity purposes and to enhance environmental awareness among schoolchildren and the general public.

The city council of a legally incorporated municipality can declare the town a bird sanctuary by resolution drawn up by the city attorney. For an unincorporated community, the resolution must be passed by the board of county commissioners. For a housing subdivision, a majority vote of the property owners' association can declare the area a bird or wildlife sanctuary. Such a declaration is meaningless, however, without accompanying publicity, educational efforts, and appropriate signs.

Florida's Nongame Wildlife Program

Prior to the 1980s, the primary efforts of the Florida Game and Fresh Water Fish Commission dealt with the management of game species—deer, hogs, turkey, and quail—although it also conducted research on several endangered nongame species (Bald Eagle, Sandhill Crane, Red-cockaded Woodpecker, and several other species of birds, mammals, and reptiles), and numerous nongame wildlife benefitted from game management. In the early 1980s, the legislature established a nongame wildlife program and the Nongame Wildlife Trust Fund to finance the program. Trust fund monies are derived chiefly from a $4.00 first-time auto registration fee paid by new residents who transfer their vehicle registrations from another state. Current citizens of Florida may also contribute to the fund by adding $1.00 to their annual auto registration renewals. The fund also accepts donations from the public.

The program provides a nongame wildlife biologist and a nongame wildlife education specialist in each regional office. In addition, in cooperation with the University of Florida, three urban wildlife specialists work with municipalities on urban wildlife problems and opportunities. The program publishes *The Skimmer*, a newsletter featuring articles and news about nongame wildlife as well as a section for children. The newsletter is free to anyone asking to be placed on the mailing list. The program has also published checklists of Florida birds, mammals, and reptiles and amphibians, also available on request at regional offices or from Tallahassee.

ENDANGERED AND THREATENED SPECIES

In 1972 the Florida Audubon Society and Florida Defenders of the Environment founded the Florida Committee on Rare and Endangered Plants and Animals (FCREPA). The committee was to prepare a list of the species in Florida that were endangered, threatened with endangerment, or otherwise of special concern. Six special subcommittees of biologists covering each major group—plants, invertebrates, fishes, amphibians and reptiles, birds, and mammals—were organized to perform the work. The end products of this effort were the volumes of the *Rare and Endangered Biota of Florida* series, published between 1978 and 1982 by the University Presses of Florida. These volumes, some of which are now out of print, are being revised by FCREPA and will begin appearing in late 1990.

Rare and Endangered Biota of Florida (Gainesville: University Presses of Florida)

Vol. 1. *Mammals*, edited by James N. Layne (1978)
Vol. 2. *Birds*, edited by Herbert W. Kale II (1978)
Vol. 3. *Amphibians and Reptiles*, edited by Roy W. McDiarmid (1978)
Vol. 4. *Fishes*, edited by Carter R. Gilbert (1978)
Vol. 5. *Plants*, edited by Daniel B. Ward (1979)
Vol. 6. *Invertebrates*, edited by Richard Franz (1982)

In 1975, the Florida Game and Fresh Water Fish Commission adopted the FCREPA list with several modifications. Ever since, the list has been reviewed annually and revised as needed under Florida Administrative Code, Chapter 39, Rules 39-27.003 (endangered species), 39-27.004 (threatened species), and 39-27.005 (species of special concern). As of 1989, the list included a total of 117 species, 44 of which are also on the federal list. The Commission publishes this list annually, showing the state status, federal status, and CITES (Convention on International Trade of Endangered Species) status. A copy of this list may be obtained from the Commission's Division of Wildlife.

Because recovery of the state's endangered species depends upon the knowledge and actions of the people who visit or live in Florida, we briefly discuss here some of these species and their special problems.

Wood Stork

This species thrives in wetland habitats that undergo periodic flooding and drying. During wet periods, fish populations spread out, reproduce, and grow. In dry seasons, the fish concentrate in pools and are available to many wading species of birds. Because of overdrainage of wetlands and the manipulation of water levels by man, the stork population has declined from a high of about 75,000 in 1930 to a current low of 4,000–5,000 breeding pairs of birds. Continued loss of wetlands and improper management of water levels can only result in continued decline of this species.

Snail Kite

This species, formerly called the Everglade Kite, depends for its very existence on a single food source, the Apple Snail (*Pomacea paludosa*). The snail is widespread throughout the Florida peninsula but is available to the kite only in open freshwater marshes that retain water throughout the year. When a marsh dries out, as occasionally happens in drought periods, the snails disappear and the kites must move elsewhere; but if they cannot find suitable habitat with snails, the kites are doomed. With the drainage of much of south Florida's wetlands and the unnatural manipulation of water levels in the remaining marshes, the kite population fluctuates widely from year to year. Once a marsh dries out, even if only temporarily, it may take several years of adequate water levels to replenish the snail population so that kites can return to the marsh. The kite population fluctuates from 200 to 700 birds, depending on water conditions the previous nesting season. In 1988, 500 kites were recorded in central and south Florida.

Bald Eagle

Outside of Alaska, more Bald Eagles occur in Florida than in any other state: about 400 nesting pairs and 1,000 immatures and subadults. These numbers represent about 40% of Florida's original eagle population, but they have remained fairly constant through the 1970s and 1980s. Unfortunately, Florida's growing human population and development efforts across the state are continually encroaching on the eagle's nest sites. The U.S. Fish and Wildlife Service and the Florida Game and Fresh Water Fish Commission have recently issued guidelines for the protection of eagle nests. These guidelines provide for an inviolate primary zone with a 750–1,500 foot radius, as well as a secondary zone with certain use and activity restrictions covering a one-mile maximum radius. Because a nest tree can be felled in minutes, and a primary zone bulldozed in several hours, citizen vigilance is important for the protection of eagle nests. Learn where eagles are nesting in your area and be alert to any proposed development plans near these sites. Contact the Game Commission if any threat appears imminent.

Crested Caracara

Formerly called Audubon's Caracara, this species once occurred from Volusia south to Collier County but is now restricted for the most part to the Kissimmee Prairie region from Osceola County south to Lake Okeechobee and Hendry County. It has been declining in recent years as native prairie habitat has been converted to citrus and improved pasture. The Florida population now numbers about 400 birds. If landowners were encouraged to leave patches of native prairie and scattered stands of cabbage palms when converting to improved pasture, it may be possible to retain this magnificent species in the Florida landscape.

American Kestrel

Florida is an important wintering area for American Kestrels from the north; they may be seen on utility poles and wires along most state highways from October through April. But the resident breeding population, the Southeastern Kestrel, which is smaller in size than its northern cousin, is relatively scarce and is declining in most parts of the state. The chief reason for the decline in central Florida is believed to be a reduction in the number of dead trees and snags that are the kestrel's nest sites. An intervention that may help increase the kestrel population is the installation of nesting boxes in suitable habitat throughout the state. This would be a good project for local Audubon chapters and Eagle Scouts.

Florida Sandhill Crane

The resident race of the Sandhill Crane occurs throughout most of the Florida peninsula in wet prairies, marshy lake edges, and low-lying pastures wherever it can find food, suitable nesting habitat, and low human disturbance. This crane will tolerate some human proximity, but not near nest sites. They can survive on improved pasturelands as long as isolated shallow-water ponds and marshes are not destroyed.

Snowy Plover

This inhabitant of Florida's Gulf coast requires expansive, dry sandy beaches for breeding and both dry and tidal sand flats for foraging. Increased human activity, vehicles, and pet dogs and cats on beaches, especially near passes and inlets during spring and early summer when the plovers nest, have caused a great reduction in the number of Snowy Plovers in Florida. It is estimated that only 100–200 remain in the state.

Least Tern

This tern appears in Florida in middle to late March to breed, then returns to South America by mid-September. It preferes to nest on sandy or shelly islands, isolated beaches, and sand spits where vegetation is sparse or absent. Such sites are also preferred by humans for many recreational activities. In recent years, the Least Tern has been hard-pressed to find sufficient ground nesting habitat. Fortunately, it has found substitute nesting sites on flat, gravel-covered roofs of shopping plazas, warehouses, schools, and apartment buildings. These sites are relatively free of disturbance by humans and their pets, raccoons, and tidal flooding, although they present other hazards (temporary flooding after heavy downpours, unfenced drop-offs, and roofing tar). The terns nest only on lightly-colored substrates (white crushed limestone pearock, and cream, yellow, or tan river pebbles) and avoid roof areas covered with gray crushed traprock.

Tern colonies on beaches, dunes, and causeways can often be protected from humans by posting the site with stakes, engineering tape, and signs identifying the colony and requesting people to remain away during the nesting season. Your regional nongame wildlife biologist can assist in posting the site and providing the proper signs. Rooftop colonies do not require posting, but it is a good idea to contact building owners or managers and encourage them to allow the birds to remain undisturbed. Where rooftop colonies are causing a nuisance, refer to Chapter 9 for possible solutions.

Red-cockaded Woodpecker

This highly specialized woodpecker, found only in open, mature pine forests, requires old, living trees (60–120 years or older) in which to excavate a nest cavity. Most commercial forests in Florida are harvested on rotations of only 20–40 years; hence the Red-cockaded has been on a steady decline for the past several decades while most of the older timber stands are being harvested. It is only in our national and state forests and refuges that this species has a chance to escape extinction, and then only if the forests are managed in such a way to enhance woodpecker survival. Unfortunately, public forest policy has been mostly directed toward maximum harvest rather than protection of wildlife. In recent years, especially after lawsuits brought by environmental organizations, this attitude has been gradually shifting. Whether or not new management practices will be sufficient and timely remains to be seen. Meanwhile the Red-cockaded Woodpecker continues to decline. Because there is little hope of preserving any woodpeckers on privately owned commercial forest lands, management efforts must be conducted in our publicly owned forests, and this will not happen without strong public support and vigilance.

Florida Scrub Jay

This jay is a threatened species because its oak scrub habitat is prime land for development into housing subdivisions, shopping malls, and citrus groves. In fact, the Florida scrub is becoming the most endangered habitat in the state. The largest colonies of jays occur on public lands on Merritt Island National Wildlife Refuge and at Cape Canaveral Air Force Station, Ocala National Forest, and Archbold Biological Station near Lake Placid. The jay will survive at these sites only if the habitat is periodically burned to maintain certain stages of the oak scrub community. The Florida Game and Fresh Water Fish Commission is developing guidelines for keeping jay populations on developed lands, but we will likely lose all of these populations now on private lands.

Anyone observing Scrub Jays on public lands outside of the previously mentioned sites, or on privately owned lands, is urged to report the sighting to the Florida Audubon Society in Maitland, a local Audubon chapter, or to a regional nongame wildlife biologist from the Florida Game and Fresh Water Fish Commission.

Cape Sable Seaside Sparrow

This small, olive-gray subspecies of the Seaside Sparrow occurs in Everglades National Park where it should theoretically be secure and well protected. Unfortunately, the park is threatened by all the forces impacting natural waterflows from the northern Everglades region. Dikes, canals, impoundments, water diversion, and agricultural pesticides and fertilizers all make tenuous the future well-being of the park. Although original plans were to monitor this population every two years, no complete survey has been conducted since 1981. The Dusky Seaside Sparrow became extinct in the 1980s, and the Cape Sable Seaside may only be a decade behind it.

Dusky Seaside Sparrow

We will conclude this chapter with the Dusky Seaside Sparrow, a population no longer considered to be endangered, but only because it is now extinct. First discovered in 1873 near Salt Lake in the St. Johns River valley in Brevard County, it was considered a separate species until 1973 when, based on biological evidence, it was designated a subspecies, or race, closely related to all the other Seaside Sparrows on the Atlantic and Gulf coasts. It was the most distinctive race of Seasides because of its black and white streaked undersides, and it occurred only in the marshes of northern Merritt Island and the St. Johns River valley west of Titusville.

Adverse impacts of man's activities on the Dusky probably began with early efforts to drain marshes in the 1920s. In the late 1940s DDT was sprayed on Merritt Island marshes, and in the late 1950s these marshes were diked and impounded for mosquito control, which effectively destroyed the Dusky's habitat. State and county road construction and canal excavation by General Development Corporation destroyed more habitat in the St. Johns marsh. Governmental inertia in restoration of habitat and the invasion of shrubby vegetation due to overdrainage intensified wildfires set by ranchers each winter to improve cattle pasturage.

These cumulative adverse impacts over five decades finally brought the Dusky to the edge of extinction and by 1979 only seven males remained in the marsh. Six of these were captured in 1979-80 and brought into captivity. Over the next several years, in a cooperative effort involving the Wildlife Research Laboratory of the Florida Game and Fresh Water Fish Commission, the Santa Fe Community College Teaching Zoo, the Florida Museum of Natural History, Florida Audubon Society, and Walt Disney World's Discovery Island Zoological Park, the Duskies were mated with female Scott's Seaside Sparrows, a closely related subspecies from the Gulf coast. Although a few young were produced, it was a matter of too little, too late, and the last Dusky Seaside Sparrow died on June 16, 1987.

BIRD/HUMAN PROBLEMS AND SOLUTIONS

As Florida becomes more developed with each passing year, interactions between birds and humans increase. Some of these are simply temporary annoyances, such as a noisy bird singing outside a bedroom window at night, but others can be more serious, for example a woodpecker persistently drilling holes into the wooden siding of a house. In many cases the problem is short-term or can easily be solved. That night-singing bird may be a Northern Mockingbird—the state bird of Florida—singing a song of passion for his beloved during a few moonlit nights in spring. Or it may be a Chuck-will's-widow who doesn't need any moonlight to stimulate his loud song in April, May, and June. As passions cool, so does the singing. And the flocks of noisy grackles or Red-winged Blackbirds that suddenly descend on a lawn in late winter will be there only a day or so before moving on. Patience and a concern for the welfare of wildlife, both in short supply in the modern world, help to minimize many of these "problems."

Many times, it is the bird that experiences the problem. For example, the windows of many new office buildings are coated with a highly reflective material to reflect heat and light. Surroundings—sky, clouds, trees—are also reflected, and flying birds can strike these windows.

The following paragraphs discuss several of these problems. One solution that we do not recommend is the killing of problem birds. In addition to being illegal, unless a permit has been issued for this by both state and federal agencies, it is often only a temporary solution because sooner or later another bird will appear to replace the removed bird. For problems that you are not able to solve peacefully, we urge you to contact the nongame wildlife biologist at your regional office of the Florida Game and Fresh Water Fish Commission. (Refer to chapter 7 on Bird Conservation for a list of addresses and phone numbers in each region.)

Birds and Noise

In Florida, grackles, frogs, and mockingbirds—like cockroaches and mosquitoes—are ever-present facts of life. For humans who can't stand the presence and noise of nature, whether it be the noise of a flock of grackles, a chorus of frogs, or a lone, midnight-singing mockingbird, we seriously recommend that they consider moving to an upper floor of an apartment or condominium building.

For those who really don't mind living in the midst of nature, but still would like to get that persistent singer just outside their bedroom window to move off a bit, we recommend the following. In the evening, at dusk, when birds are going to roost, stand by the tree or shrub where the singer roosts and create enough disturbance to discourage the bird from using that site. You may need to do this several evenings in a row. A helium-filled balloon with an eye painted on it tied to the roost tree might be sufficient to discourage the bird from roosting there.

Second (or you might try this first), tie a line to one or two of the leafy branches and extend this into your house through the nearest window or porch. You might tie a helium-filled balloon containing a few grains of round gravel or unpopped corn to this line. When the bird begins singing, yank the line a few times. The disturbance should succeed in making the bird move to another tree.

A third solution is to close up the house and turn on your air conditioning.

Chimney Swifts

Chimney Swifts, as their name suggests, usually nest in chimneys. Formerly, they nested in hollow trees, and perhaps still do in some localities where chimneys are absent. They build delicate nests of tiny twigs fastened together and to the inside wall of the chimney with a sticky saliva that hardens into a secure glue. (Bird nest soup is made from the nest of a swift in China.) After the young hatch, they become quite noisy when being fed by the parents. To an unsuspecting person down in the living room, the sound can suggest a rattlesnake in the chimney! The birds do no damage; indeed, they eat thousands of flying insects daily and are valuable to have about. We suggest that you close the damper just above the fireplace to reduce the noise and to prevent any young accidentally falling into the room. (If you have ever chased a soot-covered fledgling around the house you can appreciate this advice). After about two weeks or so the birds should fledge and leave the chimney.

If you would prefer not to have the swifts in your chimney in the future, we suggest that you have a cover of 1″ × 2″ weldwire cloth placed over the top of your chimney in early winter after the swifts have departed for South America.

Woodpeckers

Generally, woodpeckers pose no problems to humans, but once in a while an individual woodpecker begins excavating holes in the wood sidings of buildings, most often a relatively new building. The first thing to do is check the wood for the presence of insects. If the wood is infested with wood borers, for example, the woodpecker is simply responding to the presence of a food source. Getting rid of the insects should solve the problem.

Sometimes the bird is damaging the wood framing of a window. This could be a response to the woodpecker he sees in his reflection in the window. The destruction of wood is a displacement response to that intruder who refuses to leave. Try covering the window with some material, plastic or cardboard, so he does not see his reflection.

Perhaps the woodpecker is excavating a hole in the siding for a nest or roost cavity. In this case, cover the damaged area with a sheet of opaque plastic and allow it to flap loosely in the breeze. This is the kind of plastic used at construction sites to cover wood and other supplies, and used by painters as a cover cloth. It is too smooth for the woodpecker to grasp, and the free flapping end should help discourage further pecking. Another possible solution is to attach helium-filled balloons, with a large eye painted on each balloon, near the site. Another item that may work is a plastic toy pinwheel fastened so that it faces into a prevailing breeze and spins.

Be sure that there are sufficient natural nesting sites in your neighborhood. Woodpeckers excavate cavities in dead snags or branches of living trees and in trunks of dead trees. This is a good reason to leave a few dead trees, or at least a ten- to twenty-foot section of the trunk of the tree, standing—as long as it will not damage buildings or vehicles when it finally does fall. Red-bellied Woodpeckers, Red-headed Woodpeckers, and Northern Flickers will nest in bird houses, and the placement of one or more of these in your yard and neighborhood may encourage them to nest there instead of in your house.

Most woodpeckers "drum" to announce territory and to attract a mate, usually during the spring months. Like any drummer, they seek a good surface that will resonate well. Utility pole condensers and the metal flashing on chimneys and roof peaks make excellent surfaces and sounds, except, of course, to the human in the bedroom below at 6:00 A.M. Covering the site with opaque plastic with a free end to flap in the breeze, or attaching one or two one-eyed balloons may solve the problem. Or perhaps you could reschedule your wake and sleep cycle in the spring months to coincide with that of your romantic neighbor.

Domestic Ducks

When residences are built around lakes in Florida, sooner or later someone decides that the lake needs some ducks. There may already be some native Wood Ducks living on the lake, but these may not be sufficiently visible or tolerant of human activity. The only ducks available for stocking are usually domesticated mallards or Muscovy Ducks, or combinations thereof. After several years, as both the duck and human populations increase, the neighborhood fights begin over those who love and feed the ducks and those who complain about aggressive drakes and messy guano in driveways and swimming pools.

The best means of population control is to find nests and remove eggs. Do not remove all the eggs; allow one or two to remain and hatch. Otherwise the female will quickly renest and lay another full complement of eggs, and this time you may not find the nest. Not every young duckling grows up to become a pet or pest. Our lakes are also home to fish, turtles, and alligators, all of which consider a baby duck as fair game, and, occasionally, a hawk or an otter will take a duckling. As distressing as this may seem, it is all part of the game of life. (You might think about this the next time you enjoy a piece of fried chicken.)

Do not capture the ducks and transport them to another lake. It is illegal to release any exotic species into the wild in Florida, even if you captured the birds in the wild initially. The ducks and their fresh eggs are edible and could be donated to shelters to provide food for people or other animals.

Bird Roosts

Some species of birds usually gather into large flocks at the end of the day and roost together in large concentrations. In Florida we have all seen crows or gulls or herons flying to roost in the evening. Most of these roosts are not too near human centers and do not cause any problems. Roosting blackbirds usually do not present the problems in Florida that they do farther north in Tennessee and Kentucky, where roosts containing a million or more birds—chiefly Starlings, Red-winged Blackbirds, Common Grackles, and Brown-headed Cowbirds—often appear in winter near human habitations. Generally, an active roost does not pose any problems to humans, but there can be some health problems associated with disturbance of the ground under an abandoned roost weeks or months afterwards.

If a blackbird roost, or any roost for that matter, is causing some concern, the first thing to do is call on the expertise of the U.S. Fish & Wildlife Service. Each roost is unique and requires individual study to determine its potential threat, if any, to human welfare.

Birds and Windows

Large picture windows and windows coated with reflective materials can cause injury or death for birds, especially during spring and fall migration. The vast expanses of reflective glass on modern office buildings look just like open sky to a flying bird, or, closer to the ground, like the surrounding landscape. What can be done to reduce the incidence of strikes? Anything that masks the reflection will help. In some instances, wide mesh netting can be hung over the glass. This can appear decorative and is not as aesthetically objectionable as opaque plastic sheeting. Silhouettes of an avian predator, e.g., a falcon, or cutouts of large "eyes," can be strategically placed on windows.

Dark or bronze-colored window coatings tend to be more visible and less reflective than the silver-colored coatings, and fewer birds strike these darker windows. This fact should be brought to the attention of those involved in planning and construction of buildings.

Most injuries received from window strikes are concussions and are usually fatal. Occasionally a bird will be found in lethargic condition under a window. If placed in a small box for an hour or so and kept in a quiet place, it may recover and be released. If it has not recovered within several hours then it should be taken to a wildlife rehabilitator for care. Dead birds should be given to the nearest museum or university biology department.

Roof-nesting Tern Colonies

We have already discussed efforts needed to protect and encourage tern colonies in Florida (see Chapter 7 on Bird Conservation) on both beaches and rooftops. Occasionally, rooftop colonies can cause some problems for people living or working below or next door to the colony. For example, a colony of 100 or 200 terns can deposit a large number of droppings on automobiles parked in an adjoining lot, or into a swimming pool of a condominium or motel.

Once a colony has become established nothing can be done legally to remove the terns from the roof and the best course of action is to grin and bear it for a few more weeks. Their droppings are not a health menace and the only damage done is the temporary inconvenience of putting up with them and cleaning them up. A colony that forms in early May should end breeding for the most part by the end of June or early July, if the colony cycle has not been disrupted by disturbance and egg loss. If attempts are made to destroy or remove eggs, the terns will persistently renest and the period of colony activity will be extended several weeks.

This was dramatically illustrated several years ago by two adjacent roof-top colonies near Daytona Beach. One colony atop a three-story condominium was inaccessible from the roof and, although the condo owners complained about droppings in their pool area (fortunately, their automobiles were protected by a covered roof), they were not sufficiently agitated to overcome the roof access problem and they left the terns undisturbed. Within two or three weeks after they had called for help, most of the young had fledged and the problem disappeared.

Next door was a rental apartment complex with a rooftop colony of terns next to an uncovered parking lot. The apartment manager responded to his tenants' complaints by going onto the roof and removing the eggs. He continued to do this periodically and each time the terns would renest, so that three weeks after the undisturbed terns on the next-door condominium had vacated, the terns atop the apartment complex were still going strong. (Sometimes, as the TV margarine ad states, it doesn't pay to mess with Mother Nature!)

As precarious as the Least Tern's status is, we would hope that most owners or managers of buildings suitable for rooftop nesting would welcome the chance to host a colony. However, if it is important to prevent a colony from forming on a particular roof, then several actions can be taken prior to the arrival of the terns in early spring.

Since the terns will not nest on a dark substrate—for example, black, gray, or green—we recommend the stones or gravel on the roof be sprayed a dark color. If this is not a feasible option, then place several helium-filled balloons, each with a large eye painted on it, at several locations on the roof. Or, stretch several lengths of clothesline across the roof and drape these with flapping plastic flags, the kind seen in automobile dealer lots.

At the same time you are taking steps to discourage nesting on a rooftop, take some positive actions to encourage the birds to nest elsewhere. Is there another roof nearby that could be enhanced to provide the terns with an alternate site? Is there some open vacant land nearby that could be scraped of vegetation and fenced to exclude dogs, raccoons, and people?

All colonies of Least Terns, both natural and rooftop, should be reported to your regional nongame wildlife biologist and he or she should be contacted if the terns present any problems or are faced with any threats. (See Chapter 7 for addresses and phone numbers of regional offices of the Florida Game and Fresh Water Fish Commission.)

Pigeons

Pigeons in North America are the feral population of the domesticated form of the Old World Rock Dove. Pigeons were brought to the New World by early colonists for food, for pets, as a means of communication, and for recreational racing (homing pigeons). Pigeon racing is still pursued by many people and two national organizations, the American Racing Pigeon Union and the International Federation of Homing Pigeon Fanciers, foster the sport. Even though the pigeon is an exotic species, hence does not enjoy the full protection of the Migratory Bird Treaty Acts, at least the fact that some free-flying pigeons may belong to someone should make one pause before harming one. In most instances an owned pigeon will bear one or more obvious leg bands.

Pigeons cause nuisance problems when they become too numerous in a particular site—entrances to public buildings, schools, warehouses, feedlots, etc. They perch and nest on horizontal surfaces such as eaves, gables, and ledges, and their droppings fall on the ground below. They can sometimes be forced to move elsewhere by blocking or covering these perch/nest sites with chicken wire or any material that will prevent perching.

The population can be reduced by trapping and removing the birds. However, because they are homing pigeons they cannot be released elsewhere as they will promptly return to the capture site. Occasionally, birds held in captivity for several weeks at a site far from the capture point will "home" in on the new site. Sometimes a pigeon fancier may be willing to take the birds. Or there may be no alternative except to humanely dispose of the birds. We do not recommend the use of drugged baits to capture pigeons because of the danger of native species coming to the bait.

10

EXOTIC SPECIES

South Florida's climate is subtropical and with the massive development of cities, numerous tropical species of flowering and fruiting trees and shrubs have been planted in landscaping around homes, subdivisions, and parks, providing a niche for animals from other lands. With a large pet trade to provide a source of birds, it is not surprising that numerous species have been released, or escaped, and now survive in south Florida. Some of these species are reproducing; others may simply be populations of long-lived individuals living out their lifespan without breeding. A number of species are successfully breeding and expanding their populations. At least 16 species of Psittacines (parrots and parakeets), three species of mynas, a bulbul, and an oriole (see list below) now breed in the Miami area. Several of these have spread elsewhere in the state and we have included these in our species accounts, but for the most part we omit the relatively recent exotic species that have been introduced by man, either deliberately or accidentally. As time passes we learn of more additions to the list of exotic avifauna now breeding in the state. With many tourist attractions featuring live birds, occasional escapes happen and these too may survive for a time in the wild. Hence, the sighting of a Scarlet Ibis (*Eudocimus ruber*), or a King Vulture (*Sarcoramphus papa*), or an Egyptian Goose (*Alopochen aegyptiacus*) in central Florida should not be too startling or unexpected nowadays. One or more guides to the exotic avifauna of Florida are now in preparation and these will be welcome additions to the libraries of bird watchers.

Introduced Exotic Birds Breeding in Florida
    Rock Dove or Domestic Pigeon *(Columba livia)*
    Eurasion Collared-Dove *(Streptopelia decaocta)*
    Ringed Turtle-Dove *(Streptopelia 'risoria')*
    Budgerigar *(Melopsittacus undulatus)*
    Rose-ringed Parakeet *(Psittacula krameri)*
    Chestnut-fronted Macaw *(Ara severa)*
    Red-masked Parakeet* *(Aratinga erythrogenys)*
    Dusky-headed Parakeet* *(Aratinga weddellii)*
    Black-hooded Parakeet or Nanday Conure *(Nandayus nenday)*
    Green-cheeked Parakeet *(Pyrrhura molinae)*

*also known as Conure

Monk or Quaker Parakeet *(Myiopsitta monachus)*
Canary-winged Parakeet *(Brotogeris versicolurus)*
White-fronted Parrot** *(Amazona albifrons)*
Red-lored or Yellow-cheeked Parrot** *(Amazona autumnalis)*
Red-crowned or Blue-cheeked Parrot** *(Amazona viridigenalis)*
Yellow-headed Parrot** *(Amazona oratrix)*
Yellow-crowned Parrot** *(Amazona ochrocephala)*
Orange-winged Parrot** *(Amazona amazonica)*
Red-whiskered Bulbul *(Pycnonotus jocosus)*
Spot-breasted Oriole *(Icterus pectoralis)*
House Sparrow *(Passer domesticus)*
European Starling *(Sturnus vulgaris)*
Common Myna *(Acridotheres tristis)*
Crested Myna *(Acridotheres cristatellus)*
Hill Myna *(Gracula religiosa)*

**also known as Amazon

INDEX AND CHECKLIST

Boldface page numbers refer to illustrations; italic page numbers refer to species accounts. Those species marked with an asterisk (at the common name) breed in Florida. (Some exotic species breeding in Miami are not listed.) Species marked (a) are accidentals. Species marked (e) are now considered extinct.

Your personal checklist of Florida birds is incorporated into the index. A box is placed before the common name of each species. Accidental, pelagic, and rare species that you may wish to include on your checklist, but which are not covered in the text, are listed on page 288.

ADDITIONAL CHECKLIST

Pelagic
- [ ] Yellow-nosed Albatross
- [ ] Black-capped Petrel
- [ ] Cory's Shearwater
- [ ] Greater Shearwater
- [ ] Sooty Shearwater
- [ ] Manx Shearwater
- [ ] Audubon's Shearwater
- [ ] Wilson's Storm-Petrel
- [ ] Leach's Storm-Petrel

Accidental
- [ ] Pacific Loon
- [ ] Least Grebe
- [ ] Red-necked Grebe
- [ ] Eared Grebe
- [ ] Scarlet Ibis
- [ ] White-faced Ibis
- [ ] Greater White-fronted Goose
- [ ] White-cheeked Pintail
- [ ] Cinnamon Teal
- [ ] Common Eider
- [ ] King Eider
- [ ] Harlequin Duck
- [ ] Northern Goshawk
- [ ] Swainson's Hawk
- [ ] Ferruginous Hawk
- [ ] Rough-legged Hawk
- [ ] Mountain Plover
- [ ] Bar-tailed Godwit
- [ ] Sharp-tailed Sandpiper
- [ ] Curlew Sandpiper
- [ ] Great Skua
- [ ] Franklin's Gull
- [ ] Little Gull
- [ ] California Gull
- [ ] Thayer's Gull
- [ ] Iceland Gull
- [ ] Glaucous Gull
- [ ] Sabine's Gull
- [ ] Dovekie
- [ ] Common Murre
- [ ] Thick-billed Murre
- [ ] Razorbill
- [ ] Atlantic Puffin
- [ ] Key West Quail-Dove
- [ ] Flammulated Owl
- [ ] Northern Saw-whet Owl
- [ ] Lesser Nighthawk
- [ ] White-collared Swift
- [ ] Vaux's Swift
- [ ] Antillean Palm Swift
- [ ] Cuban Emerald
- [ ] Bahama Woodstar
- [ ] Black Phoebe
- [ ] Say's Phoebe
- [ ] Ash-throated Flycatcher
- [ ] LaSagra's Flycatcher
- [ ] Couch's Kingbird
- [ ] Cassin's Kingbird
- [ ] Loggerhead Kingbird
- [ ] Fork-tailed Flycatcher
- [ ] Cuban Martin
- [ ] Violet-green Martin
- [ ] Bahama Swallow

- [ ] Rock Wren
- [ ] Northern Wheatear
- [ ] Varied Thrush
- [ ] Bahama Mockingbird
- [ ] Sage Thrasher
- [ ] Thick-billed Vireo
- [ ] Bell's Vireo
- [ ] Black-throated Gray Warbler
- [ ] Townsend's Warbler
- [ ] Golden-cheeked Warbler
- [ ] Kirtland's Warbler
- [ ] MacGillivray's Warbler
- [ ] Bahama Yellowthroat
- [ ] Stripe-headed Tanager
- [ ] Western Tanager
- [ ] Black-headed Grosbeak
- [ ] Lazuli Bunting
- [ ] Black-faced Grassquit
- [ ] Black-throated Sparrow
- [ ] Lark Bunting
- [ ] Chestnut-collared Longspur
- [ ] Tawny-shouldered Blackbird
- [ ] Western Meadowlark

Rare
- [ ] Yellow Rail
- [ ] Upland Sandpiper
- [ ] Baird's Sandpiper
- [ ] Stilt Sandpiper
- [ ] Buff-breasted Sandpiper
- [ ] Ruff
- [ ] Wilson's Phalarope
- [ ] Red-necked Phalarope
- [ ] Red Phalarope
- [ ] Pomarine Jaeger
- [ ] Parasitic Jaeger
- [ ] Long-tailed Jaeger
- [ ] Black-legged Kittiwake
- [ ] Arctic Tern
- [ ] Short-eared Owl
- [ ] Olive-sided Flycatcher
- [ ] Horned Lark
- [ ] Warbling Vireo
- [ ] Philadelphia Vireo
- [ ] Yellow-green Vireo
- [ ] Bachman's Warbler
- [ ] Blue-winged Warbler
- [ ] Golden-winged Warbler
- [ ] Nashville Warbler
- [ ] Cerulean Warbler
- [ ] Kentucky Warbler
- [ ] Connecticut Warbler
- [ ] Mourning Warbler
- [ ] Canada Warbler
- [ ] Clay-colored Sparrow
- [ ] Lark Sparrow
- [ ] Harris' Sparrow

Extinct
Passenger Pigeon
Carolina Parakeet
Ivory-billed Woodpecker
Dusky Seaside Sparrow